Classroom Companion: Economics

The Classroom Companion series in Economics features fundamental textbooks aimed at introducing students to the core concepts, empirical methods, theories and tools of the subject. The books offer a firm foundation for students preparing to move towards advanced learning. Each book follows a clear didactic structure and presents easy adoption opportunities for lecturers.

Bryan Cheang · Tom G. Palmer

Institutions and Economic Development

Markets, Ideas, and Bottom-Up Change

 Springer

Bryan Cheang
King's College London
London, UK

Tom G. Palmer
Atlas Network
Arlington, VA, USA

ISSN 2662-2882   ISSN 2662-2890 (electronic)
Classroom Companion: Economics
ISBN 978-981-99-0843-1   ISBN 978-981-99-0844-8 (eBook)
https://doi.org/10.1007/978-981-99-0844-8

This Springer imprint is published by the registered company Springer Nature Singapore Pte Ltd.
The registered company address is: 152 Beach Road, #21-01/04 Gateway East, Singapore 189721,
Singapore

Acknowledgements

I would like to express my appreciation to numerous individuals who made this volume possible. I first thank various scholars whose insights have deeply influenced mine. Peter Boettke's framework of 'getting the prices, institutions, and culture right' is in my opinion the right way of thinking about development and has shaped the structure of this volume. I thank Paul Dragos Aligica for making known to me the crucial linkage between the philosophical theory of value pluralism and modus vivendi and the polycentric governance literature, a most significant theme I wish to explore further in future. Steve Davies also provided crucial feedback on Chap. 5, which made the final product much stronger than it was. I also thank Mikayla Novak for her insightful comments on early drafts. I am grateful to William Easterly and Paul Lewis for their generous endorsements and comments, and the constant support by the Institute for Humane Studies.

Very importantly, a volume like this would not be possible without research and editorial assistance. On this front, I wish to thank Maximilian Neo, Hanniel Lim, Daniel Ho, Sarah Tan and Duncan McClements for their input. Special mention must be given to Maximilian for coordinating the various interviews with the humanitarian and pro-development organisations showcased in the book. Last but not least, I thank the many 'community-based organisations' and local change agents who gave their time to be interviewed for this volume. This book is about the work that you do to make life better for ordinary people across the globe.

London, UK   Bryan Cheang

Praise for *Institutions and Economic Development*

"This marvellous handbook displays an impressive grasp of the vast literature on economic development, highlighting the crucial role of liberal ideas of freedom for economic success. The handbook masterfully summarizes debates on free markets, institutions, and culture as causes of development. This is the best textbook treatment of liberalism and development that I have ever seen."

—William Easterly, *Professor of Economics at New York University (NYU) and Co-director, NYU Development Research Institute*

"Read this book and learn why countries that are rich are composed of people who are free to follow their own bottom-up rules of order in society and economy."

—Vernon Smith, *Nobel Laureate and Professor of Economics, Chapman University*

"Cheang and Palmer offer a clear, lively and engaging introduction to the liberal perspective on one of the key questions in political economy: why are some nations richer, and more highly developed, than others? Their answer, which draws on the work of authors such as Douglass North, Friedrich Hayek, and Elinor Ostrom, emphasises the importance of trade, entrepreneurship and innovation, along with the ideas and institutions that facilitate such activities. This handbook will be read with profit by students of economic development, whether they are of a liberal persuasion or not."

—Paul Lewis, *Professor of Political Economy, King's College London*

"*Handbook of Liberal Institutions and Economic Development* by Bryan Cheang and Thomas Palmer is an outstanding tool for teaching economic development and political economy at both the undergraduate and graduate level. It is written in clear and straightforward prose so widely accessible, but also carefully researched and presents the various perspectives fairly and comprehensively. This work represents a great contribution to the literature, and should be widely adopted in classrooms and beyond."

—Peter Boettke, *Professor of Economics and Philosophy, George Mason University*

"What is the nature of economic development? What are its consequences? Answering these questions poses a vital task in a modern world which has achieved immense gains in living standards over recent generations but is yet to entirely throw off the vestiges of material deprivation. In this book, Bryan Cheang and Tom Palmer present an unremittingly liberal vision of economic development. They illustrate the profound contributions of human agency and enterprise toward economic development, powerfully revealing how freedom underpins productive forces of change. Cheang and Palmer further explain how the freedom to develop is best secured within a quality institutional framework of laws and norms constraining political domination and exploitation. This *Classroom Companion* is an indispensable, state-of-the-art source outlining a humane pathway to development, one that secures a more prosperous and just world for all."

—Mikayla Novak, *Senior Fellow, Mercatus Center*

Contents

Development and Progress

1

Arguably, the most important question in Economics and probably in social science is 'why are some nations rich, and others poor?' Not only is this an interesting theoretical question, it has practical relevance to human living. According to the World Bank, 9.4% of the global population are still living below the poverty line of US$1.90-a-day (The World Bank, 2020). Understanding the factors that contribute to a nation's economic development will help clarify the path forward for development policymaking.

This Companion will explore the phenomenon of economic development and review the leading theories explaining why it is present in some nations and absent in others. Such a task will necessarily require one to be selective, as development studies is a complex field involving various disciplines with no easy answers. Even today, development economists debate the causes of development and how to foster it in poor nations, if at all possible.

Before diving into development theories, however, this chapter will first define some basic concepts and establish general facts. The subsequent sections will pin down the concept of 'economic development' and provide factual information about changes in living standards over time. We show that a real and sustained improvement in living standards has indeed occurred—called the 'Great Enrichment' which started in the late eighteenth century onwards. Accordingly, we explore the deep determinants of this development and focus on the rules and values in society which have facilitated this improvement in living standards.

Why Care About Development?

It is important to first establish why we should care about development. Some today argue that societies ought to move past an obsession with economic growth, and particularly a fixation with Gross Domestic Product (GDP). Growth is said to be unsustainable, driving environmental problems such as global warming and

© The Author(s), under exclusive license to Springer Nature Singapore Pte Ltd. 2023
B. Cheang and T. G. Palmer, *Institutions and Economic Development*,
Classroom Companion: Economics, https://doi.org/10.1007/978-981-99-0844-8_1

resource depletion. The Intergovernmental Panel on Climate Change (2021) estimates that a global warming level of 1.5 °C is inevitable under the current growth trajectory of a carbon-based economy. Untrammelled growth also aggravates social divide and polarisation. This is why some experts and countries are emphasising the importance of non-material aspects of well-being, beyond a narrow fixation with growth. Michael Spence, an American economist and Nobel Laureate, has called for a focus on other factors that determine the quality of life such as education, economic opportunities and access to basic services (Semuels, 2016). Others, such as ecological economist Giorgos Kallis, go further and argue for zero or even negative GDP growth to limit the environmental damage dealt to our planet (Kallis, 2017). Thus, there is a need to clarify some basic terms, especially the concepts of 'growth' and 'development'. Economic growth simply refers to the increase in a nation's gross domestic product (GDP), which is defined as the total market value of all goods and services produced within a territory in a given year. Seen this way, economic growth reflects the level of material production of a nation, i.e. how much goods and services its residents enjoy.

It is granted that growth does not guarantee development. Economic development is a more holistic concept and is generally understood to include growth, plus other aspects that define a good life. Reasonably, economic development also includes measures such as literacy rates and education standards, access to health care, quality and availability of housing, and life expectancy. Recently, aspects of social progress have also been emphasised, such as a nation's environmental quality and gender equality.

Wealth Liberates People

We acknowledge that growth is no guarantee of development. Surely, possessing more money in and of itself does not mean one is happier. However, growth is nonetheless a necessary, though insufficient condition, for development. A high growth nation is not necessarily a developed one, but no nation can be considered developed if it is unable to facilitate growth in incomes for a broad swathe of its population. Thus, all major developed nations today are also those with high incomes, measured in terms of real GDP per capita.

What is also important is that economic growth enables people to pursue the goals that matter to them. Wealth allows one the financial empowerment to pursue non-material goals, whether those are environmental objectives, the pursuit of social justice activism or some deeper sense of meaning. In fact, available data shows that richer nations are those that fare well on a variety of non-material indicators too. Wealth liberates people to focus on higher levels of Maslow's Hierarchy of Needs. People are free to care about deeper things in life if money is no longer a pressing issue.

According to the environmental Kuznets curve, economic growth may cause a deterioration of the natural environment at early stages but will help improve it after some point (see Yandle et al., 2002 and Dasgupta et al., 2002 for evaluations). It is accepted that in the early stages of development, as industries are created and consumption increases, environmental outcomes may be worse. But after a certain point, economic growth can also benefit the environment by generating the resources necessary for transitioning to renewables and investing in green technologies, by shifting the values of people towards post-material aspects including environmental preservation and by fostering a healthy civil society that allow for environmental activism. Additionally, market-driven growth also facilitates environmental entrepreneurship (Huggins, 2013).

This does not mean that richer countries have no responsibility towards the environment or that they do not contribute to climate change, but it is to say that growth need not be seen as the enemy to environmentalism.[1] Data from the Yale Center for Environmental Law and Policy show a strong correlation between GDP per capita and a nation's performance on the Environmental Performance Index (EPI), which measures ten variables from air quality to carbon emissions (Wendling et al., 2020). This relationship is shown in Fig. 1.1. Moving away from a macro-view, which may obscure individual-level factors, it must also be pointed out that whether growth hurts or helps environmentalism depends on the institutional quality, governance and the policy design of specific nations (Sterner et al., 2019). To improve the environment, improve governance.

Richer countries also do better on various measures of social progress, the subject of growing interest in developed nations. Today, people care not just about money, but about issues of gender equality, sexual orientation, racial equality and fairness and social justice more generally. Interesting, there is strong association between economic growth and social progress. Data from the Social Progress Imperative in Fig. 1.2 show a close connection between GDP per capita and the Social Progress Index, which captures outcomes related to 17 Sustainable Development Goals, including personal rights, personal choice and inclusivity.

Admittedly, not all rich nations do well when it comes to social progress. The Social Progress Imperative has made clear, for example, that countries in the Gulf such as UAE and Saudi Arabia, for example, have high GDP but poor results in social progress, especially when it comes to inclusiveness (Kioes & Pfeiffer, 2015). There are also many countries today which enjoy high rates of income growth, but fall short when it comes to civil liberties and human rights, with China being the prime example. That being said, it is nonetheless clear that economic growth, while an insufficient condition for development, is a necessary one.

The philosopher Brian Kogelman (2022), in a recent and intriguing paper, argued that 'we must always pursue economic growth'. For poor countries, it is clear why growth is a moral imperative. A small increase in national income can mean the difference between life and death. But for richer countries where most

---

[1] The authors of the 2022 Environmental Progress Index for instance have usefully shown that some nations are not pulling their weight in climate action. Yale Center for Environmental Law & Policy (2022). *Environmental Performance Index 2022*. Yale University. https://epi.yale.edu/downloads/epi2022policymakerssummary.pdf.

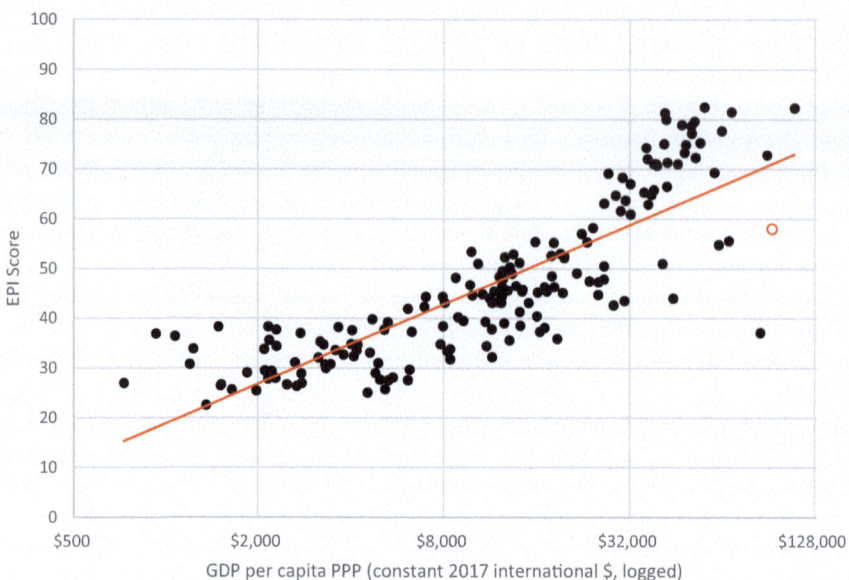

Fig. 1.1 Environmental Performance Index against GDP per capita *Source* Yale Center for Environmental Law (Wendling et al., 2020)

Fig. 1.2 Social Progress Index against GDP per capita *Source* World Bank, Social Progress Imperative (2022)

material needs are satisfied, some scholars have argued against endless growth, whether due to the problems of increased acquisitiveness, social decay or being a distraction from achieving higher, post-material goods like art, culture and leisure (Keynes, 2010; Rawls, 1971, p. 290). Brian Kogelman (2022) argues against these points and explains that growth typically occurs naturally once the underlying conditions giving rise to it (which we will explore in this handbook) are in place, and that to limit this growth would involve morally objectionable actions: turning institutions extractive, reducing dignity for entrepreneurs or to censor the spread of ideas and technology.

But Prosperity is not Inevitable

We do not of course promote a naive Pollyannaism. Economic progress may have occurred on a dramatic scale, but it has been uneven and is never guaranteed. We need to learn what contributes to economic progress and avoid that which stifles it.

The disparity in economic conditions today is clear. Certain regions of the world have not experienced the same levels of economic growth that most of the Western world now takes for granted. Average income per capita in Middle East & North Africa and sub-Saharan Africa is $6,534 and $1,501, respectively. By contrast, the income per capita of North America and Europe & Central Asia is $61,502 and $23,955, respectively, several times larger than that of Middle East and Africa. World Bank Data clearly shows the disparity in terms of 2020's GDP per capita, with the Africa being the poorest region as shown in Fig. 1.3.

A historical analysis since 1960 will also reveal uneven progress in growth rates, shown in Fig. 1.4. In this period, the dramatic rise of North America, Europe & Central Asia deserves much attention. Latin America, East Asia and the Middle East & North Africa have made modest strides but still lags far behind Western countries. Unfortunately, sub-Saharan Africa has barely budged from their income level of 1960.

Economic progress is also not guaranteed. Even though the past few centuries saw a dramatic increase in living standards, this progress was disrupted by major world events of the twentieth century. World War I saw the deaths of about 20 million military personnel and civilians (Mougel, 2011). World War II was much worse, with some estimates counting up to 60 million deaths. Between both World Wars were economic disruptions, largely arising from the Great Depression, which led to mass unemployment in numerous countries, and a decline of international trade of up to 60% (Office of the Historian, 2017).

The interwar period saw the rise of extreme political ideologies in the form of Fascism, Nazism and Communism, all of which would wreak havoc in the decades to come. While Fascism and Nazism were relatively short-lived, it did culminate in the Holocaust, which claimed the lives of 11 million people (Paul, 2020). Far

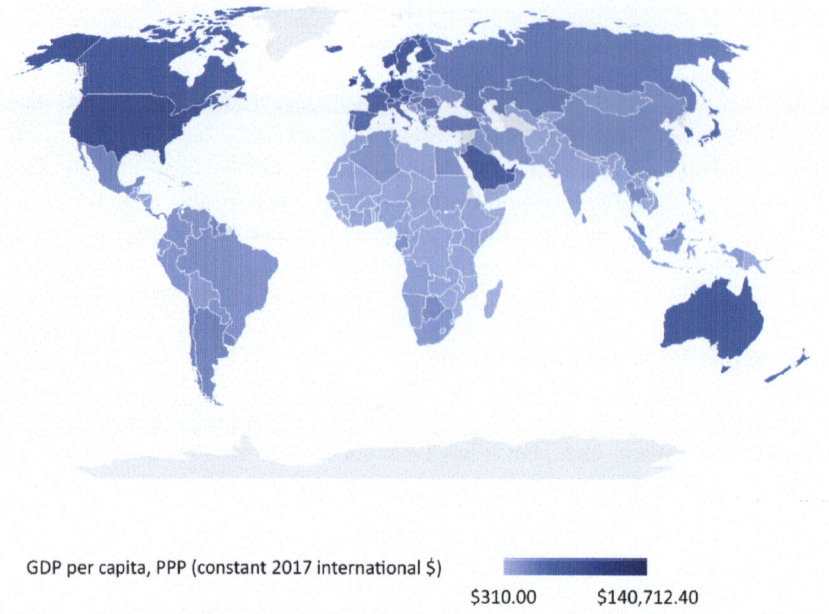

GDP per capita, PPP (constant 2017 international $)

$310.00 $140,712.40

Fig. 1.3 GDP per capita by countries, 2020 *Source* World Bank (2020)

worse, however, has been the legacy of state-sponsored communism.[2] It has been estimated that approximately 100 million people have been killed by communist regimes due to political killings and economic mismanagement, the biggest culprits being Stalin's USSR and Mao's China (Albert et al., 1999). On a larger level, it has also been found that about 262 million people were killed by authoritarian and totalitarian governments in the twentieth century (Rummel, 1997).

These tragedies, understandably, led to a slowdown in economic development and stalled human progress. They also stand as warnings against certain institutions and ideas that are inimical to development, a theme that this book will return to.

The urgency of economic development is clear today. In fact, recent developments have increased poverty. It has been reported that in 2020, global extreme poverty rose for the first time in more than 20 years, due to the disruptions brought about by COVID-19 and governmental responses to it (The World Bank, 2020). Estimates show that about 100 million more people today are living in poverty since the pandemic struck (Mahler et al., 2021).

---

[2] It should also be clarified though that the communist regimes mentioned are large-scale, state-sponsored attempts at socialism, and should not be conflated with a variety of Marxist or socialist positions taken today. There are indeed a number of reasonable positions in this regard, for example, analytical Marxism (see Leopold, 2022), and recent proposals of democratic socialism or liberal solidarity (Hodgson, 2021).

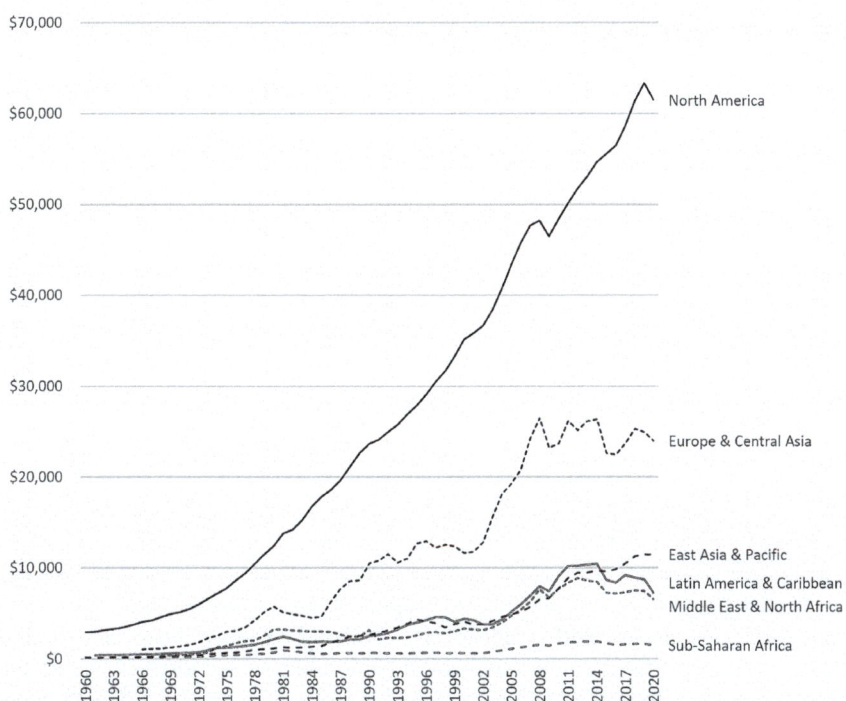

Fig. 1.4 GDP per capita by regions, 1960–2020 *Source* World Bank (2020)

Explaining Development

The principles of economics help us understand why some nations are rich and others poor. We need to first interrogate the simplest of questions: how is wealth created? To answer this, we have to investigate how goods and services are produced for the benefit of consumers.

The most elementary concept to understand in development economics is that of the Production Possibilities Curve (PPC), which helps distinguish a high growth society from a low-growth one.

A nation that has a larger PPC from the origin is one that is capable of producing a greater amount of goods and services, and thus able to satisfy the material wants of its citizens. Economics also teaches that an outward shift of the PPC (Fig. 1.5) is possible through an increase in the quantity and quality of factors of production. These factors of production in turn include land and natural resources, physical capital, labour, human capital as well as entrepreneurship. These are the immediate ingredients of economic growth.

The most basic resource is land, coupled with other natural resources found in the natural world. Most firms rely on physical premises (though there's the rise of online businesses today) and have to transform some natural resource when

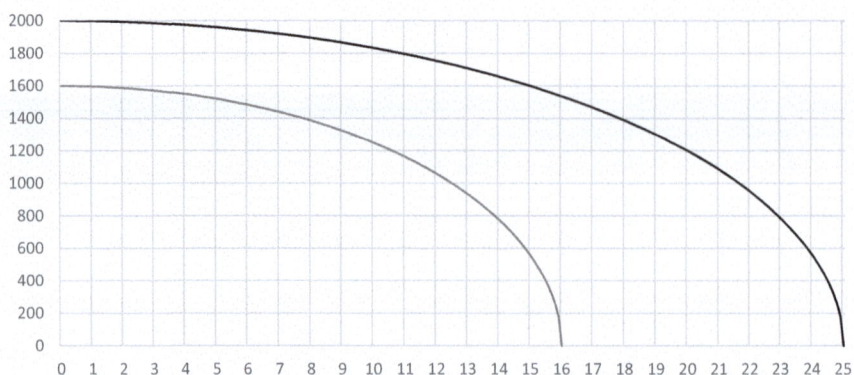

Fig. 1.5 Shift of the PPC curve

producing goods and services. This on the surface suggests that the greater the availability of natural resources, the greater the potential for production.

Labour is important because they are productive assets used by firms. Workers are needed to serve customers, operate capital, manage business processes, etc. Therefore, population growth is generally considered a positive factor in stimulating economic growth. An important aspect to consider is not just labour, but the wider category of human capital. Labour is the physical asset of the human body, while human capital refers to the skills, knowledge and experience that labour possesses. An increase in human capital means that on net, the workforce is more productive, and hence, material production may be increased. Human capital in turn is dependent on expenditures on education, on the job training programs, medical care and more.

Physical capital is also another ingredient of an economy's productive capacity. Capital consists of physical goods that are used in the production of other goods and services for consumer benefit, i.e. machines, factories, equipment, etc. Capital is accumulated in an economy when people save and invest. Rather than enjoying present consumption, funds are directed towards investing in capital goods. Capital goods are essential for high levels of material production because without them, we would not go very far. Capital goods allow workers to be more productive than they otherwise would be. Greater investments in capital translate into greater productive capacity.

The most important aspect of production, however, is entrepreneurship, which is often neglected in most mainstream accounts of economics. Entrepreneurship involves the act of creating business ventures to achieve commercial profits but is much broader than business. Entrepreneurs, in our definition, are those who discover and seize profit opportunities. Entrepreneurship is an important driver of growth insofar as it promotes efficiency and innovation through 'creative destruction', a la Joseph Schumpeter. New businesses compete with old ones, and this incessant competition replaces long-standing practices with new and productive ones that will result in better products at lower prices (Caballero, 2010).

In sum, it is by increasing the quantity and quality of these resources will nations be able to sustain the production of material goods and services for its people. The Production Possibilities Curve will be shifted outward, illustrating the greater combinations of goods and services that can be produced.

It is important to remember, however, that the above account is incomplete. Ultimately, goods and services are produced within an economy for the benefit of consumers. We thus need to look at consumers and their pursuit of economic value. Production is intimately tied to consumption. A consideration of consumption then behooves us to reflect on specialisation and the division of labour, both of which fulfil human wants, and to which we now turn.

Imagine that you are stranded on an island with some other strangers. In order to survive, you will need to meet your basic needs of eating and drinking. If you tried to gather food and drink on your own, it may be possible, but highly inefficient. One would have to forage for food from the earth, but then will encounter the difficulty of transforming them into edible products: we need tools to cut fruit, hunt animals and prepare food. How will we make tools? Where would we look for the minerals needed to form tools? All this for a simple meal. At this point, we should be able to realise that any community that relies purely on self-sufficiency will not be capable of mass production and high standards of living.

Gains from Trade

Consequently, one of the most basic insights of Economics is the importance of specialisation, exchange, and the division of labour. Rather than trying to do everything on your own, you may simply specialise in one activity, let's say being a farmer. You become very good at this and produce agricultural produce for society, in return for money which you then use to exchange for other goods and services you desire. If everyone in society engaged in such specialisation and exchange based on the division of labour, society will be able to produce much more than was possible under self-sufficiency. This basic insight was most popularly advanced by Adam Smith in 1776 with his *Wealth of Nations and* remains ever-important today.

Economists have an important principle called 'comparative advantage', which is when one can produce a certain good or service at a lower opportunity cost than someone else. When people specialise in what they have a comparative advantage in and trade with others, both parties can consume beyond what is possible in its absence. If we didn't trade with others, we would have to give up more resources to achieve a certain outcome, but in trade, we take advantage of someone else's relative efficiency and mutually gain in the process. What is true for an individual is true for a nation. When nations produce what they have a comparative advantage in, they manage to transcend the confines of their PPC. Thus, economies stand to gain from trade in terms of greater production and consumption possibilities. In the late twentieth century, the opening up of many developing nations like China and India to global trade was a big factor behind their rapid economic development

(Panagariya, 2019). Today, it is estimated that the total value of free trade around the world is $28.5 trillion (UNCTAD, 2022).

Trade should not just be seen in terms of goods and services. The free movement of labour around the world promises to bring about even greater prosperity. As it is today, severe restrictions on immigration mean that talent is locked up in places where little use is made of them. When we allow people to move freely, we unlock their potential. The economist Michael Clemens (2011) likens the gains from free immigration to 'trillion-dollar bills on the sidewalk'. So large is this gain that 'eliminating those (immigration) barriers amount to large fractions of world GDP—one or two orders of magnitude larger mount to large fractions of world GDP—one or two orders of magnitude larger than the gains from dropping all remaining restrictions on international trade' (Clemens, 2011, p. 84).

Gains from Innovation

Closely accompanying gains from trade are also the gains from innovation.

Innovation is another critical key to understanding economic development. There are two components. First, 'product innovation' refers to the introduction of new types of goods and services and the improvements in quality of existing products. This is an important aspect of economic development, because material well-being does not just mean having higher incomes, but access to better quality products. Political elites throughout history, like Kings and Queens, enjoyed wealth, but never had the same access to the technologies, gadgets and appliances of today.

This is complemented with 'process innovation' which refers to the introduction of new ways of producing goods and services and the improvements in commercial practices. This may include managerial practices, organisational processes and the improved uses of various factor inputs. Process innovation results in greater productivity. Goods and services can be produced cheaper and faster, saving resources for other uses instead. It is process innovation that makes new products become widely available to the masses, even if they may be limited to the elite few in the beginning. Process innovation also helps us reimagine the possibilities of business. Today, business activities transcend physical distance and can operate remotely across continents. The extent of the market has tremendously been extended due to the discovery and use of new production techniques.

The benefits of innovation are significant. Technological progress for one has allowed us to enjoy better product quality at reduced prices. A good example is personal computing. Personal computing has not always been a luxury accessible to most people. In 1972, the most basic model, HP 3000, costs a whopping $95,000, equivalent to half a million in today's dollars. Today, the cheapest model goes for a few hundred dollars and possesses capabilities beyond the wildest dreams of computer scientists back in the 1970s. The prices of other consumables have also fallen dramatically. The decline in the price of televisions

(96%), software (67%) and toys (69%) is a testament to the immense potential of technological revolutions (see Roser & Ritchie, 2013b).

The gains from specialisation, coupled with the gains from innovation, improve material living standards, allowing the average individual to enjoy a greater range of ever-improving goods and services.

Entrepreneurship the Driving Force

Trade and innovation, however, are not mechanical processes. They are fundamentally driven by entrepreneurs, who are central players on the economic stage. Entrepreneurs make use of the various factors of production and synthesise them into a coherent plan of action. Without them, capital, labour, land and other resources would have no economic value to consumers whatsoever.

The role of entrepreneurs, however, is often neglected in mainstream economics, including in the field of development. Early theories of growth tended to emphasise greater inputs into an economy's production function, which in turn generates outputs. Economic growth, however, is not delivered the same way a factory machine produces clothes. The economy is an organism comprising human action. When we unpack this 'black box', we observe the crucial element of entrepreneurship.

Entrepreneurship is often difficult to define. It certainly must be distinguished from business management, which is primarily centred around the smooth oversight of the firm's operations. We take entrepreneurs here to be anyone who discovers and seize profit opportunities (Holcombe, 2006). Sometimes, entrepreneurs help bring the market into equilibrium, and in other times, they disrupt the status quo. The equilibrating and disruptive functions of entrepreneurship cohere with the intellectual contributions of economists Israel Kirzner (1973) and Joseph Schumpeter (1942), respectively.

Gains from trade are tied to entrepreneurial action. Entrepreneurs, either by themselves or within firms, are alert to profit opportunities around them. They seize these opportunities by developing production plans to satisfy their consumers. Of course, some entrepreneurs are more successful than others, and they are guided in their endeavours by the feedback mechanism of profit-loss, which rewards firms that are best able to value-add to the customers they serve.

The gains from innovation also must be understood in relation to entrepreneurship. Entrepreneurs, as part of their constant process of learning, sometimes discover new goods and services, and new production techniques worth employing. They then pursue these new innovations and disrupt the status quo in the process. The disruptive actions of these entrepreneurs constitute the process of 'creative destruction' that the economist Joseph Schumpeter (1942, p. 83) described as 'the essential fact about capitalism'. This is the same process that has radically transformed our lives, especially in the past few decades which witnessed exponential technological progress. It was entrepreneurial insight that conceived Uber, the smartphone and the mRNA vaccines, and soon, spaceflights for the ordinary man. Today, many growth models in economics recognise the centrality of entrepreneurship and creative destruction (see Aghion & Howitt, 1992, 2008).

The benefits of innovation accrue to ordinary consumers and are not simply concentrated in the hands of the elites. This was the subject of empirical research by Nobel Laureate William Nordhaus (2004), who showed that from 1948 to 2001, most of the benefits of technological progress in the United States were received by consumers rather than by the producers themselves.

It should also be noted that today, there are numerous criticisms against the corporatisation of business. Arguably, large corporations dominate the economy, forming an economic oligarchy. Economic wealth may also translate into political influence, undermining the democratic process. Those who play down the severity of market dominance point to how the large firms and billionaires of the 1990s are no longer around today, a testament of creative destruction (Bourne, 2019). However, given the unprecedented nature of Big Tech and the network effects they enjoy, a new era of anti-trust regulations and corporate governance reforms may be sorely needed (Zingales, 2014; Fukuyama et al., 2021).

Institutions and Ideas Matter

Economies become wealthy by exploiting gains from trade and gains from innovation, which are in turn made possible by entrepreneurship. Both mechanisms allow greater levels of production, and a broader range of consumer wishes to be satisfied. However, some nations have not been able to take advantage of these processes. They lack some fundamental ingredients that are needed to engage in successful economic production. We need to understand why. Increases in productive inputs and the gains from trade and innovation are all part of the explanation but remain proximate causes of growth. Hence, there is a need to turn to more fundamental explanations of growth, as opposed to proximate accounts.

There have been generally four schools of thought in the analyses of fundamental factors of growth. The first is the geography school, which holds that a nation that enjoys favourable geographical conditions is one that will ultimately thrive, or at least derive a significant headstart. The second is the cultural school, which focuses on the favourable cultural traits that predispose a nation towards economic production and progress. The third is the leadership school, which focuses on the actions of enlightened political leaders in enacting good policies. Last of all is the notion that 'institutions matter', which is the idea that the prevailing rules in any society influence economic behaviour, and hence outcomes (Fig. 1.6).

In this book, we primarily focus on the role that institutions and ideas play in generating positive economic outcomes. Institutions, i.e. the rules and norms in a society, as well as the ideas that underpin them, have a fundamental impact on a nation's growth prospects. This is not to say that they are the only factors that matter, but rather that they are most central to any understanding of long-run development.

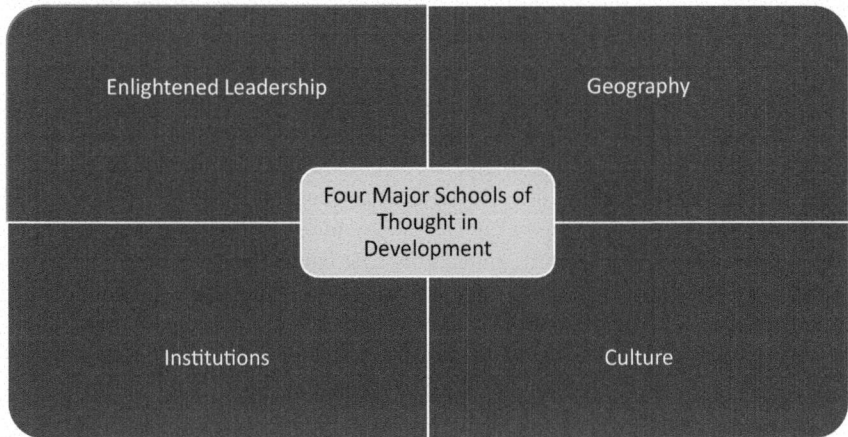

Fig. 1.6 Four Major Schools of Thought in Development

The idea that institutions are of great importance is today taken for granted in the social sciences (Rodrik et al., 2004; Acemoglu et al., 2005; Acemoglu & Robinson, 2012, 2020). This was not previously the case. For much of the twentieth century, however, various post-war theories of development either assumed the presence of good institutions or downplayed their importance.

Economic Theories

In the post-war period, development theory heavily emphasised the importance of capital accumulation. According to what is now known as 'capital fundamentalism', poor nations needed to mobilise domestic savings and welcome overseas investments in order to kick-start economic growth. Seen this way, the problem with poverty is a lack of capital investment, which can be solved through an injection of such funds. Closely associated with capital fundamentalism was the theory by Walt Rostow of the 'linear stages of growth', which posited that developing countries are in the backward stages of modernisation and thus may advance through the following stages: traditional society, preconditions for take-off growth, economic take-off, the drive to modernity and the age of mass consumption (Rostow, 1960). Rostow's modernisation theory also rested on the belief that developing nations sorely needed capital, without which they would not be able to bring about industrial development and catch-up growth.

The emphasis on capital accumulation thus dovetails with the emphasis in development circles on foreign aid. Poor countries should, according to this perspective, foster domestic savings for investment purposes, including initiatives such as tax incentives and government investment in domestic industries. One theory in this vein of thought is by the development economist Paul Rosenstein-Rodan who believed that there was a minimum scale for savings, investments and demand that must be reached for growth to take-off. Accordingly, the state should embark on a 'big-push', to catalyse growth through large, infrastructure and similar spending projects (Murphy et al., 1989; Rosenstein-Rodan, 1943). If domestic efforts are inadequate, then external injections of foreign aid may be necessary. If poor countries lacked capital, then it would make sense for richer nations or world organisations to inject such capital into these countries through aid programs.

While these theories correctly pointed out that capital investment is key to any nation's growth story, the heavy emphasis on capital meant that the deeper problems of governance were neglected. Poor countries may not have a functioning state bureaucracy with which to foster investments or attract them (Bardhan, 1990). In the absence of proper and functioning institutions, external foreign aid programs may in turn be mired in inefficiency and corruption at worst. As will be shown in the later chapters, such foreign aid programs sidestepped the deeper question of how to reform domestic institutions in a manner that promoted market-based development.

In the later twentieth century, two other economic theories of development came to the fore: endogenous growth theory and the neoliberal-Washington Consensus. Both theories also sidestepped institutional questions. In the 1980s onwards, as part of the rise of 'neoliberal' ideas, a set of policy reforms, known as the Washington Consensus, became part of the dominant paradigm in development. These policies emphasised macroeconomic stability, fiscal restraint and balanced budgets, as well as market policies like privatisation and liberalisation (Williamson, 2009). The Washington Consensus framework has been controversial and subject to much debate till today. One important strand of criticism is that it failed to recognise that market reforms required certain institutional pre-requisites, which many post-communist nations did not possess at the time (Rodrik, 2006).

Endogenous growth theory emerged in part to fill the gaps in neoclassical economics, emphasising the interplay of internal factors that would lead to technological and productivity improvements (Romer, 1994). An important ingredient in endogenous growth theory is investments in human capital and the knowledge spillovers that such investments will lead to. Consequently, an implication of this perspective is that the state has a role to play in promoting and creating incentives for human capital improvements and technological research, since private firms may under-invest in them (Cypher & Diaz, 2008).

While both Washington Consensus and endogenous growth theory pointed to important insights, that of the importance of markets and human capital respectively, the focus on the institutional environment was not central. Economists today generally agree that the quality of a nation's governance should be the first question of development. Poor governance, or the absence of healthy governance institutions, will mean that markets cannot function properly, or that the requisite investments in technology are not forthcoming.

Geography and Culture

In addition to economic theories of development, there have also been other theories that place a premium on culture and geography. In these perspectives, institutions are also not the central actor. The geography school argues that development is mainly dependent on a nation's geographical location and natural conditions. Understandably, there's a wide variety of theories within the rubric of geography, with some emphasising climate (Bloom et al., 1998), the access to waterways (Sachs et al., 1995), its role in generating uneven development (Harvey, 2005), as well as the nature of the factor endowments present. A well-known, albeit very long-run theory drawing from an emphasis on factor endowments is by Jared Diamond (1997), who identified initial favourable conditions such as the East–West axis and favourable animal and plant endowments in the Eurasian landmass, all of which provided a head start in the race to develop.

The relationship between geography and institutions is complex and disputed. Some variants of geographical theories may be more deterministic, suggesting that natural conditions may pose a severe barrier to development, trapping nations in poverty (Bloom et al., 2003). A leading proponent of the geographical school, Jeffrey Sachs, has claimed explicitly that institutions are not fundamental causes of development: 'for much of the world, bad climates, poor soils and physical isolation are likely to hinder growth whatever happens to policy' (Gallup et al., 1999).

This is not to say that institutions do not matter at all; in fact, the claim is that geography may in fact have an indirect effect on the nature of institutions that are created. The leading institutional economists today, Daron Acemoglu and James Robinson, acknowledge that geographical factors have an indirect, historical influence on the type of institutions that colonies inherited during colonialism, which in turn led to path-dependent effects over the long run (Acemoglu et al., 2002). While those like Jeffrey Sachs place more weight on geography and the barriers it poses, Acemoglu and Robinson emphasise institutions.

The notion that 'institutions matter' is of course more complicated than it sounds. Institutional economics is an internally diverse school of thought, which includes an older tradition in America featuring the likes of Thorstein Veblen, John Commons, Wesley Mitchell and John Kenneth Galbraith, as well as 'New Institutional Economics', its standard bearers being Ronald Coase, Douglass North, Elinor Ostrom, among others (see Hodgson, 2004 and Menard & Shirley, 2005 for an excellent coverage of both sub-traditions). One, though by no means the only, theme that unifies all institutionalists is the belief that economics cannot be reduced to an analysis of individual utility maximisation and rational behaviour, a cornerstone of mainstream economics today. Individuals are shaped by their culture, habits-of-mind, history, politics and more. Economic behaviour is thus far more complex and is situated within socially embedded rules. The agenda of institutional economics thus broadens our field of vision, refocuses attention onto the myriad factors that influence human action, and contributes to an interdisciplinary approach to development studies. By examining insights from other disciplines beyond the narrow confines of economics, one better understands the nature and causes of the wealth of nations.

Accordingly, 'culture', something that is typically sidestepped in mainstream economics but central to sociology, is crucial for development studies. On this aspect, prominent economic historians have shown how the prosperity of the Western world is in large part a product of its values. A number of accounts emphasise the Protestant work ethic of Max Weber, whereby protestant Christianity is said to promote hard work, a sense of thrift and values conducive to capitalism. The historian David Landes (1995) is one example of such a proponent. A related argument is by Joel Mokyr (2016), who focused his argument on the culture of innovation that arose in the Western world due to intellectual figures such as Francis Bacon, all of whom disseminated an ideology of progress. What such accounts have in common are unique cultural traits that explain Western prosperity.

A question that arises from such accounts is whether then pro-development values are basically rooted in the West. Does development require Westernisation then? A useful cultural account of development is by Lawrence Harrison, who outlined some universal values that are conducive to progress. Pro-growth cultures are those that have religious beliefs that encourage rational thought, material progress, forward-thinking and practicality (Harrison, 2006). Such cultures also see in trade a positive-sum game and the possibility of mutual gain. Seen this way, poor countries require a cultural transformation in order to attain development.

In our perspective, culture is an important ingredient in development and is one that works in close tandem with institutions. Institutions, being the rules that govern human life, are connected with the prevailing cultural norms and beliefs. The beliefs we hold shape and are in turn shaped by the rules of society and the way we are collectively governed. We argue that economic progress and development require societies to have a set of rules and values that reward economic exchange, production, and innovation. In subsequent chapters, we explain why the institutions of market capitalism, as well as the liberal values that underpin them, are essential for nations to experience progress.

Institutional economists, in the tradition of Douglass North, have acknowledged that both culture *and* formal institutions influence behaviour and shape development outcomes. This is not new. Yet, ongoing questions remain as to how, when and why is it that culture influences institutions and vice versa. It has been said that culture has been treated as a black box in institutional analysis (Acemoglu & Johnson, 2005). The link between culture and institutions is complex and is the subject of ongoing research.

Another major challenge in development theory is how societies can indeed transition to and acquire the set of institutions and values that reward progress. It is one thing to know what these ingredients are and a totally different task altogether of the actual implementation. Indeed, Western nations have tried to socially engineer Western-style institutions in poor nations, with mixed success. For every South Korea, there is an Iraq that undercuts the 'Western Institutions' argument. It is also difficult to see how cultural change can take place, especially in the context of top-down development policies implemented by global organisations.

The Great Enrichment Tells Us That Prosperity is Possible

Achieving economic development is indeed an important objective to work towards. History also shows that economic progress is possible. One of the most important facts in history is the Great Enrichment, which refers to the sudden and enormous improvements in living standards in the nineteenth century. This is best represented in Fig. 1.7, which depicts what has famously been called the 'hockey stick' graph of development.

What this graph illustrates is that first and foremost, human beings have been poor for most of history. This data, gathered from the work of British economist Angus Maddison, tells us that people from the past were much poorer than we are today. Estimates tell us that the average income per person in 1820 was around $1100 a year. People living in the decades and centuries before were no richer than this.

The amazing breakthrough occurred only very recently in human history (the blade of the hockey stick), beginning in the nineteenth century onwards and which accelerated in the 2nd half of the twentieth century. During this period, the average national income of Western Europe rose by 517% percent. In the same period, average American GDP per person rose by 581% percent and life expectancy by 28 years. In Asia, average GDP per person rose by 96% percent between 1913 and

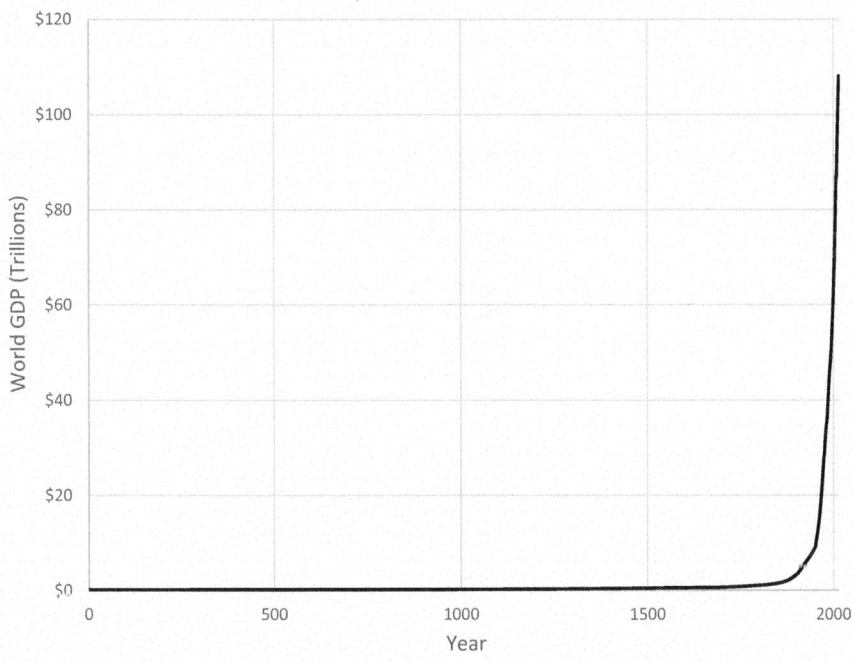

Fig. 1.7 World GDP over the last two millennia *Source* Maddison Database (2010)

1999. Today, the average GDP per capita is approximately $15,000, more than 15 times the average of the past (Roser, 2013).

The economic historian Deirdre McCloskey, in her Bourgeois trilogy, has shown how this Great Enrichment dramatically increased incomes by a factor of 30, or in other words, 3000%. This is a significant turning point in history, one that we should appreciate, study, and seek to sustain. For the first time in recorded human history, half of the world is middle class or richer. Research by the Brookings Institution published in 2018 shows that we have reached a 'global tipping point', where some 3.8 billion people now live in households with enough discretionary expenditure to be considered 'middle class' or 'rich' (Kharas & Hamel, 2018) (Fig. 1.8).

Significantly, the middle class is fast growing and is projected to reach more than 4 billion people by the end 2020 and 5.3 billion people by 2030. Compared to today, the middle class in 2030 will have 1.7 billion more people, while the vulnerable groups will have 900 million fewer people (Fig. 1.9).

It cannot be overemphasised that economic growth has benefitted not just the 1%, but the very poor among us. Data shows that the number of people living in poverty and absolute poverty has been slashed. Since 1820, the number of people *not* living in extreme poverty has gone up to more than 7 billion (Figs. 1.10 and 1.11).

A major contributing factor to this dramatic reduction in poverty was the rise of Asia in the twentieth century, especially India and China. East Asian economies

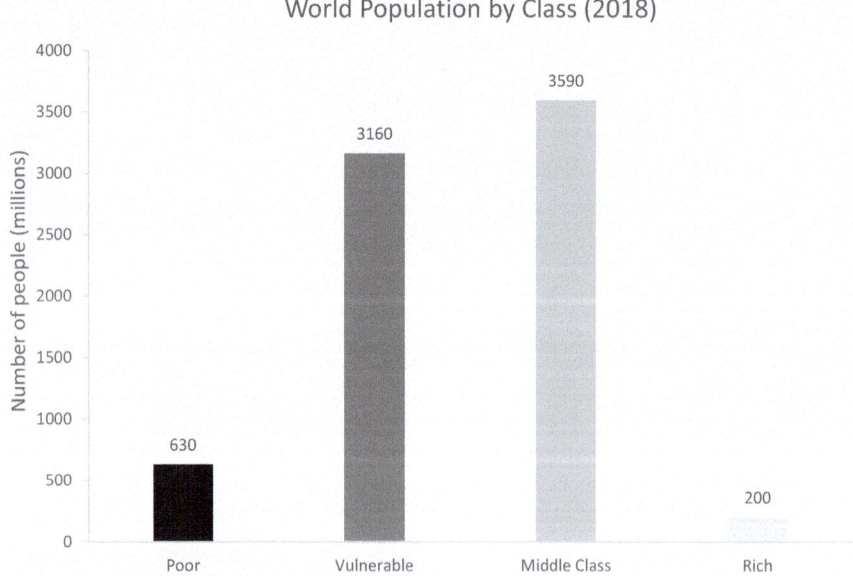

Fig. 1.8   World Population by class in 2018 *Source* Calculations by World Data Lab as Reported by Brookings Institution (Kharas & Hamel, 2018)

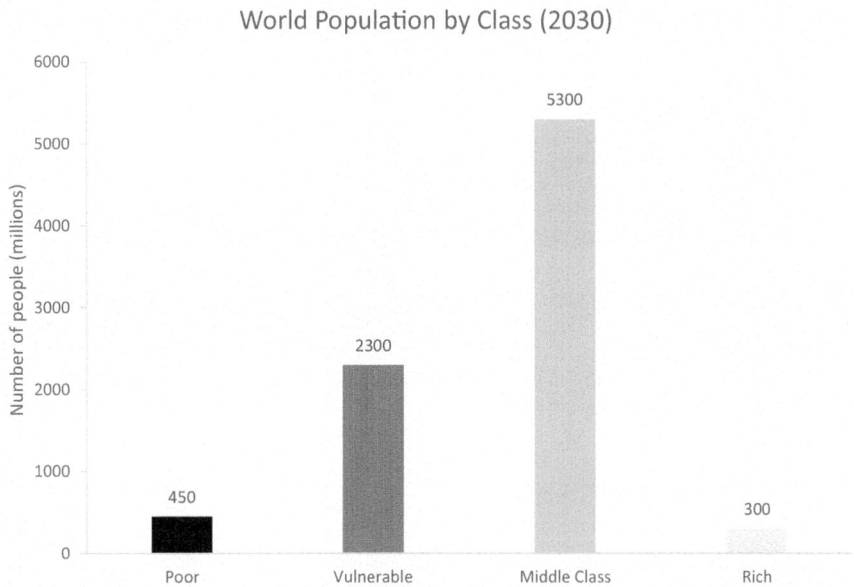

Fig. 1.9 World Population by class in 2030 *Source* Calculations by World Data Lab as Reported by Brookings Institution (Kharas & Hamel, 2018)

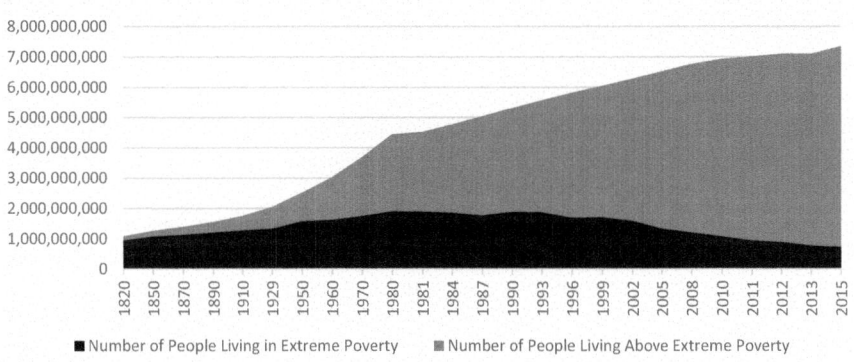

Fig. 1.10 World population living in extreme poverty, 1910–2015 *Source* World Bank; for details see Ravallion (2015)

like Japan, South Korea, Singapore, Taiwan and Hong Kong industrialised and caught up to the West within one generation. China and India's growth have also been significant, to the point of reducing global income inequality. According to investigations by Christoph Lakner, a consultant at the World Bank, and Branko Milanovic, senior scholar at the Luxembourg Income Study Center, global income inequality fell for the first time since the Industrial Revolution, in the period from 2008 to 2014 (The World Bank, 2019).

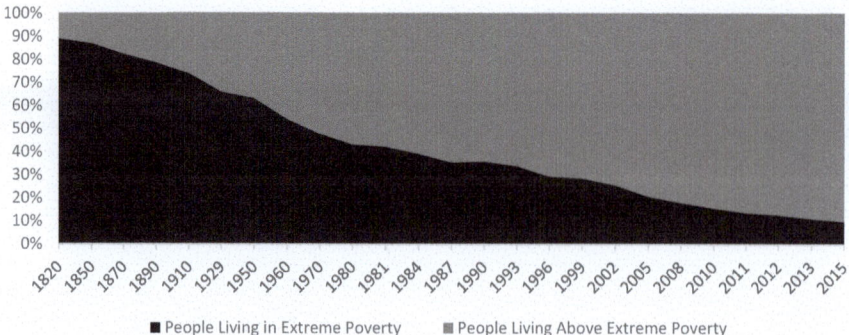

Fig. 1.11 Proportion of world population living in extreme poverty, 1910–2015 *Source* World Bank; for details see Ravallion (2015)

Access to Essential Goods

Of course, the high living standards that most people enjoy today are not just denoted in monetary terms. Economic prosperity has also allowed nations to provide for basic needs, namely access to food and water, health care, and education.

Access to food has seen tremendous improvements in the past 60 years. Daily caloric supply has increased 31% since 1961, according to the UN Food and Agriculture Organisation. The global per capita supply of protein has also increased similarly by about 33%, from 61 g in 1961 to 81 g in 2014. However, these trends vary tremendously across the world's regions. The daily per capita caloric supply in North America is 3,471 cal while that of Africa is only 2,311. Protein supply tells the same story. In 2014, per capita protein supply in North America is 40% higher than in Africa (Roser & Ritchie, 2013a).

Progress in the access to safe and reliable water supply is also seen. As of 2020, about three of our four people have access to safe drinking water, with an upward though slow trend of progress in the last ten years. Household sanitation levels have also improved markedly over the past two decades with more than half of the households gaining access to 'safely managed' sanitation facilities where excrements are safely disposed of (Unicef, 2020).

Access to education is also a key aspect of economic development, of which we have made great strides. In 1900, 78.6% percent of people aged 15 years and older were classified as illiterate. In 2016, that number has dropped to under 14% percent. Primary school enrolment has also increased over the past century from 72% in 1970s to 91% today (Roser & Ortiz-Ospina, 2016).

We are also living longer and healthier lives today. In 2017, the average life expectancy in the world was 71.7 years. Just around 150 years ago, it was 29.7 years (Roser et al., 2019). Notwithstanding the impact of COVID-19, there have been great improvements in the past two decades in healthcare access and quality, due to gains in low- and middle-income countries. This is according to recent data from the Global Burden of Disease study published in *The Lancet*. In 2016, the global average healthcare access and quality score was 54.4, increasing from 42.4 points in 2000 (Fullman et al., 2016).

On Sustainability

While the core focus of this handbook is on the nature and the causes of the wealth of nations—economic development—no discussion of it would be complete without some brief mention of sustainability. Today, sustainability is a highly valued objective in business, society, and public policy. From the perspective of development, the key concept is that of 'sustainable development', which we may simply define as an approach to development that is cognisant of wider environmental impacts, and which aims to limit these harms to the natural world. This is because economic growth may proceed at too fast a pace or may be driven by environmentally unfriendly strategies. Thus, sustainable development calls for an approach to growth sensitive to these green objectives.

One initial step in the sustainability project is to better capture these objectives, which are said to be neglected in national income indicators. Gross domestic product and its variants are focused on the measurement of material income generated from the production of goods and services. So, a narrow obsession with these indicators may blind societies to the negative effects of growth. There are of course a variety of environmental indicators that one may track, but one specific indicator that synthesises both traditional growth aspects with environmental goals is that of 'Green GDP', which subtracts losses to biodiversity and climate costs (Stiglitz et al., 2009). An influential and recent indicator is the Sustainability Development Index, which modifies the HDI by also considering 'ecological overshoot', i.e. 'the extent to which consumption-based CO2 emissions and material footprint exceed per-capita shares of planetary boundaries' (Hickel, 2020).

The proper relationship between growth and environmental objectives is complex, because it is dependent on deeper normative commitments.[3] It should be pointed out that there are a variety of environmentalist positions (see Schmidtz & Shahar, 2019 for a comprehensive volume). One of which is 'deep ecology', or radical environmentalism, which holds that the natural world possesses intrinsic value in itself, and thus deeply rejects anthropocentrism in most mainstream environmentalism (Naess, 1971). Other radical positions trace environmental problems to deeper ideological roots of Western society, such as capitalism, neoliberalism, patriarchy and industrialism. If such a radical position is taken, then many contemporary environmental proposals, which operate within the framework of industrial capitalism, are rejected. This rejection may take the form of eco-socialism, the paradigm of de-growth (Jackson, 2016; Victor, 2019) or even a wholesale rejection

---

[3] We recommend reading Michael Hulme's (2021) latest book on climate change, which transcends the narrow scientism in mainstream discourse and shows how normative commitments, social meanings and the humanities shape climate discourse.

of the basic tenets of modern life. On another end, some extreme anthropocentric humanists reject environmentalism for being fundamentally incompatible with human flourishing (Biddle, 2011).

We obviously cannot settle this debate, which understandably features a wide range of positions beyond those just stated. The point we wish to make is that if economic growth and environmentalism are both seen as desirable—and there are good reasons to believe so—then there should be a reasonable compromise on both sides. Many mainstream environmentalists propose solutions, such as carbon taxation and investment in green energy, which are not only compatible with growth, but may even contribute to growth and its material benefits. These win–win proposals are to be encouraged. Arguably, the paradigm that most befits such a position is 'ecomodernism', which seeks to decouple growth from its environmental impacts and alleviate environmental problems through modern, smart, and technologically driven solutions (Asafu-Adjaye et al., 2015; Symons, 2019). As with all positions, ecomodernism has its share of criticisms. We, however, broadly share its basic premises: climate change is a serious problem and a consequence of modernity, but rather than dismantling the inherited institutions of modernity, lets reform them (Hulme, 2021, Chap. 3).

This handbook ultimately is not about environmentalism but endorses the basic idea that growth and environmental objectives need not be at loggerheads. Growth, especially its pace and the approach used, may have to be modified, especially in the transition to renewables. Such policies and compromises should be supported. But growth itself should not be entirely rejected. There is also a strong relationship between growth and environmentalism (see Fig. 1.1 abovementioned again), such that wealthier nations, on balance, can better afford to invest in renewables, are more climate-resilient, and tend to have more vibrant civil societies where environmental activism flourishes. In fact, many leading economists have begun to incorporate environmental concerns into growth analyses and outline their mutual compatibility—most notably William Nordhaus, whose work has 'brought us considerably closer to answering the question of how we can achieve sustained *and* sustainable global economic growth' (emphasis mine) (Royal Swedish Academy of Sciences, 2018).

In the spirit of institutionalist thinking, the task of achieving sustainable development may also be considered as a challenge of governance. What sort of institutional arrangements and what reforms to existing institutions may be achieved if green objectives are to be met? Seen this way, the constraints of political economy, such as incentive compatibility, bounded rationality, and collective action problems, need to be considered in environmental governance (Sterner et al., 2019; Fleck & Hanssen, 2016)). Accordingly, environmental governance may also benefit from the insights of polycentric, bottom-up theories of governance explored in this handbook, especially the way in which these foster experimentation in environmental adaptation strategies—an approach to climate change embraced by Nobel Laureate Elinor Ostrom herself (see Pennington, 2008; Ostrom, 2012; Kahn 2021; Turnheim et al., 2018).

So What?

The tremendous human progress that occurred, so clearly documented above, bears several important lessons. First, it tells us that poverty, not prosperity, has been the norm in human history. Most of us are born into a developed nation, with clean water, access to food, health care, and modern amenities. We typically take these for granted as if they always were. This was never the case. One should therefore not take for granted the modern living standards that have become so common everywhere. Consequently, this means that we ought to be focused on explaining prosperity, not poverty. Poverty is obvious and common. Prosperity is the puzzle to explain. The importance of development economics, and this book, becomes clear.

Second, there is more room for optimism than we initially thought. It is easy to look around the world and be filled with pessimism. The media contributes, in no small part, to the Mean World Syndrome, a psychological phenomenon first coined by Dr George Gerbner in the 1970s to describe our impression that the world is more dangerous than it really is (Gifford, 2020). The nature of news reporting is that it will always report on events that happened, rather than those that did not. While there are both good and bad things that happen in the world, our headlines are always flooded with reports on war, epidemics, and other crises due to our natural inclination towards negative information (Pinker, 2018). This constant stream of bad news plays on our primal fears and contributes to our pessimism.

Human welfare may also be understood in subjective terms, in relation to individual happiness, rather than the attainment of goods and services related to welfare (such as income and essential goods abovementioned). Does growth necessarily lead to greater happiness? Are people happier today than they were before? The famous insights by Richard Easterlin (1974, 1995) provide a negative answer. Through time-series data that track happiness levels as incomes rise, it has been shown that in Europe, United States and even in Asia, higher levels of income do not correspond with higher levels of happiness (Easterlin, 1995). If we consider subjective happiness, we also have cause for concern about the rise of mental health problems in many countries today.

We cannot settle these disputes definitively. Some scholars have, for example, insisted that happiness has indeed increased, if happiness is understood in its cultural contexts, or if different measurement approaches are used. What is important to note for our purposes is that the timeframe of analysis matters. A longer timeframe demonstrates greater levels of progress, but a shorter timeframe will naturally give us more cause for concern. Optimists of human progress point to how we are living in the most peaceful time in human history today (Pinker, 2011) Relative to centuries ago, this may be true. However, at the time of this writing, the first major war since 1945 has broken out in Europe. This Ukraine crisis is also connected with a severe energy crisis and inflationary pressures sweeping major economies. The stagflation of the 1970s seems to be recurring at present times. The timeframe of analysis is critical.

The facts of the Great Enrichment, however, give us room to be optimistic. We are much better off than our ancestors of centuries past, at least on a good many indicators. The question is 'why?', and how we can sustain this.

Liberal Political Economy and Institutional Entrepreneurs

In our book, we show that liberalism is the prime force for material development and human well-being. Liberal policies, institutions, and ideas provide a framework for individuals to enrich themselves through trade, exchange, and innovation. It is the basis for nations to achieve economic prosperity. Beyond just wealth, liberalism also accords the freedom to individuals to fulfil their wishes, and what they believe to be a good life. This freedom is not just an ingredient necessary for growth, it is also a moral end in itself worth striving for. Put this way, the purpose of development is not merely about increasing national income, reducing poverty, creating jobs—as important as these all are—but allowing people to actualise their potential as free beings.

Liberalism is of course contested on numerous levels. There are debates about what actually constitutes liberalism and also concerns about the ill-effects of liberalism in society. For us, we take liberalism in its classical sense, a rich tradition including esteemed figures like Adam Smith, David Hume, John Locke, John Stuart Mill and in the twentieth century Ludwig von Mises, Milton Friedman, Karl Popper, Friedrich Hayek, Elinor Ostrom and more (see Schmidtz & Brennan, 2010). This is the political philosophy that emphasises the importance of individual freedom, the maintenance of general rules in the social order, the rule of law, and competition as a key organising principle. It is the same set of ideas that contributed to the growth of Western society in the nineteenth century and the birth of constitutionalism in the West.

The recognition of the contribution of liberalism to material development and human welfare is by no means original to us. Adam Smith, the father of modern economics, first posited that it was liberalism that led to the wealth of nations. Some development economists in the twentieth century, against the grain of mainstream thinking, also emphasised market liberty rather than development planning, individuals such as Peter Bauer, William Easterly, Hernando de Soto, and Deepak Lal. Today, prominent figures such as Deirdre McCloskey have unveiled the humane face of liberalism and how it accords dignity, equality, and liberty to the least well-off and oppressed among us.

We present an account of market liberalism that is distinct from the confines of neoclassical economics, which lies at its heart man as a rational utility maximiser, with fixed preferences and who possesses all relevant information, and which models markets from the perspective of competitive general equilibrium. Liberalism, in our account, is presented from the perspective of institutional economics, which takes the rules and social influences of human interaction seriously.

Accordingly, the liberal institutionalism of Douglass North, F.A. Hayek and Elinor Ostrom forms the guiding thread in this handbook.[4] Importantly, these trio of scholars adopt what may be called a 'culturally-situated' form of individualism, which allows us to explore the important role of cultural values in influencing national development prospects.[5]

Our account of liberal institutions and values is heavily influenced by Douglass North, F.A. Hayek and Elinor Ostrom. The insights of Douglass North are especially crucial because of the historical institutionalism he employed, where he showed how certain ideas can stand the test of time and influence economic performance far into the future, for better or for worse (see Galiani & Sened, 2014 for a comprehensive review of his legacy). His writings, with Barry Weingast (1989) also revealed the importance of liberal institutions of property rights and limitations on power to improvements in living standards in eighteenth-century England. Similarly, Hayek is also relevant to us because of his non-neoclassical, evolutionary defence of the market order, which is the approach we take in Chapter 3. Hayek's liberalism also allows us to defend the market order on culturally agnostic grounds—one that accepts value pluralism rather than a monistic social system, thus addressing the East Asian cultural challenge that we take seriously (see Chapter 6). Elinor Ostrom has significant contributions to institutional economics that we explain in Chapter 4. Her work encourages scholars to examine the rules in use, rather than the rules in form, and this opens us up to a range of property rights institutions, from state, to private, to communal to open access. We also draw on her vision of a polycentric social order and connect this to value pluralism—which is a novel defence of liberalism we present in Chap. 6.

The 'culturally-situated' individualism of North, Hayek and Ostrom also explains our emphasis on the role that institutional entrepreneurs play in reforming governance and the intellectual climate of opinion. Institutional entrepreneurs are individuals, organisations or coalitions that seek, advocate, and enact governance reforms and ideological change. Governance reforms include new policies, the reform or abolishment of existing government policies that may be harmful, as well as larger legal, political or constitutional rules that may hinder civil freedoms. Such reforms are at times coupled with ideological change, which is also crucial, since ideas (and not just random policies) have a life of their own and a deep effect

---

[4] The inter-connections and overlaps between all three of them are vast and interested parties should consult other sources to understand them better. We recommend the following accounts. Boettke, P. J., & Mitchell, M. D. (2017). *Applied Mainline Economics*. Mercatus Center. Aligica, P. D., Boettke, P. J., & Tarko, V. (2019). *Public governance and the classical-liberal perspective: Political economy foundations*. Oxford University Press.

[5] Notwithstanding internal differences, all three scholars generally do not subscribe to a hard form of methodological individualism and allow for an analysis of how social structures, cultures and belief systems influence individual preferences and decision-making. For example, Hayek's defence of the liberal order rests neither on the poles of methodological individualism or methodological holism, but on a middle way: a 'holistic individualism', as explained by Paul Lewis (2014).

on the course of history. Their role is especially felt in certain critical junctures of time, when political leadership plays a big role in setting the future course of society (Beaulier & Smith, 2015).

The role of institutional entrepreneurs has often been neglected in past development studies, as many of the well-intentioned governance reforms were often imposed without an appreciation of the local context and participation. Institutions and ideas cannot be easily engineered from afar but evolve gradually as people in their own communities press for change. Throughout this book therefore, we present original interviews, case studies and stories of agents of change and how they have helped to further human development.

We acknowledge that market liberalism subject to much criticism. In the context of development, it is said that a heavy reliance on markets may be unwise. There are various voices in this regard. Many economists emphasise the pervasiveness of market failures, which is supposedly worse in developing nations, and hence a need for active government intervention. Dependency theorists and Marxist-based theorists emphasise the exploitation of poor nations by rich countries or the exploitative effects of transnational capital. Critics of Washington Consensus policies also point to evidence that 'neoliberal reforms' have failed when they were applied by transitioning economies after the Cold War. We will in this book take these criticisms seriously and discuss them in the various chapters.

Structure of the Book

Some clarifications on our approach are in order. Our primary target audience is the intelligent lay reader, undergraduate and graduate students, and policymakers. As such, there will be little technical analysis of various growth models, which interested readers may find elsewhere. This is not to say that the quantitative analyses of growth in mainstream economics are unimportant, but that rather we choose to expand our inquiry to wider questions that are often obscured. We therefore adopt an interdisciplinary approach and focus on the 'big ideas' within development thinking, one that incorporates issues of culture, history, ethics, institutions and politics. Notably, such themes are often sidestepped in conventional mainstream economics, which is unfortunate for anyone interested in development, because these are important variables that affect a nation's progress (Boettke, 1994).

The limitation of a purely quantitative approach is that humanistic considerations that are crucial to any rich consideration of human flourishing are omitted (McCloskey, 2021; 2022; Smith & Wilson, 2019). Economics also cannot be divorced from politics, especially when we consider the intimate role that power exerts in determining economic outcomes (Ozanne, 2016). Many of these factors, culture, ethics, power and the like cannot be easily modelled within the confines of mainstream economics and requires a broader field of vision.

In this handbook, therefore, we approach development from the interdisciplinary lens of *political economy*, in terms of examining the interaction between states and markets in generating economic outcomes, and the effects of these shifting institutional boundaries. We place these issues within a wider context of *ethics*, where we consider what it means to live in a good society, one where the freedom and equality of individuals are respected. We premise our case on the belief that to live a full life requires protecting the rights of free and equal citizens under the rule of law.

We also provide a disclaimer that any handbook such as this will necessarily be incomplete, considering the voluminous literature on development, both past and present. There are understandably some concepts or ideas that will be omitted in this handbook. We provide references to both primary and secondary sources that the reader is fully encouraged to reflect on. In line with the spirit of good social science, we also encourage the reader to critically evaluate (and even disagree with) the arguments that we make.

Chapter 2 will start with a brief historical survey of key thinkers in the field of development economics. We start with the classical development economists of the twentieth century and proceed to explore the contributions of several contemporary thinkers on major development issues: Jeffrey Sachs, Amartya Sen, Robert Solow, and Paul Romer. This chapter also provides an interesting contrast between two 'anti-establishment' figures in the form of Peter Bauer and Ha-Joon Chang, who themselves occupy different ends of the debate over the merits of markets. Both individuals, despite their contrasting ideological perspectives, illustrate the importance of examining development from a perspective.

A political economy analysis will confront the central question on the proper role of state and markets in resource allocation and economic coordination. Crucially, state-market relations are also embedded within a wider web of institutional arrangements and cultural environment. The framework we adopt for the subsequent chapters is summarised by the phrases 'getting the prices right' (Ch 3), 'getting the institutions right' (Ch 4) and 'getting the culture right' (Ch 5), all of which if aligned produce positive development outcomes.[6]

We provide a liberal political economy answer to the central institutional question of 'what are the rules, norms and arrangements necessary for progress?'. To that question, we focus on the importance of markets, especially the institutions and values that sustain them. Crucially, in this handbook, we will also consider leading objections to markets in the development context, in order to provide nuance. For example, Chap. 3 will consider market failure theory and dependency theory. Chapter 6 will consider the tough challenge posed by the East Asian developmental state paradigm.

Accordingly, Chap. 3 will explore the nature of markets and its necessity in the context of development. We argue here that economic freedom is an essential requirement of any nation that wishes to achieve growth, and widely shared prosperity. We acknowledge that in the development establishment, pro-market reforms

---

[6] I wish to acknowledge that this helpful tri-fold classification is obtained from Peter Boettke et al. (2005).

have often been pursued by global organisations in a top-down manner without due regard for local knowledge. Through specific case studies and interviews conducted, we show how such reforms are best implemented in a bottom-up manner by local actors who provide crucial contextual knowledge. This chapter considers the criticisms of market failure theorists and dependency theorists against markets, more specifically neoclassical economics, and their relevance today. An alternative paradigm of understanding markets in the form of market process theory, best associated with the economist Israel Kirzner, is also introduced.

Chapter 4 will first provide a brief review of the field of institutional economics. It will show that there is much overlap between old and new institutional economics, and that the key distinguishing feature of this field is that it rejects the notion of the 'given individual' in mainstream economics and instead places a premium on the wider influences on human decision-making. Institutional economics is thus highly relevant to development studies in its interdisciplinary emphasis. Accordingly, the second part of the chapter focuses on the institutional regulation of markets, namely legal institutions that uphold the rule of law and property rights protections. Political economists have consistently stressed the way markets, and economic behaviour in general, are necessarily embedded in political, social and cultural institutions, which if neglected would render any analyses incomplete. We show that these legal institutions, which are the bedrock of any healthy market economy, are instrumental in facilitating productive wealth creation. We will also review past approaches to development pursued by international organisations, such as foreign aid and Washington Consensus policies, and show how a neglect of institutions hampered their effectiveness.

Chapter 5 will explore the importance of cultural values as a determinant of economic progress. Beginning with a discussion of the prominent cultural scholar Lawrence Harrison, we proceed to explore the specific cultural values that hinder or contribute to development, particularly focusing on individualism, and the extent to which commercial activities are socially honoured. The importance of culture is seen by the fact that many economic reforms of the past, while well-intentioned, did not succeed since they were foreign impositions, for example: many Washington Consensus policies failed because they were exogenously imposed (Boettke et al., 2008). Thus, a consideration on culture and values helps us understand why certain reforms succeed, and why others fail, and also helps us appreciate how local actors translate principles of development into successful and concrete programs on the ground.

We also present arguments from economic historians who documented the role that culture-as-ideas played in the historic development of Western societies, particularly how a mentality of innovation, improvement and market-tested betterment facilitated a Great Enrichment. We argue that a liberal, pro-enterprise culture is essential for economic development and helps hasten the process of building inclusive economic and political institutions. However, such a position must also be tempered, because culture-as-ideas are transmitted in specific times and places by cultural entrepreneurs, and the outcome of such transmission and cultural competition is fundamentally uncertain.

In these chapters, we also explore challenges to liberalism, such as dependency theory and market failure economics. In this post-Cold War era, the intellectual pendulum has swung back against market liberalism, especially after the Great Financial Crisis of 2008. Marxist-inspired theories of development remain popular, decades after dependency theory first came on the scene in the 1960s. The criticism against global capitalism continues to touch on the way capital exploits labour, siphons natural resources from the poor and concentrates wealth and power in economic elites (Ghosh, 2019; Patnaik & Patnaik, 2021). Recently, Western capitalism is also said to be founded on historic racism and systemic injustice. Less radical positions emphasise the imperfections of markets and thus the necessity of strong government intervention to create markets, regulate businesses or provide the basic conditions for development (Stiglitz & Greenwald, 2014).

Our general response to these criticisms is that markets are by no means perfect, especially if judged against a benchmark of efficiency as in neoclassical economics. Markets do fail and have also been rigged by political elites at the expense of others. Western history is not unblemished. We, however, argue that these imperfections notwithstanding, markets remain the best possible mode of economic organisation and is also one that is most consistent with human dignity. Our case studies will show how markets are not just Western constructions, but very much desired by local communities themselves in their search for better lives. We will show how liberal change agents in developing countries pursue market reforms and the widely shared prosperity that it fosters.

Chapter 6 will focus on the topic of state capacity and political leadership in the context of development. State capacity, understood as the existence of centralised political authority and the ability of said authority to enforce its will, levy taxes and provide public goods, is identified by many scholars to be crucial for development. Some also go one step further and insist that technocratic political leadership is also desirable. This argument says that astute and wise political leadership is sufficient for positive economic development, and how good institutions are merely secondary to and follow such leadership.

This perspective is one that resembles our belief in the importance of leadership but differs in its emphasis on state power in fostering development. In this view, it is strong, enlightened political leaders who lead their nations to prosperity, rather than those who pursue liberal ideas. The prime example often used here is that of Singapore, seen as a successful benevolent dictatorship and technocracy. We will also discuss the China model of state capitalism, which is also, notably, one that is largely inspired by the success story of Singapore (Ortmann & Thompson, 2014). These are two countries who on the surface seem to contradict our position, since they achieved economic growth while maintaining authoritarian and illiberal political institutions.

Our response is that strong, enlightened leaders can sometimes have a positive impact on society, but such power should also at the same time be constrained. State capacity is indeed an ingredient in development but must also be tempered by *state constraints*. These are constraints on the exercise of power and involve checks and balances and the rule of law. Civil society organisations and social movements therefore play an important role in acting as a bulwark against state power, through their political activism and challenges to state injustice. Additionally, state capacity itself does not exist in a vacuum, and often (as we will show through examples), the state gains such capacity through its collaborations with these civil society organisations, who provide relevant policy knowledge and advice to state officials.

Chapter 6 also seeks to address the East Asian cultural challenge, which challenges the universality of Western liberal democracy. In response, we draw insights from political philosophers who defend value pluralism and the literature on polycentric governance and show that ultimately, a liberal social order may be defended on culturally agnostic grounds. A social system that grounded on pluralism, rather than an agreement on moral truths, and one that affords a scope for decentralisation, best accommodates the great diversity of social life we see in today's world.

We conclude our book in the last chapter. This chapter will focus on the theory of institutional change, with a special emphasis on institutional evolution and how it is driven by local actors. Most institutionalists, while acknowledging that institutions matter, are at a loss of how to actually establish good institutions. The practical task of achieving good institutions is a challenge for both academic theoreticians and world organisations. Here, we suggest that community-based organisations and intellectual entrepreneurs are especially crucial in improving institutions by promoting new ideas and reforms. This book thus ends on an optimistic note by making a case that progress in institutional reform is very much alive and possible.

Discussion Questions

1. What is the difference, if any, between economic growth and economic development?
2. How important are material wealth and prosperity in living a good and full life?
3. To what extent has human history experienced progress (or regress) in the past few centuries?
4. In what ways are we living better lives than people of the past? And in what ways have life become worse?
5. What is the relationship, if any, between material aspects of development and non-material components such as equity, sustainability and justice?
6. What is the difference between proximate and fundamental causes of growth, and how do we distinguish them?

References

Acemoglu, D., & Johnson, S. (2005). Unbundling institutions. *Journal of Political Economy, 113*(5), 949–995. https://doi.org/10.1086/432166.

Acemoglu, D., & Robinson, J. (2012). *Why nations fail: The origins of power, prosperity, and poverty.* Crown Business.

Acemoglu, D., Johnson, S., & Robinson, J. A. (2002). Reversal of fortune: Geography and institutions in the making of the modern world income distribution. *The Quarterly Journal of Economics, 117*(4), 1231–1294.

Acemoglu, D., Johnson, S., & Robinson, J. A. (2005). Institutions as a Fundamental Cause of Long-Run Growth. In P. Aghion, & S. N. Durlauf (Eds.), *Handbook of economic growth* (Vol. 1, pp. 385–472). Elsevier.

Aghion, P., & Howitt, P. (1992). A Model of Growth Through Creative Destruction. *Econometrica, 60*(2), 323–351. https://doi.org/10.2307/2951599.

Aghion, P., & Howitt, P. W. (2008). *The economics of growth.* MIT Press.

Albert, G. P., Courtois, S., Werth, N., Paczkowski, A., Panné, J. L., Bartosek, K., & Margolin, J. L. (1999). *The Black book of communism: Crimes, Terror.* Repression.

Bardhan, P. (1990). Symposium on the state and economic development. *Journal of Economic Perspectives, 4*(3), 3–7.

Beaulier, S., & Smith, D. (2015). On your mark, get set, develop! In P. Boettke, & C. Coyne (Eds.), *Oxford handbook of Austrian economics.* Oxford University Press.

Bloom, D. E., Canning, D., & Sevilla, J. (2003). Geography and poverty traps. *Journal of Economic Growth, 8*(4), 355–378. https://doi.org/10.1023/A:1026294316581.

Bloom, D. E., Sachs, J. D., Collier, P., & Udry, C. (1998). Geography, demography, and economic growth in Africa. *Brookings Papers on Economic Activity, 2,* 207–295.

Boettke, P. J., Coyne, C. J., Leeson, P. T., & Sautet, F. (2005). The new comparative political economy. *The Review of Austrian Economics, 18*(3), 281–304. https://doi.org/10.1007/s11138-005-3113-0.

Bourne, R. (2019). *Is this time different? Schumpeter, the Tech Giants, and Monopoly Fatalism.* Cato Institute.https://www.cato.org/publications/policy-analysis/time-different-schumpeter-tech-giants-monopoly-fatalism.

Caballero, R. J. (2010). Creative destruction. In S. Durlauf & L. Blume (Eds), *Economic Growth* (pp. 24–29). Palgrave Macmillan. https://doi.org/10.1057/9780230280823_5.

Clemens, M. (2011). Economics and emigration: Trillion-dollar bills on the sidewalk? *Journal of Economic Perspectives, 25*(3), 83–106. https://doi.org/10.1257/jep.25.3.83.

Cypher, J., & Diaz, J. (2008). *The process of economic development.* Taylor and Francis.

Dasgupta, S., Laplante, B., Wang, H., & Wheeler, D. (2002). Confronting the environmental Kuznets curve. *Journal of economic perspectives, 16*(1), 147–168. https://doi.org/10.1257/089 5330027157.

Diamond, J. (1997). *Guns, germs, and steel.* Norton.

Fleck, R. K., & Hanssen, F. A. (2016). Environmental Policy for the Anthropocene: Information, Incentives, and Effective Institutions. In *Environmental Policy in the Anthropocene* (pp. 39–52). Property and Environment Research Center. https://www.perc.org/wp-content/uploads/2016/10/EnvironmentalPolicy_RFleckAHanssen.pdf.

Fukuyama, F., Richman, B., & Goel, A. (2021). How to save democracy from technology: ending big tech's information monopoly. *Foreign Aff., 100,* 98.

Fullman, N., Yearwood, J., Abay, S. M., Abbafati, C., Abd-Allah, F., Jemal Abdela, A. A., & Adeso, R. (2016). Measuring performance on the Healthcare Access and Quality Index for 195 countries and territories and selected subnational locations: A systematic analysis from the Global Burden of Disease Study 2016. *The Lancet.*

Gallup, J. L., Sachs, J. D., & Mellinger, A. D. (1999). Geography and economic development. *International Regional Science Review, 22*(2), 179–232. https://doi.org/10.3386/w6849.

Ghosh, B. N. (2019). *Dependency theory revisited.* Routledge.

Gifford, B. E. (2020). *What is mean world syndrome?*. Happiful.https://happiful.com/what-is-mean-world-syndrome/.

Hamilton, B., & Whalley, J. (1984). Efficiency and distributional implications of global restrictions on labour mobility. *Journal of Development Economics, 14*, 61–75. https://doi.org/10.1016/0304-3878(84)90043-9.

Harrison, L. (2006). *The Central Liberal Truth*. Oxford University Press.

Harvey, D. (2005). *Spaces of neoliberalization: towards a theory of uneven geographical development* (Vol. 8). Franz Steiner Verlag.

Hickel, J. (2020). The sustainable development index: Measuring the ecological efficiency of human development in the anthropocene. *Ecological Economics, 167*.

Hodgson, G. M. (2004). *The Evolution of Institutional Economics: Agency, Structure and Darwinism in American Institutionalism*. Routledge.

Hulme, M. (2021). *Climate Change*. Routledge.

Huggins, L. E. (2013). *Environmental Entrepreneurship: Markets Meet the Environment in Unexpected Places*. Edward Elgar Publishing.

Holcombe, R. (2006). *Entrepreneurship and economic progress*. Routledge.

Jackson, T. (2016). *Prosperity without Growth*. Routledge.

Kahn, M. E. (2021). *Adapting to Climate Change*. Yale University Press.

Kallis, G. (2017). *Degrowth (the economy key ideas)*. Agenda Publishing.

Khan, M. (2018). Oxfam: sex scandal or governance failure? *Lancet, 391*(10125), 1019–1020. Lancet. https://www.thelancet.com/journals/lancet/article/PIIS0140-6736(18)30476-8/fulltext.

Kharas, H., & Hamel, K. (2018, September 27). *A global tipping point: Half the world is now middle class or wealthier*. Brookings Institution. https://www.brookings.edu/blog/future-development/2018/09/27/a-global-tipping-point-half-the-world-is-now-middle-class-or-wealthier/.

Kogelmann, B. (2022). We Must Always Pursue Economic Growth. *Utilitas*, 1–15. https://doi.org/10.1017/S0953820822000358.

Kioes, G., & Pfeiffer, T. (2015). *Social Progress Index (SPI) Measuring more than just GDP*. Deloitte.

Keynes, John Maynard. (2010). Economic Possibilities for our Grandchildren. In L. Pecchi & G. Piga (Eds.), *Revisiting Keynes: Economic Possibilities for our Grandchildren* (pp. 17-26). MIT Press.

Landes, D. (1995). *The wealth and poverty of nations: Why some are so rich and some so poor* . Little, Brown.

Maddison Database. (2010). Maddison Historical Statistics. https://www.rug.nl/ggdc/historicaldevelopment/maddison/.

Mahler, D. G., Yonzan, N., Lakner, C., Aguilar, R. A., & Wu, H. (2021). *Updated estimates of the impact of COVID-19 on global poverty: Turning the corner on the pandemic in 2021?* World Bank Blogs. https://blogs.worldbank.org/opendata/updated-estimates-impact-covid-19-global-poverty-turning-corner-pandemic-2021.

McCloskey, D. N. (2021). *Bettering humanomics: A new, and old, approach to economic science*. University of Chicago Press.

McCloskey, D. N. (2019). *Why liberalism works: How true liberal values produce a freer, more equal*. Yale University Press.

Mokyr, J. (2016). *A culture of growth—the origins of the modern economy*. Princeton University Press.

Mougel, N. (2011). *World war i casualties*. Reperes.

Murphy, K. M., Shleifer, A., & Vishny, R. W. (1989). Industrialization and the Big Push. *Journal of Political Economy, 97*(5), 1003–1026.

Nordhaus, W. D. (2004). Schumpeterian profits in the American economy: Theory and measurement. *National Bureau of Economic Research*. https://doi.org/10.3386/w10433.

Office of the Historian. (2017). *Protectionism in the interwar period*. Office of the Historian, United States of America. https://history.state.gov/milestones/1921-1936/protectionism.

Ostrom, E. (2012). Nested externalities and polycentric institutions: must we wait for global solutions to climate change before taking actions at other scales?. *Economic theory, 49*(2), 353–369. https://doi.org/10.1007/s00199-010-0558-6.

Ozanne, A. (2016). *Power and neoclassical economics: A return to political economy in the teaching of economics.* Springer.

Panagariya, A. (2019). *Free trade and prosperity: how openness helps developing countries grow richer and combat poverty.* Oxford University Press.

Patnaik, P., & Patnaik, U. (2021). *Capital and imperialism: Theory, history, and the present.* Monthly Review Press.

Paul, A. (2020). *Holocaust memorial day 2020: What is it and how many lives have been lost to genocide?* Metro.https://metro.co.uk/2020/01/27/holocaust-memorial-day-2020-many-deaths-genocide-12125183/.

Pennington, M. (2008). Classical liberalism and ecological rationality: The case for polycentric environmental law. *Environmental Politics, 17*(3), 431–448. https://doi.org/10.1080/096440108 02055659.

Pinker, S. (2018). *The media exaggerates negative news: This distortion has consequences.* The Guardian. https://www.theguardian.com/commentisfree/2018/feb/17/steven-pinker-media-negative-news.

Ravallion, M. (2015). The economics of poverty: History, measurement, and policy. Oxford University Press.

Rodrik, D. (2006). Goodbye Washington consensus, hello Washington confusion? A review of the World Bank's economic growth in the 1990s: Learning from a decade of reform. *Journal of Economic Literature, 44*(4), 973–987. https://doi.org/10.1257/jel.44.4.973.

Rodrik, D., Subramanian, A., & Trebbi, F. (2004). Institutions rule: The primacy of institutions over geography and integration in economic development. *Journal of Economic Growth, 9*(2), 131–165. https://doi.org/10.1023/B:JOEG.0000031425.72248.85.

Romer, P. (1994). The origins of endogenous growth. *Journal of Economic Perspectives, 8*, 3–22. https://doi.org/10.1257/jep.8.1.3.

Rosenstein-Rodan, P. N. (1943). Problems of industrialisation of eastern and south-eastern Europe. *The Economic Journal, 53*(210/211), 202–211. https://doi.org/10.2307/2226317.

Roser, M. (2013). *Economic growth.* Our World in Data. https://ourworldindata.org/economic-growth.

Roser, M., & Ortiz-Ospina, E. (2016). *Global education.* Our World in Data. https://ourworldindata.org/global-education#citation.

Roser, M., & Ritchie, H. (2013a). *Food supply.* Our World in Data. https://ourworldindata.org/food-supply.

Roser, M., & Ritchie, H. (2013b). *Technological progress.* Our World in Data. https://ourworldindata.org/technological-progress#exponential-technological-progress-goes-with-exponential-decreases-in-costs.

Roser, M., Ortiz-Ospin, E., & Ritchie, H. (2019). *Life Expectancy.* Our World in Data. https://ourworldindata.org/life-expectancy.

Rostow, W. (1960). *The stages of economic growth: A non-communist manifesto.* Cambridge University Press.

Rummel, R. J. (1997). *Death by government.* Transaction Publishers.

Sachs, J., Warner, A., Åslund, A., & Fischer, S. (1995). Economic reform and the process of global integration. *Brookings Papers on Economic Activity, 1*, 1–118.

Schmidtz, D., & Shahar, D. C. (2019). *Environmental ethics: what really matters, what really works.* Oxford University Press.

Schumpeter, J. (1942). *Capitalism, socialism, and democracy* (3rd ed.). Harper and Brothers.

Semuels, A. (2016). *Does the economy really need to keep growing quite so much?* The Atlantic. https://www.theatlantic.com/business/archive/2016/11/economic-growth/506423/.

Shirley, M. (2005). Institutions and Development. In C. Menard & M. Shirley (Eds.), *Handbook of new institutional economics* (pp. 611–638). Springer.

Sterner, T., Barbier, E.B., Bateman, I. et al. Policy design for the Anthropocene. *Nat Sustain* 2, 14–21 (2019). https://doi.org/10.1038/s41893-018-0194-x.

Stiglitz, J., Sen, A., & Fitoussi, J.-P. (2009). *Report by the Commission on the Measurement of Economic Performance and Social Progress.* European Commission.

Stiglitz, J., & Greenwald, B. (2014). *Creating a learning society: A new approach to growth, development, and social progress.* Columbia University Press.

Symons, J. (2019). *Ecomodernism: technology, politics and the climate crisis.* Polity Press.

Turnheim, B., Kivimaa, P., & Berkhout, F. (Eds.). (2018). *Innovating climate governance: moving beyond experiments.* Cambridge University Press.

The World Bank. (2019). *Yes, Global Inequality Has Fallen. No, We Shouldn't Be Complacent.* World Bank. https://www.worldbank.org/en/news/feature/2019/10/23/yes-global-inequality-has-fallen-no-we-shouldnt-be-complacent.

The World Bank. (2020). *Poverty and shared prosperity 2020: Reversals of fortune.* The World Bank.

UNCTAD. (2022). *Global trade hits record high of $28.5 trillion in 2021, but likely to be subdued in 2022.* UNCTAD. https://unctad.org/news/global-trade-hits-record-high-285-trillion-2021-likely-be-subdued-2022.

Unicef. (2020). *Households.* JMP Global Database, World Health Organisation. https://washdata.org/data/household.

Victor, P. A. (2019). *Managing without growth : slower by design, not disaster.* Edward Elgar Publishing.

Wendling, Z. A., Emerson, J. W., Sherbinin, A. D., & Esty, D. C. (2020). *Environmental performance index 2020.* Yale Center for Environmental Law & Policy.

Williamson, J. (2009). A short history of the Washington consensus. *Law & Business Review American, 15*(7).

World Bank. (2020). World Development Indicators. World Bank. https://datacatalog.worldbank.org/search/dataset/0037712/World-Development-Indicators.

Yandle, B., Vijayaraghavan, M., & Bhattarai, M. (2002). The environmental Kuznets curve. *A Primer, PERC Research Study*, 2(1). Property and Environment Research Center. https://www.perc.org/wp-content/uploads/2018/05/environmental-kuznets-curve-primer.pdf.

Zingales, L. (2014). *A capitalism for the people: Recapturing the lost genius of American prosperity.* Basic books.

A Brief History of Modern Development Thinking

2

The purpose of this chapter is to provide a brief historical overview of the field of development economics, through an analysis of key development thinkers. It should be noted at the outset that the field of development economics, as with most other fields, defies easy categorisation. We are also unable to provide a comprehensive review of every school of thought in development economics, which is highly varied, ranging from classical development economics, structural change theories, Marxist and dependency theories, neoclassical and Washington Consensus, and institutionalist theories (see Dutt & Ros, 2008).

Our chapter here focuses on three groups. We first focus on the early classical development economists of the mid-twentieth century, which include figures like Paul Rosenstein-Rodan, Ragnar Nurkse, Albert Hirschman and Arthur Lewis, and their emphasis on capital accumulation, increasing returns to scale and big-push industrialisation. Classical development economics is worth exploring, considering its significant historical influence. Additionally, these classical theories, being wedded to a 'market failure paradigm', put a high premium on government activism in the development process, which, as the following chapters will show, has problematic implications.

After which, we also explore other major development economics in the postwar era who have shaped development theory and practice in various ways, from neoclassical growth theory of Robert Solow to Jeffrey Sach's far-reaching impact on actual development aid practices, to Amartya Sen's political economy analysis of freedom in development. Third, we explore two interesting scholars who very much 'rebelled' against the conventional wisdom, albeit for very different reasons: Peter Bauer and Ha-Joon Chang. Both individuals rejected the development orthodoxy but arrived at different conclusions on the proper role of the state in development policy, which illustrates the ongoing relevance of this question that we will return to in subsequent chapters.

© The Author(s), under exclusive license to Springer Nature Singapore Pte Ltd. 2023
B. Cheang and T. G. Palmer, *Institutions and Economic Development*,
Classroom Companion: Economics, https://doi.org/10.1007/978-981-99-0844-8_2

Classical Development Economics

Development economics as we know it today was very much shaped by several scholars in the mid-twentieth century, which include key figures like Paul Rosenstein-Rodan, Hans Singer, Ragnar Nurkse, Albert Hirschman and Arthur Lewis. Central to their approach to development is the belief that poor nations could find themselves stuck in sub-optimal equilibria, depending on initial conditions, and which require a 'big-push', often involving state-led industrialisation (Krugman, 1992). Classical development thinkers like them often rely on the concepts of 'increasing returns to scale' and the problem of 'surplus labour' to explain the problems of under-development and the ingredients needed to reverse it (Ros, 2008). The problem of under-development typically stems from the fact that poor nations are stuck in low-productivity and labour-intensive sectors, and once certain conditions are achieved and a 'critical threshold' was passed, a virtuous cycle of development may be kick-started and sustained.

In the latter half of the twentieth century, classical development economics is said to have given way to other schools of thought. Paul Krugman (1994) explained that the rise of technical modelling in economics displaced this earlier classical influence. Others, however, have lamented the rise of Washington Consensus and neoliberal theories as the culprit for this decline and insist that in fact, liberal theorists like Adam Smith had recommended state-led industrialisation just like classical development economists did (see Kattel et al., 2016). Subsequent chapters will further elucidate the role that markets, in our opinion, play in the development process, but at this point we turn to understand these classical scholars and their contributions.

Paul Rosenstein-Rodan (1902–1985)

Paul Rosenstein-Rodan was a Polish economist who emigrated to Britain in 1930. His writings on development issues significantly contributed to the rise of the discipline of development economics following World War II.

He is best known for his 1943 article which originated the 'Big-Push' theory of development (see Rosenstein-Rodan, 1943). This model argues that large-scale investment programs are needed to jumpstart industrial development in poor countries, as opposed to what he called a wasteful 'bit-by-bit' approach to investment. Just as an airplane taking off needs to hit a certain critical groundspeed, a developing country needs to achieve a 'critical mass' of investment in order to experience an economic take-off (Rosenstein-Rodan, 1961). This big-push model has since been developed by other economists (see Murphy et al., 1989).

The need for this big-push is in turn related to the concept of 'external economies of scale', also called 'pecuniary externalities'. This can be understood through the following scenario: the growth in scale of a certain firm (or industry) also contributes to the growth of other related industries. The growth of Silicon Valley, for instance, is intimately connected with the rise of a whole variety of service and tech-intensive firms in the wider ecosystem of California. According to economic theory, to achieve external economies of scale, an industry needs to acquire a certain minimum scale in order for the cost savings to be enjoyed by other industries and firms (due to the presence of 'indivisibilities' in production). When an industry grows in size, individual firms within it benefit from lower costs (agglomeration) and also generate improvements in human capital—all of which are spillover effects.

Infrastructure projects are especially subject to indivisibilities. Infrastructure, like highways, roads, flood control systems, telecommunications networks, typically involves high initial capital outlays, a long gestation period and a minimum scale for it to actually have an impact. A railroad servicing only a narrow slice of the country defeats the purpose of transport infrastructure; it is only when the rail infrastructure connects various significant points of a country will its true benefits be unlocked.

Accordingly, the required investments necessary to jumpstart development will be underestimated by the private sector, as the market would fail to account for the abovementioned externalities. Firms are also oriented around a short time horizon and will not undertake the necessary long-term investments in infrastructure, what he called 'social overhead capital'. Therefore, the role of the state is necessary in catalysing the 'big-push', to get the airplane of development off the ground.

The interconnectedness of firms and industries also relates to his belief in a 'balanced theory of growth' (see also 'Ragnar Nurkse'). A firm may be a supplier or a client of another firm. Rosenstein-Rodan used the following illustration: if there were some new shoe factories being built, there would be an increased production of shoes and higher incomes for the factory workers, but for development to take place, these shoe factories also needed customers and its workers need an outlet for their wages to be spent. These complementarities mean that the government's development planning should be balanced across various industries, especially consumer goods industries.

There are of course limitations of this big-push theory of development. The first is that it has a bias towards industrialisation, which must be tempered by the realisation that many developing countries remain wedded to agricultural sectors. Development may not always necessitate a focus on industrial sectors to the exclusion of others. Roseinstein-Rodan's emphasis on large-scale breakthroughs in the development process, however, seems to have pre-empted East Asia's rapid and sudden take-off, which many have attributed to state-led industrial policy (Sauer et al., 2003). However, state-led industrialisation may also lead to problems of over-investment, miscoordination, and wastage of resources, as seen in the former Soviet Union. This is in our opinion one of the chief weaknesses of this approach, which is that it assumes too much state capacity in developing countries which is typically absent, and the necessary institutions for judicious investments to be made.

Ragnar Nurkse (1907–1959)

Ragnar Nurkse was an influential Estonian development economist of the twentieth century and contributed significantly to the big-push and balanced theory of growth that is also associated with Paul Rosenstein-Rodan.

Central to this balanced theory of growth is the idea that poor countries need to achieve a certain 'critical mass' in order for the development process to be jumpstarted (see Nurkse, 1970). Once this process has commenced, there will be increasing returns to scale, which is a positive feedback process that generates yet further returns, in this case development benefits. The problem that developing countries face is that they are stuck in a 'poverty trap' and have not managed to achieve this critical threshold.

Poor nations are stuck in this trap for many reasons, but a significant one for Nurkse is the fact that they have a small market size. This is a 'vicious cycle', which can be understood with a simple observation: people in poor countries have low incomes, and if this is so, there is low purchasing power and thus a small size of the market. If the market is small, then there is a lack of propensity for firms to invest (and a limited pool of savings from which investments may be made), which in turn leads to low level of capital goods and low productivity. How then can poor nations have higher incomes if they lack productivity? This is a dilemma that poor nations need to break out of.

Just like Paul Rosenstein-Rodan suggested, Nurkse (1970) believed in the need for a 'big-push', state-led investment program to break this cycle. Through large-scale investments into various industries (balanced growth), the size of the market thereby expands. With higher incomes generated, capital investments are then induced and productivity grows; the vicious cycle above is replaced by a positive 'virtuous' cycle of growth.

Importantly, the need for government intervention here is once again understood in reference to market failure. In a poor country with a small size of the market, it is unsurprising that firms are either unable or unwilling to make the necessary investments. This is a gap that governments must fill, in order to break poor nations out of a sub-optimal equilibrium they find themselves in. The contributions of classical development economists like Paul Rosenstein-Rodan and Ragnar Nurkse, among others, thus help us understand the push towards massive foreign aid programs in the post-World War II period, where funds were channelled into poor countries in hopes of catalysing development (Snowdon, 2009). Interestingly, however, Nurkse (1957) did paint a pessimistic picture about the efficacy of foreign aid programs, believing that 'domestic effort is always the first prerequisite. Without it even the most lavish foreign aid could not achieve economic development'.

Once again, this model assumes that central planners either possess the necessary incentives or knowledge to correctly make the investments into simultaneous industries to catalyse growth (see Beaulier & Subrick, 2006a, 2006b). Many times, state predation is itself a barrier to growth in poor countries and needs to be corrected. Nurkse also strongly opposed export-led growth, believing that balance of payments problems would arise, or that foreign investors or countries would exploit the nation's resources. Additionally, the fact that developing nations typically specialise in agricultural goods or primary commodities means that a reliance on such exports preclude the necessary capital investments needed to break the economy out of the poverty trap. Evidently, the fact that many countries did rely on export-led growth, especially export-oriented industrialisation in the late twentieth century, provides some reason to cast doubt on his pessimism towards exports.

Albert Hirschman (1915–2012)

Albert Hirschman was an influential thinker of the twentieth century who contributed to fields ranging from development economics, political economy and political theory.

His contributions to development economics are based on his conceptualisation of an 'unbalanced theory of growth', contra that of Paul Rosenstein-Rodan and Ragnar Nurkse. Hirschman believed that it was often unrealistic to expect developing countries to muster the large-scale simultaneous investments advocated by balanced theories of growth. After all, poor countries lack the resources in the first place: 'if a country were ready to apply the doctrine of balanced growth, then it would not be underdeveloped in the first place' (Hirschman, 1958, p. 53). Unbalanced growth theory was also advocated by others such as Hans Singer, Paul Streetan and another more prominently, Walt Rostow, proponent of the 'stages of growth' approach to development.

Key to understanding Hirschman's theory, best articulated in his seminal 1958 book, is to disaggregate investments into two classes: investments into 'socially overhead capital' ('SOC', or also called divergent series of investment), which essentially refers to infrastructure like telecommunications, railways and health care, and investments into 'directly productive activities' ('DPA', or also called convergent series of investment), which unlike the first category, lead directly to an increase in goods and services for consumption. Due to a paucity of resources, investments should be targeted, considering that investments into SOC will lead to an automatic inducement in DPA investments and vice versa. Let's use an analogy: if investment in electricity and power generation is made (SOC), then this would automatically induce capital investments in power-intensive industries (DPA), such as manufacturing. Hence, investment spending need not be simultaneous and total, but be strategic, since investment projects possess complementaries that affect one another.

Another concept that explains such complementarities is Hirschman's distinction between 'backward linkages' and 'forward linkages'. Backward linkages occur when an investment into an industry or firm induces investments into earlier stages of production; for example, the growth of electric vehicles today has also stimulated the growth of lithium ion batteries needed to power these vehicles. Forward linkages, by contrast, occur when an investment project induces investment in later stages of production. The existence for such linkages means that development policy should be strategically focused on 'leading sectors', identifying projects which have the greatest sum total of linkages.

Hirschman's contribution here is significant, because it contributes to present-day discussions on industrial policy, where the state seeks to target investments into strategic sectors with the most knock-on benefits. Theories of the entrepreneurial state and industrial policymaking today therefore owe some intellectual debt to the theory of unbalanced growth (see Oqubay, 2015; Andreoni & Chang, 2016). However, one problem with Hirschman's account is the difficulty of the government to identify the specific investment path that would yield the greatest linkages or the ideal sequencing of investment projects. Hirschman did express a preference for an 'unbalancing' with SOC, i.e. emphasis on public investment in infrastructure before that in directly productive activities. But this also raises the important question of how the state is expected to invest suitably in the right infrastructure, and do so in a cost-effective manner, which is a task that many developing nations have faced.

Arthur Lewis (1915–1991)

Arthur Lewis was an influential British economist who won the Nobel Prize in Economics in 1979. His career spanned several decades over a number of leading institutions such as London School of Economics and Princeton University.

Lewis developed a 'dual sector' model, in an attempt to explain the persistence of under-development in some countries, relying on the concept of surplus labour. According to Lewis (1954), workers in poor countries are largely found in the low-productivity, traditional and labour-intensive agricultural sector, and the fact that there is an excess supply of such workers prolongs under-development. These workers are understandably attracted by higher wages in the capital-intensive modern sectors, which usually are found in urban centres. The movements of such workers into higher productivity growth sectors keep wages low, up until the point where such surplus labour is exhausted and fully absorbed by the modern sector.

Why is there excess labour in the primary sector in the first place? Importantly, these sectors, which are mainly agricultural, rely on labour-intensive processes, whose productivity is subject to diminishing marginal returns. These agricultural workers do not enjoy the benefit of capital machinery, and their productivity is constrained by the fixed nature of the land they work on. At a certain point therefore, there are a certain proportion of workers in these industries who are not contributing to the total output, which has reached its limit. They are the excess labour that will gradually move into the modern sector.

As excess labour moves into the modern sector, wages are initially depressed, but will increase over time as capital accumulation takes place. The profits in modern sectors are usually reinvested into capital, and subsequent rounds of such investment will gradually raise the marginal product of labour in these industries, thus improving their wages and general welfare. This transition process continues till the point where the excess supply of labour is fully absorbed, and when the wage rates between both sectors are equalised.

The benefit of Lewis' model is to point attention to the existence of these dual sectors in poor countries, and how historically, development has indeed seen a greater reliance towards capital-intensive industrialisation. It has been said that China's industrialisation, and that of many Asian countries in the twentieth century, saw a move away from subsistence agriculture, towards manufacturing and industrial activities, a testament to the Lewis model (Islam & Yokota, 2008; Whitehead, 2005). His model has also been criticised on several grounds, first in terms of its 'broad-brush' nature and unclear policy prescriptions, and second in terms of its failure to explain why capital investments are not exclusive to large industrialists, but also features of small entrepreneurs, migrants and even agriculturalists themselves (see Bauer, 1956). Arthur Lewis, just like many other classical development economists, also did envision an active role for government to stimulate entrepreneurship and industrialisation (1954, p. 199, 349), an assumption we wish to challenge in following chapters from a political economy perspective.

Walt Rostow (1916–2003)

Walt Whitman Rostow was an influential American economist and who advised several post-war administrations, namely John F Kennedy and Lyndon Johnson. We acknowledge that he is not typically considered within the family of classical development economists (explored above), but arguably, his concepts of economic take-off, in our opinion, resemble the notions of 'critical mass' and 'scale economies' that they relied on.

In the context of development studies, Rostow (1960) is most well known for his 'stages of growth' theory (also called modernisation theory), which posits that a developing country undergoes modernisation in five stages: traditional society, preconditions for take-off, economic take-off, a maturing stage, and the stage of mass consumption. Significantly, this book was written in the early years of the Cold War and served as a blueprint for America's anti-communist efforts in the developing world.

According to modernisation theory, many countries at the time (and still today) are stuck in the first two stages and thus need to move up. Traditional societies are those with a high reliance on subsistence agriculture, and therefore, a low level of material production. There is limited use of technology and a lack of centralised political authority responsible for the investment of public goods. Importantly, power is concentrated in the hands of feudalistic landowners rather than any kind of centralised nation state. Some nations may manage to move out of this stage and enjoy the preconditions for economic take-off: there is an increasing shift towards industrial activities away from agrarianism, increasing trade and division of labour, and increasing investments. An important precondition for take-off is a shift away from traditional mindsets, to a modern one that embraces science, rationality, risk-taking, and enterprise.

Economic take-off is the third important stage in Rostow's account and is best exemplified by Britain's industrial revolution in the eighteenth century, and which many other Western nations have undergone since then. In this stage, not only has industrialisation occurred, there is an increasing use of technology and urbanisation in society. In the cultural and political sphere, a developed country is also one with a modern political system with a rational bureaucracy, and where people in society secure power through open means of competition rather than through the acquisition of privileges as in ages past.

Beyond this third stage, there is then a 'drive to maturity', where the use of modern technology is now widespread across economic activities. There is also economic diversification, where a wide range of industries form and creative destruction sets in. The economy starts to acquire a strong presence in the international economy. Additionally, a wide swathe of the population experiences a clear improvement in transportation and modern infrastructure. This then culminates in the last stage which is the 'age of mass consumption'. As the name suggests, people in society enjoy mass consumption of goods and services, especially luxuries previously unaffordable. Since the satisfaction of material wants is no longer a pressing concern, people start focusing on post-material goals, such as equity, sustainability and various forms of self-actualisation and cultural gratification.

Rostow not only provided the abovementioned roadmap for development, but was interested in the policy implications: what could government do to encourage modernisation? This was especially crucial to prevent developing nations from falling to communism and thus out of the American sphere of influence. In a striking resemblance of the earlier big-push theories, Rostow's writings contributed to the rise of official development assistance (i.e. foreign aid) by the Western world (Pearce, 2001). Massive amounts of foreign aid have been provided by the West to lift poor nations out of poverty, but also with a political motive in mind of establishing influence in sensitive regions.

What is especially valuable is that Rostow seems to have provided a very useful classification that distinguishes the state of developed and underdeveloped countries. Indeed, many countries today, since Rostow's publication of the book, have experienced rapid economic take-off and today are either in a mature stage of enjoying mass consumption. East Asia, for example, is arguably in the later stages of Rostow's account, with many of them becoming trade powerhouses in their own right, and contributing significantly to world culture.

This theory understandably has its share of criticisms. First, it seems to posit a linear path to development from traditional societies all the way to the age of mass consumption. This fails to recognise that some nations may revert to earlier stages, and the growth process may not be as self-sustaining as Rostow envisioned. It is said, for example, that Argentina's growth spurt in the early twentieth century was negated by negative growth in the later decades, culminating in its disastrous 2001 debt crisis (Todaro & Smith, 2020, pp. 143–144). Additionally, Rostow is also criticised for being ethnocentric, assuming that the Western model of development is necessarily the ideal for poor nations. Some traditional societies may reject materialistic mass consumption, and indeed, many have happily pursued alternative development of their own. Authoritarian development (as in the case of China and Singapore) is also a challenge to Rostow; these countries have rejected Western liberalism but managed to achieve economic take-off. This raises the question: must development necessitate Western modernisation?

For us, a significant issue with Rostow's stages of growth theory is that despite its many advantages, it may not be adequate in providing specific policy advice. How may countries actually move from one stage to another? Historically, as abovementioned, Rostow's stages of growth theory have validated massive foreign aid programs to poor countries, but as this study has explained, such programs have been subject to many problems and often done more harm than good.

Rostow's theory may also be fruitfully contrasted with the writings of economic historian Alexander Gershenkron, who is known for his discussions of industrialisation *in the context of economic backwardness.* Unlike Rostow, Gershenkron did not believe that modern economic growth—which involves industrialisation—proceeded in linear stages and in fact varied from country to country. The specific trajectory and nature of such growth depended in part on the degree of 'economic backwardness' the country finds itself in relation to already-industrialised nations (Gershenkron, 1962). He believed that the more backward a nation is, the greater its political impetus would be to close this gap, and also its ability to learn from frontrunners. In this way, Gershenkron helps us understand the 'latecomer effect', why later-industrialising nations underwent a much faster process of growth than earlier ones, and how they often borrowed technology in the process. His value is also much more methodological and points to the importance of temporal sequencing in history: 'every historical event that takes place changes the course of all subsequent events' (Gershenkron, 1962, p. 41).

Importantly, Gershenkron's theory has political economy implications: the more backward a nation, the greater the need for the state to compensate for the country's lack of 'pre-requisites' for industrial development. While Great Britain could industrialise in a relatively free market manner, later European powers like France and Germany and Russia would need more active interventions to achieve the same outcome. Understandably, theorists of the interventionist East Asian model have drawn from Gershenkron's thesis (see Chang, 2019). If this is true, does this mean that African nations today, who are least developed, would require a strong dose of intervention to achieve development?

Contemporary Development Economics

We now turn to more contemporary figures in development economics. Admittedly, this selection here is limited and cannot do justice to the wide range of work currently being done today. However, we wanted to focus on several features of development thinking today: the reliance on neoclassical growth accounting, human capital, foreign aid as a development practice, as well as the importance of non-material objectives as ends of development—concepts that the following four figures are instrumental in championing.

Neoclassical Growth Theory and Robert Solow

Robert Solow is an influential American economist with significant contributions to development economics. He has been widely celebrated and is the recipient of the John Bates Clark Medal, the Presidential Medal of Freedom and the Nobel Prize in Economics.

Solow's central contribution is what is called the neoclassical growth model, which was also independently discovered by Trevor Swan and thus called the Solow-Swan model (see Solow, 1956). Mainstream development economics today is deeply shaped by this model and is thus worth our attention. Its ability to predict gross domestic product, or output, with realistic assumptions is responsible for its canonisation in modern economics.

Solow's growth model can be understood with reference to an earlier variant called the Harrod-Domar growth model, which formulates a relationship between a country's rate of economic growth as a function of the national savings and the nation's capital-output ratio: $\frac{\dot{Y}}{Y} = s/c$. (see Harrod 1939; Domar, 1946). This means that a country's growth rate is positively associated with savings (the more people save, the faster GDP will grow) and also inversely with the capital ratio (the more capital efficient a nation is, the lower the 'c', and the faster GDP will grow).

This is a useful theory that captures the widely shared intuition that savings and capital investment contribute to growth. Logically, if the constraint on development is low capital formation, then massive foreign aid injections are justified. The Harrod-Domar thus contributes to the capital fundamentalism that is dominant in post-war development thinking (see Easterly, 1999; Nugent & Yotopoulos, 1976).

The Solow Model develops the model beyond just capital and saving, using the Cobb–Douglas production function:

$$Y = K^{\alpha}(AL)^{1-\alpha}$$

where Y is national income, K is capital, A is productivity, L is labour and α is the capital elasticity of output. This has several intuitive properties, most notably constant returns to scale—doubling the stock of both capital and labour would double output—and diminishing marginal returns from all factor inputs. We will make some additional assumptions:

$$\dot{K} = sY - \delta K$$

$$\frac{\dot{A}}{A} = g$$

$$\frac{\dot{L}}{L} = n$$

$$Y = C + I$$

Intuitively, these are that our capital stock suffers a constant rate of depreciation δ, a constant proportion of output s is saved, productivity grows at a constant rate g, labor supply increases at a constant rate n and our economy neither trades nor has a government so the sum of consumption C and investment I is national income Y. Importantly, for the purposes of calculating per capita income, we implicitly assume the number of hours of labour each agent supplies remains constant with respect to time and that n strictly reflects the growth of the number of agents in our economy.

We wish to find if there is an equilibrium growth rate under the model. To do this, we take the logarithm of both sides and differentiate:

$$ln(Y) = \alpha ln(K) + (1 - \alpha)ln(AL)$$

$$\Rightarrow \frac{\dot{Y}}{Y} = \alpha \frac{\dot{K}}{K} + (1 - \alpha)\frac{\dot{A}}{A} + (1 - \alpha)\frac{\dot{L}}{L}$$

$$\Rightarrow \frac{\dot{Y}}{Y} = \alpha \frac{\dot{K}}{K} + (1 - \alpha)(g + n)$$

Therefore, as α, g and n are constant by assumption, if the rate of growth of income is constant, the rate of growth of capital must also be constant. We can again exploit this by differentiating:

$$\frac{\dot{K}}{K} = \frac{sY - \delta K}{K} = s\frac{Y}{K} - \delta$$

$$\Rightarrow s\frac{\dot{Y}K - Y\dot{K}}{K^2} = 0$$

$$\Rightarrow \frac{\dot{Y}}{Y} = \frac{\dot{K}}{K} = g_Y$$

Therefore, if our rate of growth of income is constant, it must be equal to the rate of growth of capital, denoted g_Y. We can find the value of g_Y by substituting into our earlier equation:

$$g_Y = \alpha g_Y + (1 - \alpha)(g + n)$$
$$g_Y = g + n$$

And per capita income growth g_y follows from this as our functions are exponential:

$$g_y = g_Y - \frac{\dot{L}}{L} = g + n - n = g$$

As g is likely to be roughly constant between countries, as research and development is in the long run a public good, even if in the short term patents and difficulties of imitation make it a club good, once countries have overcome any initial shortage of capital they should be expected to converge to the same growth rate, ceteris paribus, in a phenomenon known as 'conditional convergence'. Although countries can experience 'catch-up' growth in the short-run and thus achieve higher rates than g, as occurred for the East Asian Tigers of Singapore, Hong Kong, Taiwan and South Korea, in the long run they are restricted to 'cutting-edge' growth and thus now have similar rates of growth to the United States that they were once predicted to surpass.

Additionally, the result that long-run growth in our economy *only* depends on g implies the high importance of technology and ideas in enabling the economy to continue to grow. Since nations will conditionally converge on a steady state, it is differences in technology, ideas and productivity that explains much of the divergence in growth rates between countries. His early article observes that more than half of the increases in American national income are not due to capital and labour but driven by the exogenous residual representing technological innovation (Solow, 1957). Since then, development policy has increasingly channelled funds towards research and development and innovation activities.

But will our economy stay on the balanced growth path? Although we have shown that a constant growth rate in per capita income must necessarily be g, could we achieve an ever-increasing rate of growth by setting s to a high level? The key insight of the Solow model, explaining its enduring popularity, is no. To prove this, we define a variable, $\tilde{k}$, that is constant along the balanced growth path:

$$\tilde{k} = \frac{K}{AL}$$

which is constant as:

$$\frac{\dot{K}}{K} = g + n = \frac{\dot{A}}{A} + \frac{\dot{L}}{L}$$

Along the balanced growth path. We can differentiate with respect to time to find that:

$$\dot{\tilde{k}} = \frac{\dot{K}AL - K\dot{A}L - KA\dot{L}}{(AL)^2}$$

$$= \frac{\dot{K}}{AL} - \frac{K}{AL}\frac{\dot{A}}{A} - \frac{K}{AL}\frac{\dot{L}}{L}$$

$$= \frac{sY - \delta K}{AL} - g\tilde{k} - n\tilde{k}$$

$$= \frac{sK^{\alpha}(AL)^{1-\alpha}}{AL} - \tilde{k}(\delta + g + n)$$

$$= \frac{sK^{\alpha}}{(AL)^{\alpha}} - \tilde{k}(\delta + g + n)$$

$$= s\tilde{k}^{\alpha} - \tilde{k}(\delta + g + n)$$

which is always true, not merely along the balanced growth path. This differential equation has no analytical solution: however, we can discern that it is globally stable as $0 < \alpha < 1$, meaning savings per worker increase less than linearly while required investment increases linearly, so, since, by assumption, s, δ, g and n are constant over time, there will exist a steady state where $\dot{\tilde{k}}$ is zero and $\tilde{k}$ is thus constant. This can be shown graphically:

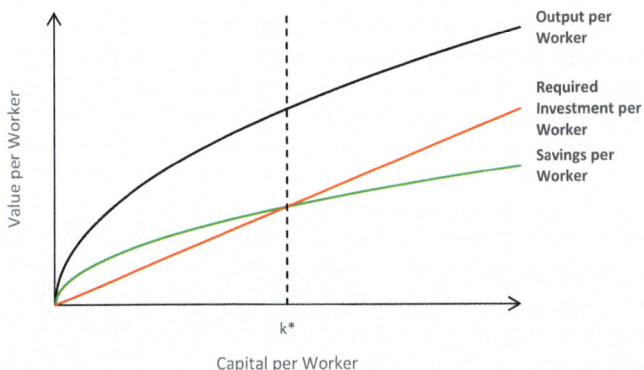

In this steady state, we can solve for $\tilde{k}$:

$$\tilde{k} = \left[\frac{s}{\delta + g + n} \right]^{\frac{1}{1-\alpha}}$$

Using the definition of $\tilde{k}$, we can find an expression for capital:

$$K = AL \left[\frac{s}{\delta + g + n} \right]^{\frac{1}{1-\alpha}}$$

Our goal is to maximise consumption, c. Consumption is the proportion of income not saved, meaning that consumption along the balanced growth path, c^*, can be expressed as follows:

$$c^* = (1 - s)s^{\frac{1}{1-\alpha}} \left[\frac{1}{\delta + g + n} \right]^{\frac{1}{1-\alpha}}$$

Differentiating with respect to the savings rate yields:

$$\frac{\partial c^*}{\partial s} = \frac{\left(s^{\frac{1-2\alpha}{\alpha-1}} \right)(s - \alpha)}{\alpha - 1}$$

which equals zero and is thus optimised when $s = \alpha$, meaning that α is the optimal proportion of output to save. This explains why developed countries generally grow more slowly: their cutting-edge growth must come from sources beyond investment. However, as developing countries have often had s set inefficiently low historically, they can benefit from raising their savings rates to experience catch-up growth.

The Solow model is useful in illustrating the ingredients needed to achieve growth: capital, labour, (especially) technology and new ideas. However, as Chap. 1 has explained, these ingredients are merely proximate factors. Under what institutional environments and under which value systems will such ingredients accumulate and be used most productively? What also is the role of government policy in achieving development? Is the state able to facilitate catch-up growth and cutting-edge growth? The answers to these questions require us to look beyond neoclassical growth accounting.

Endogenous Growth Theory, Human Capital and Paul Romer

Paul Romer is a prominent American economist who is well known for his endogenous growth theory contribution to development studies, for which he was awarded the Nobel Prize in Economics in 2018.

Endogenous growth theory can be understood with reference to the earlier Solow model which treated technological progress, or simply put new ideas, as exogenous to the economic system (Romer, 1990). That is, while new ideas, technology, and productivity affect the long-run growth of an economy, these processes are assumed to be external to and independent of the internal workings of the economy; they are akin to 'shocks' to the system that happen from time to time. The key point of endogenous growth theory is to emphasise how these processes are part and parcel of the economic growth process itself.

Endogenous growth theory thus created an economic model that echoes the intuition of many economists: that investments into capital and technology, especially that on human capital, have a strong impact on long-term growth. Firms constantly engage in such investments, and as they learn from experience and market conditions, they improve their investment projects over time. Government policies may also hamper or encourage the rate of such technological progress, through factors such as education policy, intellectual property protections and policy towards national R&D.

One implication of this emphasis is that growth can be sustained indefinitely through the accumulation of new ideas. Economies need not be stuck in a steady-state equilibrium and be subject to diminishing returns of capital accumulation. Simply accumulating more capital and labour is unsustainable, but innovation can sustain long-run growth indefinitely.

Endogenous growth theory is not just associated with Paul Romer, although he made a significant contribution to it in his seminal 1990 paper. Others such as Aghion & Hewitt (1992) and Grossman & Helpman (1991) also contributed to this body of work through an exploration of Joseph Schumpeter's emphasis on innovation and creative destruction. This theory is thus significant in stressing the central role of innovation in any nation's growth story. There are, however, further questions that must be asked here, regarding the institutional environment and cultural conditions required to encourage and maximise innovation. After all, there are some countries where, despite the efforts of government, innovation remains hampered. Simply pouring money into investments may not necessarily yield the intended results. A wider political economy analysis will be useful in highlighting the political or institutional barriers to innovation-led growth (Baumol et al., 2007). There is also a need to focus on the role of entrepreneurship, which is crucial for innovation, but which is unfortunately neglected in mainstream economics (Holcombe, 2007).

Jeffrey Sachs on Geography and Foreign Aid

Jeffrey Sachs is a renown American development economist, whose work has perhaps more than others been practised in the world of development policy. He has been a researcher, an advisor (to various governments and world organisations) and a practitioner of development economics, with many of his contributions actually being implemented on the ground.

Sachs' theoretical contributions are aplenty and cannot be done justice with limited space, but we can start by his emphasis on the importance of geography as a limiting factor. As mentioned in the introductory chapter, some scholars argue that geographical conditions, more so than other variables, limit a nation's long-run growth prospects. Thus, Sachs (2003) has argued that 'institutions don't rule', and that there are unique geographical problems, such as poor soil conditions, disease ecology, distance from the coast and other climatic factors, that have limited development in poor regions such as Africa. In line with his emphasis on geography, he is also well known for his theory on the natural resource curse, which is simply the idea that an abundance of natural resources may stifle development. His influential paper argues that economies with a 'high ratio of natural resource exports to GDP…tended to have low growth rates..' (Sachs & Warner, 1999). Looking around the world, we can certainly observe oil-rich countries, for example, such as those in the Middle East and Russia, being overly dependent on oil and resource incomes, rather than investing in the necessary infrastructure, public goods and systems needed for sustained development.

Sach's belief that 'geography rules' has its share of critics, understandably. This goes against the prevailing consensus about institutions and values, which this guidebook has emphasised. On the one hand, there are many countries with unfavourable geographical conditions that have done well. Botswana, for example, is a landlocked African nation located in the middle of the African continent, yet it has done very well, a testament to its market-based reforms and good governance (Beaulier & Subrick, 2006a, 2006b). Geography is also not destiny, as short-term changes in institutions and political leadership may overcome natural factors; certainly, the contrast between North and South Korea provides compelling evidence of this. May geography have a more indirect, long-run effect on institutions, rather than being an immediate determinant? Scholars like Daron Acemoglu et al. (2002) and Jared Diamond (2013) have shown how historical circumstances may have an indirect, long-run and known-on impacts on a country's subsequent development, in terms of the type of institutions being adopted.

Another aspect of Sach's ideas is his advocacy of foreign aid programs. This is in part because of his belief that much of Africa is experiencing a poverty trap and thus the need for foreign aid to push the economy out of it. Aid has come a long way over the past few decades. Overall aid spending has consistently increased, though the recipients of aid have varied over the years (Fig. 2.1).

Sachs is today well known for his writings on disease alleviation type aid by global organisations, notably that against malaria, as well as the Millennium Villages Project. His belief in aid has understandably put him at odds with critics of aid such as William Easterly and Dambiya Moyo, who are sceptical of its effectiveness (see Easterly, 2006; Moyo, 2009). For us, we certainly concede that foreign aid can sometimes have limited benefits, we can point to schools being built, malaria bed nets being distributed, etc. These are tangible benefits received by local peoples that should not be denied. Yet, we ought to remember that foreign aid is diverse and can include private versions by organisations as well as those administered by governments, which we believe to be less inefficient. More importantly, these achievements are insufficient in the long term if they are unaccompanied by fundamental changes in a nation's governance. Aid can help in

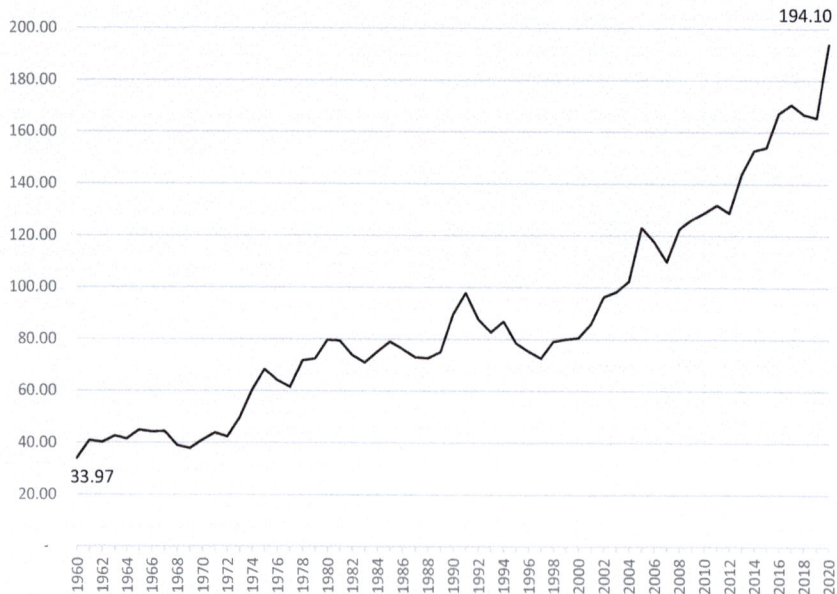

Fig. 2.1 Net official development assistance and official aid received (current US$) in billions
Source World Bank (2021)

limited cases, but it is not a panacea and not a substitute for fundamental structural reform (see Skarbek & Leeson, 2009).

Interestingly, even though Sach's advocacy of foreign aid programs today is heavily opposed by classical liberal-oriented scholars, he is well known for 'shock therapy' programs, which were rapid transitions to the market economy in former Soviet states. A 2014 book captures this irony of Jeffrey Sachs as 'Dr Shock' and 'Mr Aid' (Wilson, 2014). Indeed, we know that the transition experience of Eastern European countries was mixed. Post-Soviet Russia's privatisation programs were poorly managed, leading to the rise of kleptocracy and oligarchy. Countries like Poland, however, have done much better (see Sachs, 1994). For us (as explained in this Chapter), the problem is not with markets per se, but the poor implementation of these transition programs in ways that did not first get institutions and the cultural foundations right.

Ultimately, Jeffrey Sachs remains an influential figure in the world of development economics and his ideas provide fertile ground for debate.

Amartya Sen on Freedom and Capabilities

Amartya Sen is an Indian economist who has made significant contributions to various fields, including development studies. He is also recognised with a Nobel Prize in Economics in 1998 for his work on welfare economics.

Sen's contribution to development economics is unique in his heavy use of philosophy, which is often neglected in much of mainstream economics. Sen starts with a simple but important question of what 'development' means in the first place. Often, this is understood in material terms, i.e. the growth in national income as measured by gross domestic product. For Sen, an increase in material income, while desirable, is not the ultimate end of development. Even happiness and basic needs are inadequate. It is the increase in people's freedom, measured in terms of capabilities that matter (Sen, 1999a).

Sen's capabilities approach to development posits that the chief end of development is to expand the ability of people to actually live the lives that they value. This encompasses more than just money, because if people lack other aspects of capabilities, for example, they lack literacy or equal rights in society, their unfreedom limits their capacity to achieve their ends. A wealthy woman who lacks the equal rights to make decisions in society is not really better off.

Sen's emphasis on freedom has been significant in terms of shifting the discourse away from mere material objectives. The United Nations Human Development Index and its subsequent outputs have in part been inspired by Sen's work. Sen's exploration of the range of freedoms have led to greater attention on issues of gender quality, workers' rights in the workplace, among others (Alkire, 2002). Political freedom is particularly relevant today, because it challenges the notion of 'authoritarian development', the idea that development can be achieved without the type of liberal democratic practices championed by the West. China and Singapore are two commonly-used examples of this, where rapid increases in income have been achieved without political liberalisation (see Chap. 6 for more). For Sen, this is undesirable, because despite material wealth, people under such regimes remain unfree and so lack the full range of capabilities they need to live the lives they want. Also, as a response to 'Asian values' advocates, Sen (2017) insists that democracy is indeed a universal value and not exclusive to the Western context.

Significantly, for Sen, he views freedom in a positive way, beyond a purely negative conception of freedom as non-interference. Freedom is not just the absence of coercion from the state and others, but also entails the ability to achieve one's goals. Thus, in his later work *Development as Freedom*, Sen (1999b, p. 10) outlined five different aspects of freedom: (1) political freedoms, (2) economic facilities, (3) social opportunities, (4) transparency guarantees and (5) protective security. These are all inter-connected and valuable in their own right. Without social opportunities, for example to receive an education, one may not be able to exercise his or her democratic right to vote. In the absence of political freedoms, one's wealth and property may be insecure and subject to expropriation, as it has often been in authoritarian societies.

Freedom for Sen, is both an end and a means of development. As mentioned, something valuable is lost if freedom is traded away, or sacrificed in the name of material progress, as some authoritarian states have done. The end of development is not the instrumental achievement of material goals, but the fulfilment of the moral ideal of freedom. This principle therefore poses a strong critique of authoritarian developers like Singapore and China who seek to provide the material enrichment that people crave, but deny them the liberal freedom that they are entitled to. At the same time, of course, freedom also contributes instrumentally to high-quality development. This helps us understand Sen's (1999b, p. 16) famous declaration that 'no famine has ever taken place in the history of the world in a functioning democracy'. There are various mechanisms for this. For example, democratic leaders are more accountable to the public than authoritarian regimes are, and the open flows of information may highlight economic problems and address them before disasters ensue. As we have explained in Chap. 4, institutions of liberalism and democracy are important for development.

Overall, Sen has made a significant *political economy* contribution, by highlighting the importance of political democracy in the economic development process. This continues to be of great relevance in the world today, especially at a time when authoritarianism and various forms of unfreedom continue to be subjected on people aspiring for better lives.

The 'Rebels'

Peter Bauer

Peter Bauer was a Hungarian-born development economist who moved to Britain and who spent most his career at the London School of Economics.

The key thing to note about Bauer was that his views on development were in contrast to much of the establishment at the time. The development establishment, especially in the post-war period, strongly believed in the necessarily of big-push type projects, the need for foreign aid to developing nations (Bauer, 1976). Bauer criticised the foreign aid establishment, on the basis that aid would often do more harm than good, since they would prop up bad governments in poor nations, which was the very source of under-development. Bauer did not believe that heavy state intervention was required to stimulate growth, and advocated a Smithian recipe of limited government, the rule of law and market capitalism for poor countries. He is therefore significant in influencing the later work of classical liberal development economists such as William Easterly and other critics of aid such as Dambisa Moyo.

For Bauer, it wasn't more capital or in fact other specific factor inputs that made the difference on poverty reduction, but rather it was about the freedom and dignity of individuals (Dorn, 2002). Markets and a liberal social order must be institutionalised for such progress to take place. Freedom was not only means for progress, but also an end worth preserving, but which was often suppressed by development experts in global organisations. Bauer's view of development is thus similar to Sen, in that both believed that liberal freedom is a moral ideal worth striving for in its own right, independent of technical questions of income maximisation and the like.

Another significant point of departure from the conventional wisdom at the time was Bauer's rejection of the idea that population growth was a contributor to poverty, and that globalisation and openness to trade, especially with the Western world, were harmful. Bauer thus stood against Malthusian beliefs, which today continue to pervade environmentalism and public policy. This is not necessarily an extreme and foolish position: under the right conditions, population growth can be positive for countries, since they constitute human capital and the potential for innovation (Boettke & Coyne, 2022; Simon, 2019). To blame population growth for poverty is to obscure structural problems of governance that are at the heart of under-development (see Bauer, 1998).

His encouragement of free trade is also reminiscent of Adam Smith, particularly in clarifying the false conflation of trade and Western imperialism. Adam Smith was not an uncritical apologist of Western empires and colonialism but had rejected these practices for being inefficient *and immoral*. The benefits of markets, for classical liberals like Adam Smith and Peter Bauer, are based on the principle of consent, and thus, there should be no dichotomy between free market economics and anti-colonial ideas (see Easterly, 2021). This is an especially important insight, especially in the decades after World War II, when newly independent states, in an effort to be free from Western influence and 'neocolonialism', adopted policies of autarky and protectionism, which only hampered their development prospects (see Tarling, 1993, Chap. 8). Free trade is based on the principle of voluntary consent, and an acceptance of trade does not have to imply an acceptance of unjust historical practices of the Western world.

Peter Bauer's contributions are important and far-reaching. Perhaps because it stood in stark contrast to much of development thinking in his time, his ideas were not as popular as other thinkers. Certainly, foreign aid has continued to be a staple of global development policy (Shleifer, 2009). Additionally, some critics may also argue that functioning markets also require state capacity and in some cases, governments that go beyond the classical liberal minimal state ideal (see Chap. 6 on state capacity). The precise balance between state and markets remains contested today and may be different in various local contexts.

Ha-Joon Chang

Ha-Joon Chang is a South Korean economist who is well known for his critiques of what he believes to be the excesses of neoliberal economics. To understand Chang, we need to note that he is considered a heterodox economist rather than a mainstream one. This means that he typically rejects many of the policy prescriptions and methods of mainstream economics, whom he views as wedded to an unfounded faith in free market orthodoxy.

It is, however, crucial to note at the outset that heterodox economics need not necessarily imply left-wing ideas, as Geoffrey Hodgson (2019) has usefully clarified. The neoclassical model in mainstream economics is not synonymous with free market economics and has in fact been used to justify socialist central planning, as seen in the socialist calculation debate of the early twentieth century. Conversely, while some market economists like those in the Chicago tradition are wedded to neoclassical tenets, others, especially those in the Austrian tradition, reject them.

Nonetheless, Chang in various books and publications has popularised the idea that free market economics is not necessarily good for developing nations, and in fact may not even have been practised consistently by Western nations in the first place. Chang has argued that industrial policy, selective government interventions and infant-industry protection are all sensible for developing nations. The East Asian developmental state model provides a key piece of evidence for Chang's thesis and those of a similar persuasion (see Chang, 2006). Many East Asian economies did not follow the free market prescriptions laid out by global organisations and had often and consciously forged their own hybrid model, mixing state and market elements (see Amsden, 1994).

Chang is also well known for his denunciations of Western hypocrisy. Western countries and the global organisations they lead are often hypocritical, because they do not always practise the liberal economic policies that they preach to developing nations. They have in fact been 'kicking away the ladder' that poor countries need to climb in their development aspirations (Chang, 2002). Neoliberal advocates are thus 'Bad Samaritans', doing more harm than good (Chang, 2008).

In our opinion, Chang is an interesting thinker worth reading, even if we disagree with his conclusions. First, Chang is right to point out the many stances of hypocrisy on the part of Western nations. Even as they preach free trade, they have indeed often implemented protectionist policies that have harmed the poor. They continue to maintain barriers (such as immigration controls) to their domestic market which deprive the poor of global market access. Historically speaking, Western nations have also engaged in colonial imperialism, which is not consistent with the spirit of voluntarism in liberal democracy. Today, many global organisations, such as the World Bank and International Monetary Fund, have pursued policies that are at odds with the interests of the global poor. These criticisms must be accepted, and as the subsequent Chap. 3 shows, bottom-up reforms, rather than those engineered top-down, prove to be most sustainable.

Importantly, Chang's criticisms of neoliberalism stand on the shoulders of influential critics of the past. Chang (2012, Chap. 1) famously argued that 'there is no such thing as a free market', which is a rearticulation of the works of Karl Polanyi (1944). The basic argument here is that the rise of the market economy is historically tied to the rise of the nation state, and it was precisely the political imposition of market norms that established capitalism. The growth of capitalism, according to the Polanyian view, is typically associated with a rise of instrusive state power. Therefore, market economies are not 'natural' spontaneous orders, to use Hayek's terminologies, but are rather political creations.

On the one hand, this argument goes too far. First, this Polanyian historical account has been challenged by market-liberal economic historians like Douglass North (1977) and Deirdre McCloskey (1997), who showed the long-running existence of markets that predate nation states. Second, even if one accepts that economic institutions are structured or even enforced politically, this does not negate the real existence and benefits of economic freedom where it has been tried. There is a real difference in economic performance between and within countries when varying levels of economic freedom are tried. And while it is indeed true—as Chang suggests—that Western history is not a libertarian 'free for all', we cannot deny that individualism, entrepreneurial dignity and commerce are all important cultural values that emerged in the Anglosphere and which has made a significant impact around the world (McCloskey, 2010).

In our opinion, Chang's valuable contribution is his challenge of mainstream economists' methodological assumptions. Chang is right to point out that economic organisation is always politically embedded within a certain set of rules—in that way, markets do not exist as a *free-floating abstraction*. For us, this necessitates a wider methodological toolkit when engaging in social science, beyond the strictures of neoclassical economics. This does not mean that markets are 'unreal', or are devoid of 'rules', it just means that we ought to engage in good political economy thinking.[1] And on that note, numerous *liberal political economists* have demonstrated the importance of bottom-up social processes, on the spontaneous nature of many *governance* structures (as opposed to government), and the

---

[1] We recommend reviewing the debate over Polanyi between Blyth (2004) and Hejeebu and McCloskey (2004), where the latter accepted the need to recognise social embeddedness but nonetheless put forth a pro-market view.

rules that govern economic behaviour (Leeson, 2014; Stringham, 2015). In short, Chang's heterodox economics need not require us to throw the baby out with the bathwater.

Discussion Questions

1. What are some of the common themes and assumptions in classical development economics?
2. Are poor nations necessarily stuck in a 'poverty trap' (or equivalent), and does this in any way require a 'big-push' by the state?
3. To what extent did classical development economists consider questions of state capacity, governance and institutions? Does this matter?
4. What is the significance of considering democracy, human rights and political freedom, as Amartya Sen pointed out, in development studies? Have such ethical matters been adequately considered in contemporary development policymaking?
5. How have foreign aid programs changed over the years?
6. What do the anti-establishmentarian challenges of Peter Bauer and Ha-Joon Chang tell us about the development establishment and their approach to developing countries?

References

Acemoglu, D., Johnson, S., & Robinson, J. A. (2002). Reversal of fortune: Geography and institutions in the making of the modern world income distribution. *The Quarterly Journal of Economics, 117*(4), 1231–1294.

Aghion, P., & Howitt, P. (1992). A Model of Growth Through Creative Destruction. *Econometrica, 60*(2), 323–351. https://doi.org/10.2307/2951599.

Alkire, S. (2002). Dimensions of human development. *World   Development,   30*(2), 181–205. https://doi.org/10.1016/S0305-750X(01)00109-7.

Amsden, A. H. (1994). Why isn't the whole world experimenting with the East Asian model to develop?: Review of the East Asian miracle. *World Development, 22*(4), 627–633. https://doi.org/10.1016/0305-750X(94)90117-1.

Andreoni, A., & Chang, H. J. (2016). Industrial policy and the future of manufacturing. *Economia e Politica Industriale, 43*(4), 491–502. https://doi.org/10.1007/s40812-016-0057-2.

Bauer, P. T. (1956). Lewis' Theory of Economic Growth [Review of *The Theory of Economic Growth*, by W. A. Lewis]. *The American Economic Review, 46*(4), 632–641. http://www.jstor.org/stable/1814286.

Bauer, P. T. (1976). *Dissent on development*. Harvard University Press.

Bauer, P. T. (1998). Population growth: Disaster or blessing? *The Independent Review, 3*(1), 67–76. https://www.independent.org/pdf/tir/tir_03_1_05_bauer.pdf.

Baumol, W. J., Litan, R. E., & Schramm, C. J. (2007). *Good capitalism, bad capitalism, and the economics of growth and prosperity*. Yale University Press.

Beaulier, S. A., & Subrick, J. R. (2006a). Poverty traps and the robust political economy of development assistance. *The Review of Austrian Economics, 19*(2), 217–226. https://doi.org/10.1007/s11138-006-7349-0.

Beaulier, S. A., & Subrick, J. R. (2006b). The political foundations of development: The case of Botswana. *Constitutional Political Economy, 17*(2), 103–115. https://doi.org/10.1007/s10602-006-0002-x.

Blyth, M. (2004). The great transformation in understanding Polanyi: Reply to Hejeebu and McCloskey. *Critical Review, 16*(1), 117–133. https://doi.org/10.1080/08913810408443601.

Boettke, P. J., & Coyne, C. J. (2022). The economic logic behind the Ultimate Resource. *The Review of Austrian Economics, 35,* 303–314. https://doi.org/10.1007/s11138-022-00571-2.

Chang, H. J. (2002). *Kicking away the ladder: Development strategy in historical perspective.* Anthem Press.

Chang, H. J. (2006). *The East Asian development experience: The miracle, the crisis and the future.* Zed Books.

Chang, H. J. (2008). *Bad Samaritans: The guilty secrets of rich nations and the threat to global prosperity.* Random House.

Chang, H. J. (2012). *23 things they don't tell you about capitalism.* Bloomsbury Publishing USA.

Chang, H. J. (2019) Chapter Six. The Economic Theory of the Developmental State. In M. Woo-Cumings (Ed.), *The Developmental State* (pp. 182–199). Cornell University Press.

Diamond, J. (2013). *Guns, germs and steel: A short history of everybody for the last 13,000 years.* Random House.

Domar, E. D. (1946). Capital expansion, rate of growth, and employment. *Econometrica, Journal of the Econometric Society,* 137–147. https://doi.org/10.2307/1905364.

Dorn, J. A. (2002). Economic development and freedom: The legacy of Peter Bauer. *Cato Journal, 22*(2), 355–371. https://www.cato.org/sites/cato.org/files/serials/files/cato-journal/2001/11/cj22n2-10.pdf.

Dutt, A. K., & Ros, J. (Eds.). (2008). *International handbook of development economics.* Edward Elgar Publishing.

Easterly, W. (1999). The ghost of financing gap: Testing the growth model used in the international financial institutions. *Journal of Development Economics, 60*(2), 423–438. https://doi.org/10.1016/S0304-3878(99)00047-4.

Easterly, W. (2006). The big push deja vu: A review of Jeffrey Sachs's the end of poverty: Economic possibilities for our time. *Journal of Economic Literature, 44*(1), 96–105. https://doi.org/10.1257/002205106776162663.

Easterly, W. (2021). Progress by consent: Adam Smith as development economist. *The Review of Austrian Economics, 34*(2), 179–201. https://doi.org/10.1007/s11138-019-00478-5.

Gerschenkron, A. (1962). *Economic backwardness in historical perspective.* Harvard University Press.

Grossman, G. M., & Helpman, E. (1991). *Innovation and growth in the global economy.* MIT Press.

Harrod, R. F. (1939). An essay in dynamic theory. *The economic journal, 49*(193), 14–33. https://doi.org/10.2307/2225181.

Hejeebu, S., & McCloskey, D. (2004). Polanyi and the history of capitalism: rejoinder to Blyth. *Critical Review, 16*(1), 135–142. https://doi.org/10.1080/08913810408443602.

Hirschman, A. (1958). *The strategy of economic development.* Yale University Press.

Hodgson, G. M. (2019). *Is there a future for heterodox economics?: Institutions, ideology and a scientific community.* Edward Elgar Publishing.

Holcombe, R. (2007). *Entrepreneurship and economic progress.* Routledge.

Islam, N., & Yokota, K. (2008). Lewis growth model and China's industrialization. *Asian Economic Journal, 22*(4), 359–396. https://doi.org/10.1111/j.1467-8381.2008.00282.x.

Kattel, R., Kregel, J. A., & Reinert, E. S. (2016). *Classical development economists of the mldtwentieth century.* Edward Elgar Publishing.

Krugman, P. (1992). Toward a counter-counterrevolution in development theory. In *Proceedings of the World Bank Annual Conference on Development Economics,* Washington, DC: World Bank.

Leeson, P. T. (2014). *Anarchy unbound: Why self-governance works better than you think.* Cambridge University Press.

McCloskey, D. N. (2010). *Bourgeois dignity: Why economics can't explain the modern world.* University of Chicago Press.

McCloskey, D. N. (1997). Polanyi was right, and wrong. *Eastern Economic Journal, 23*(4), 483–487.

Moyo, D. (2009) *Dead aid: Why aid is not working and how there is a better way for Africa.* Macmillan.

Murphy, K. M., Shleifer, A., & Vishny, R. W. (1989). Industrialization and the big push. *Journal of Political Economy, 97*(5), 1003–1026. https://doi.org/10.1086/261641.

North, D. C. (1977). Markets and other allocation systems in history: The challenge of Karl Polanyi. *Journal of European Economic History, 6*(3), 703–716.

Nugent, J. B., & Yotopoulos, P. A. (1976). *The economics of development: empirical investigations.* Harper and Row.

Nurkse, R. (1957). Foreign aid and the theory of economic development. *The Scientific Monthly, 85*(2), 81–85.

Nurkse, R. (1970). *Problems of capital formation in underdeveloped countries.* Oxford University Press.

Oqubay, A. (2015). *Made in Africa: Industrial policy in Ethiopia.* Oxford University Press.

Pearce, K. (2001). *Rostow.* Michigan State University Press.

Polanyi, K. (1944). *The great transformation.* Farrar & Rinehart.

Romer, P. M. (1990). Endogenous technological change. *Journal of Political Economy, 98*(5), S71–S102. https://doi.org/10.1086/261725.

Ros, J. (2008). Classical development theory. In A.K. Dutt & J. Ros (Eds.), *International Handbook of Development Economics Vol 1 & 2* (pp. 111–124). Edward Elgar Publishing. https://doi.org/10.4337/9781848442818.00015.

Rosenstein-Rodan, P. N. (1943). Problems of industrialisation of eastern and south-eastern Europe. *The Economic Journal, 53*(210/211), 202–211. https://doi.org/10.2307/2226317.

Rosenstein-Rodan, P. N. (1961). Notes on the theory of the 'big push'. In *Economic development for Latin America* (pp. 57–81). Palgrave Macmillan, London.

Rostow, W. W. (1960). *The stages of economic growth: A non-communist manifesto.* Cambridge University Press.

Sachs, J. (1994). *Poland's jump to the market economy.* MIT Press.

Sachs, J. (2003). Institutions don't rule: Direct effects of geography on per capita income. *National Bureau of Economic Research.* https://www.nber.org/papers/w9490.

Sachs, J. , & Warner, A. M. (1999). The Big Rush, natural resource booms and growth. *Journal of Development Economics, 59*(1), 43–76. https://doi.org/10.1016/S0304-3878(99)00005-X.

Sauer, C., Gawande, K., & Li, G. (2003). Big push industrialization: Some empirical evidence for East Asia and Eastern Europe. *Economics Bulletin, 15*(9), 1–7.

Sen, A. (1999a). *Freedom as development.* Oxford University Press.

Sen, A. (1999b). *Commodities and capabilities.* Oxford University Press.

Sen, A. (2017). Democracy as a universal value. In L. May (Ed.), *Applied Ethics - A Multicultural Approach* (pp. 107–117). Routledge.

Shleifer, A. (2009). Peter Bauer and the failure of foreign aid. *Cato Journal, 29*(3), 379–390. https://www.cato.org/sites/cato.org/files/serials/files/cato-journal/2010/11/cj29n3-1.pdf.

Simon, J. L. (2019). *The economics of population growth.* Princeton University Press.

Skarbek, D. B., & Leeson, P. T. (2009). What can aid do. *Cato Journal, 29*(3), 391–397. https://www.cato.org/sites/cato.org/files/serials/files/cato-journal/2009/11/cj29n3-2.pdf.

Snowdon, B. (2009). The Solow model, poverty traps, and the foreign aid debate. *History of Political Economy, 41*(Suppl_1), 241–262. https://doi.org/10.1215/00182702-2009-026.

Solow, R. M. (1956). A contribution to the theory of economic growth. *The Quarterly Journal of Economics, 70*(1), 65–94. https://doi.org/10.2307/1884513.

Solow, R. M. (1957). Technical change and the aggregate production function. *The Review of Economics and Statistics,* 312–320.

Stringham, E. (2015). *Private governance: Creating order in economic and social life.* Oxford University Press.

Tarling, N. (Ed.). (1993). *The Cambridge history of Southeast Asia.* Cambridge University Press. https://doi.org/10.1017/CHOL9780521355063.

Todaro, M. P., & Smith, S. C. (2020). *Economic development*. Pearson UK.

Whitehead, J. (2005). The Krugman Twist and the Lewis Model: East Asian lessons for the Caribbean under globalization. *Social and Economic Studies*, 222–246.

Wilson, J. (2014). *Jeffrey Sachs: The Strange Case of Dr. Shock and Mr. Aid*. Verso Books.

World Bank. (2021). *Net official development assistance and official aid received (current US$)|Data*. World Bank. Retrieved from:https://data.worldbank.org/indicator/DT.ODA.ALLD. CD?end=2020&start=1965.

Markets and Development

3

One of the central questions to ask in development studies is as follows: what system does a society utilise in order to manage the economic problem of resource scarcity? Every society will confront the task of allocating scarce resources efficiently across a multitude of wants. As such, the debate over comparative economic systems between rival modes of organisation is a crucial one in development studies. This choice of over economic systems will determine whether the resources in society are utilised in a rational way and to the widespread benefit of individuals. This is a fundamental issue to resolve before thinking about increasing national income or wealth.

Historically, there are a multitude of systems used to manage the allocation of resources, from feudalism to tribal and communal style arrangements, to socialism and free market capitalism (see Halliday & Thrasher, 2020 for a comparative survey). Among these many alternatives however, and especially in the past century, the debate has been between central economic planning on one end, to unfettered free markets on the other. All economies in the world lie somewhere along this spectrum, and the decision over the precise form of economic governance has been controversial, politically contested and comes with far-reaching implications on human welfare. Generally speaking, the twentieth century saw the ideological paradigm shift from the central planning towards a greater reliance on market forces especially since the end of the Cold War (White, 2012). This triumphalism over the ultimate superiority of liberal capitalism has of course come under further contestation in the twenty-first century, after successive 'crises' such as the 2008 financial crisis and most recently the coronavirus pandemic, all of which have led to deep reflections over economic governance, the role of markets and states.

State-market relations is an important topic for development studies. Scholars of different orientations have advocated for different arrangements, from development planning to more laissez-faire approaches. Since the late twentieth century, international organisations have certainly recommended 'neoliberal' policy prescriptions on the developing world. Some regions of the world, most notably East Asia, chose

© The Author(s), under exclusive license to Springer Nature Singapore Pte Ltd. 2023   61
B. Cheang and T. G. Palmer, *Institutions and Economic Development*,
Classroom Companion: Economics, https://doi.org/10.1007/978-981-99-0844-8_3

to deviate from this path in favour of a more hybrid approach. In this context, this chapter will explore the case for and against markets in the development context. The first section will explain the positive contributions of greater economic freedom for facilitating economic progress. The theoretical arguments in favour of freer markets are then exemplified through five case studies of local organisations who have successfully embarked on pro-market reforms. The second section will then present some market-sceptical arguments, from two traditions: dependency theory, which highlights the unequal power relations in global development, as well as market failure theory, which challenges the neoclassical paradigm and expectation of market efficiency.

It is the hope of the present authors that this dialectical structure will better clarify the nature of market freedoms, and the extent to which they should be pursued in development. Our overall position is that markets are by no means perfect institutions (contra neoclassical economics), but on a *comparative basis* they are nonetheless essential, though insufficient conditions for economic progress. The case for markets also does not preclude significant reforms necessary in the governance of global development organisations in order to reduce the power imbalances present.

Markets and the Benefits of Economic Freedom

Chiefly, the case for markets is a moral one. When reflecting on what it means to achieve 'development' and 'progress', one cannot escape the question of what it means to live a full, rich and good life. It is our contention that a life worth living is one under conditions of freedom, where individuals pursue their goals free from domination.[1] Material enrichment is important, but on its own provokes the question: what is the point of living under a gilded cage?[2] Of course, such moral arguments are unsatisfying for some. Show us the goods! Political economists therefore provide instrumental arguments and have generally agreed that markets are essential prerequisites for economic progress, which this section will elucidate.

But it is first important to understand what 'markets' mean. A greater reliance on markets means to accord greater freedom in the economic sphere, for consumers and producers to freely exchange, invest, deploy their assets and associate (or disassociate) in ways that they so choose. Entrepreneurs and owners of enterprises should have the freedom to determine what is produced and how and on what

---

[1] There are of course legitimate questions surrounding what 'freedom' entails (see Schmidtz & Brennan, 2010 for a brief history of the idea). If freedom comprises more than simply the absence of coercion, and also the 'capacity' to act or maintain a basic standard of living, then some form of state redistribution or welfare assistance is required. It should be clarified that this is an entirely justified position that is consistent with market liberalism and the many contemporary proposals for a minimum income guarantee (see Zwolinski, 2019).

[2] Some development models, especially the one adopted by China and Singapore, seek to precisely achieve this balance: high economic growth and liberalisation without political liberalisation.

terms it is offered. Workers should have the freedom to choose their occupations and to determine on what terms their services are offered, including the right to quit employment and seek other work. Consumers should have the freedom to buy or not to buy and to determine the terms on which they seek to purchase goods and services. Investors should have the freedom to allocate their savings and assets and to cooperate with entrepreneurs and intermediary institutions and to determine the terms on which they offer to invest. At the heart of economic freedom so described is the principle of voluntary exchange, where consent, rather than coercion, is the basic characteristic defining social relations.

A market economy so described of course may look very different from one context to another. The degree of economic freedom also varies, with some governments intervening more pro-actively than others, for reasons ranging from equity, to correcting market failures, to catalyse innovation. Empirically, this degree of economic freedom can be, and indeed has been, measured, producing an aggregate ranking of all nations. The two leading indicators in this regard is the Index of Economic Freedom (IEF) as well as the Economic Freedom of the World (EFW) report.

The main argument put forward in favour of greater market freedoms is that it is positively correlated with a variety of welfare indicators, chief of which is national income per capita. Past research, as well as recent editions of EFW, has documented the strong relationship between economic freedom and income per capita (Hanke and Walters 1997; Fraser Institute, 2021). The following diagrams illustrate these points. First, when the nations of the world are segmented in terms of how economically free they are, the freer ones are much richer on a per capita basis (see Fig. 3.1). Second, the material benefits of economic freedom are also to the benefit of the least well-off. Figure 3.2 shows that the share of total income that is earned by the poorest 10% is unrelated to economic freedom. However, if we are unconcerned about shares, but focus on the actual amount of income, then Fig. 3.3 shows that the poorest 10% of the population earn higher amounts of income in countries with higher economic freedom than in those with lower economic freedom. Importantly, the same data sources also show that economic freedom is also positively associated with other non-material aspects of human welfare, such as environmental quality, social progress and global peace, most of which explored in Chap. 1 (see Berggren, 2003 for a summary).

Correlation is of course not indication of causation. Why is economic freedom a contributor to human welfare? Market liberals believe that higher economic freedom provides the incentives for people to create wealth, develop innovations and fulfil their potential. When individuals are free from state coercion and are able to make use of their persons and property as they see fit, they stand to gain from their investments, and thereby contribute to growing national wealth. The lure of profits drives competitive improvements in product choice and quality. The lure of personal enrichment drives people to work harder, improve themselves and create market value.

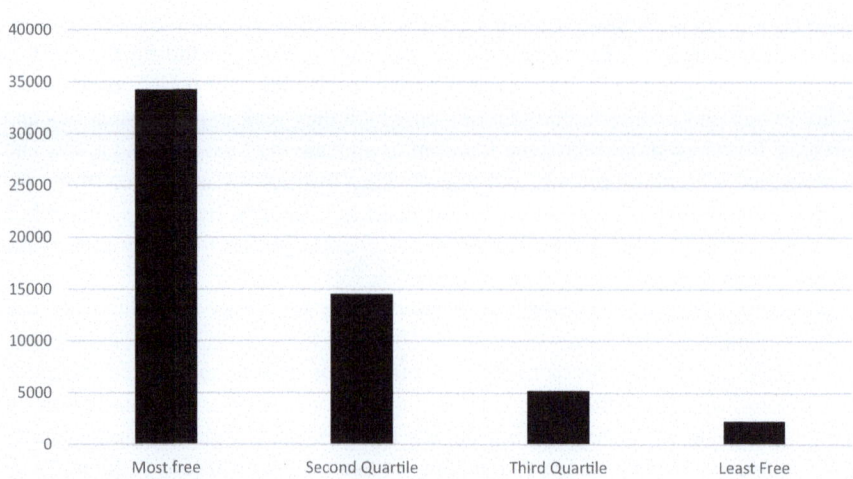

Fig. 3.1 Economic Freedom and Income Per Capita [GDP per Capita (current US$) 2020] *Source* Economic Freedom of the World: 2021 Report (Fraser Institute, 2021)

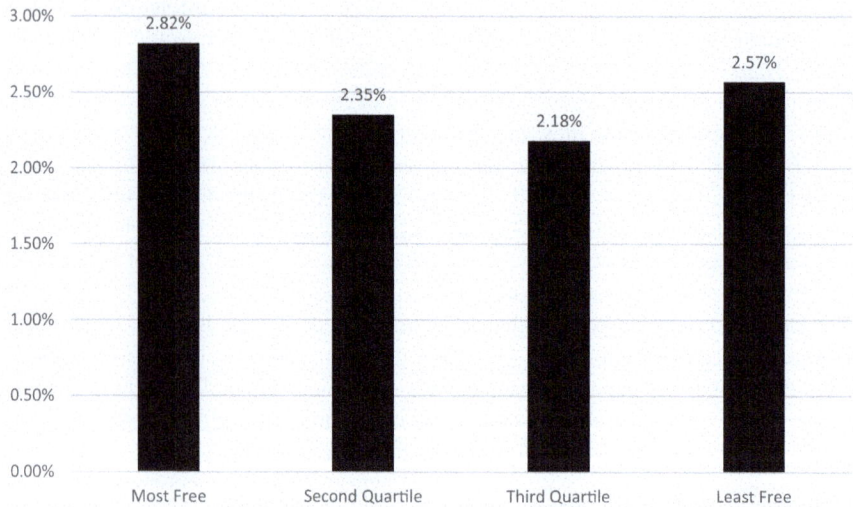

Fig. 3.2 Economic Freedom and the Income Share of the Poorest 10%. *Source* Economic Freedom of the World 2021 Report (Fraser Institute, 2021)

What about the non-material aspects? Let's take several in turn. Economic freedom is said to contribute to environmental progress because the market-driven wealth creation allows society to find ways to conserve resources, use more efficient and greener alternatives. Greener societies are generally wealthier, and more market-friendly. Economic freedom may also generate social progress, because market exchange facilitates social cooperation among persons unknown.

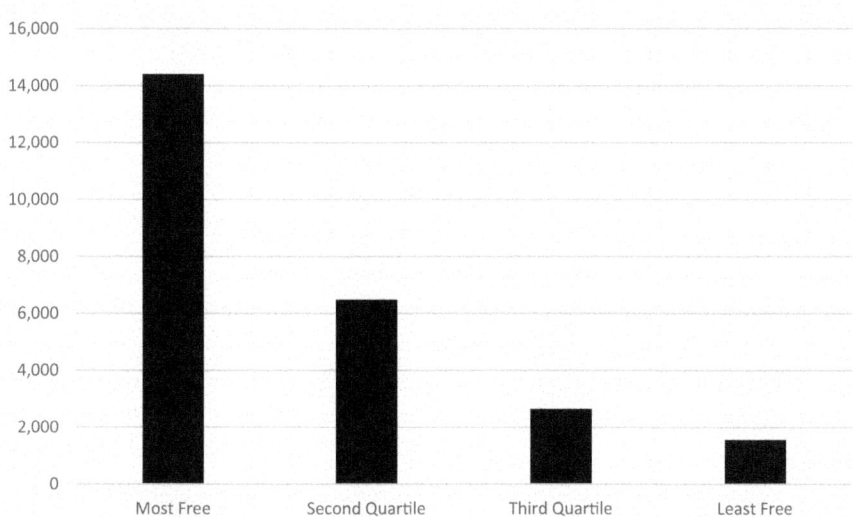

Fig. 3.3 Economic Freedom and the Income Earned by the Poorest 10% (Amount of income earned per capita in constant 2017 PPP$) *Source* Economic Freedom of the World 2021 Report (Fraser Institute, 2021)

As Voltaire famously quipped about the London Stock Exchange, 'here Jew, Mohammedan and Christian deal with each other as though they were all of the same faith, and only apply the word infidel to people who go bankrupt'. Commercial relations between men and women foster independence, tolerance and understanding, which is why some researchers have found tolerance for gender diversity and homosexuality to have been driven by historical improvements in economic liberty (Horwitz, 2015). John D'Emilio (2007) famously wrote about how capitalism created the material conditions for gay and lesbian people to live independent lives and thus successfully press for identity recognition.

Ultimately, the market-fostered social interdependence may also be expressed in the international realm between nations. A variant of the democratic peace theory, the capitalist peace theory states that nations that share capitalist relationships would be least likely to go to war (Gartzke, 2007). The simplified expression is that when money crosses borders (or goods and services), soldiers do not. The economic interdependence between nations forge close ties and acts as a powerful disincentive against warlike aggression.

The widespread benefits of economic freedom have meant that, understandably, nations have progressively opted to be plugged into the global economy. The economic transitions of China and India in the twentieth century are the most dramatic examples of such, but since then, pro-market economic reforms have also gathered pace across the world. It is important to note, however, that economic transition is never uniform, and the nature and success of which depends on local conditions, especially the participation of local people. The sheer variety of these conditions have therefore meant that there is a great 'variety of capitalism' in the world today, where the institutions of the market economy vary wildly from context to context (Feldmann, 2019; Hundt & Uttam, 2017).

It is important to note that economic freedom has generally and steadily increased in the past decades since 1945. This is simply because of the increased global integration of national economies and the market transitions of former communist nations in the 1990s. However, it is also worth noting that the degree of economic freedom has slowed in the recent past, mainly due to governmental responses to the coronavirus pandemic (Miozzi & Powell, 2022). These responses have seen governments dramatically increase their state spending, and recently deal with the economic fallout owing to the energy crisis and inflation (Economist, 2021). Therefore, one should not assume a linear and inexorable rise in economic freedom.

Market Reforms from the Bottom-Up

The nature and benefits of economic freedom are well documented by academic research. What, however, is not clear is the way that these benefits may be achieved by individual nations in their local contexts. Typically, analyses of market reforms in the development literature place global organisations at the centre, as the ones promoting such policies for the betterment of the global poor. Not only have many of these policies failed, it also obscures the agency of local actors in their own communities. It is therefore showcase here, through original interviews conducted, the efforts of local individuals and organisations in enacting market reforms and achieving the shared prosperity that it promises. The diversity of approaches to enacting market reforms once again illustrates the varieties of capitalism in the world.

Liberating Enterprise in India

The necessity of economic freedom so described, is exemplified by the Centre for Civil Society (CCS), which has carried out crucial initiatives on the regulation and dismantling of regulatory barriers for marginal entrepreneurs, such as street vendors, in India. Launched on 15 August 1997, CSS is an independent, non-profit research and educational think tank based in Delhi committed to increasing opportunity, prosperity and quality of life by reinvigorating civil society and readjusting political society. Its mission is to promote social change through public policy by being a resource for innovative community and market-based ideas for critical policy issues particularly in the areas of education, livelihoods and governance (Atlas Network, 2021).

One of the most prominent aspect of CCS' work has been their advocacy for the rights and economic conditions faced by street vendors in India. Street vendors constitute roughly 2.5%, or over 1,000,000 of India's population: apart from being a source of self-employment and entrepreneurship, street vending plays a central role in urban life by supplying affordable and essential goods to the public (Bedi, 2013; Bhowmik, 2003). Statistically, street vendors contribute towards 50% of India's savings, 63% its the Gross Domestic Product, and account for US$10,000,000 a day in transactions (Sankrit, 2015). However, by virtue of their operation in public spaces without clearly defined usufructuary rights, vendors often succumb to arbitrary abuse, extortion and harassment by local authorities (Narang & Sabharwal, 2019).

CSS has been a consistent champion for the rights of street vendors: in 2014, CCS was instrumental in securing the passage of a landmark legislation for protecting the right to livelihood for street vendors in India and has continued to monitor its progress. After 50 years of regulation by state and municipal laws that weighed against vendors, the Street Vendors (Protection of Livelihood and Regulation of Street Vending) Act 2014 (hereon referred to as 'Act') legitimised a vendor's right to livelihood and regulates urban street vending with due consideration to the social security of vendors. Pivotally, the act institutes guidelines for states to implement clear rules under which vendors can do business, such as prohibiting eviction before survey and accommodating all existing vendors, making relocation the last resort by giving due consideration to the economic conditions of vendors, and introducing participatory decision-making and giving vendors a voice in decisions that affect their livelihood (Bedi and Narang, 2020). CSS' work on this front has thus been pivotal in ensuring the security, dignity and freedom from harassment for street vendors (Atlas Network, 2021).

Implementation of the law, however, remains fragmented and remains unfinished in states around the country, since the act delegates the power to make subordinate legislation and implement its key features to state governments (Bedi and Narang, 2020). Resultantly, CCS has identified that states vary drastically in their implementation of the act: most notably, the progress of some states have stagnated, while others have implemented rules and schemes that contradict or go beyond the mandate of the Act itself, such as introducing new obligations for vendors not mentioned in the Act, or empowering state governments to remove members of the Town Vending Committees, the local bodies tasked with overseeing issues related to vendors. Given the varied states of implementation of the Street Vendors Act, CCS has created an overarching strategy to address the problem: at the policy level, CCS has turned their focus onto policy changes at the state level to bring them in line with national law, and diligently tracks the progress and weaknesses of individual states towards adopting national reform (Narang and Sharma, 2021). CCS also engages directly with legislators, and has been repeatedly recognised as an authoritative voice on the topic of street vendors: government stakeholders have invited CCS to testify to a Parliamentary Standing Committee studying the effectiveness of the Street Vendors Act and draft amendments to the act, and nominated CCS as a non-governmental representative for several Town Vending Committees (Atlas Network, 2021). Additionally, government think tanks have also consulted CCS on how the government could support vendors during the pandemic, culminating in the eventual implementation of some of the recommendations proposed by CCS.

Additionally, CCS directly engages with vendors by educating them on their legal rights through information campaigns and helping to defend them in court, thereby empowering vendors to effectively push back against fines and eviction. Sentient of the need to change public perceptions, CCS has also published opinion articles, held informational meetings with journalists and engaged directly with students to change their perspective of street vendors (Atlas Network, 2021).

Low-Tax Growth in Madrid, Spain

In a healthy market economy, government agencies and enterprises, however important they may be for strategic reasons, should not crowd out private enterprises and the fiscal spending should not impose a crushing burden on the public, nor should tax rates become so high, as they have in some societies, that incentives to invest and work become negative. One example which illustrates the impact of lowered taxes on economic growth is the Community of Madrid. In Spain, taxes are levied by the central, regional and local governments. While regional governments unilaterally administer and regulate stamp duties, transfer, wealth and inheritance taxes, they can only approve additional taxes and set the regional income tax brackets and rates, which constitute only half of the overall income tax, while the remaining half is decided by the central government (Enache, 2021).

Resultantly, taxes vary across regions: of particular interest here is the Community of Madrid, which is the region with the lowest taxes of all the Autonomous Communities in Spain. However, Madrid collects the most taxes and contributes the most (19.3%) to the national GDP. Since 2010, Madrid enjoyed the highest increase in GDP among other Autonomous Communities, with an average increase of 1.8% relative to the national average of 1.1%.

The immense economic growth Madrid has enjoyed is attributable to its government led by Isabel Díaz Ayuso, specifically the work of its Cabinet Minister of Economy, Finance and Employment, Javier Fernández-Lasquetty. A staunch supporter of classical liberalism and economic freedom, Javier has championed numerous taxation reforms, earning Madrid the distinction of the number one rank among 19 Spanish regions for tax competitiveness per the Spanish Regional Tax Competitiveness Index (RTCI) for both 2020 and 2021 (Pina, 2021; Enache, 2021). Since 2003, under the presidency of Esperanza Aguirre, the regional government of Madrid has approved tax cuts for taxes over which they have jurisdiction (i.e. personal income tax, wealth tax, inheritance and gift tax, and property transfer tax and stamp duty). For the fraction of personal income taxes that regional governments possess jurisdiction over, for example, Madrid has the lowest minimum bracket in Spain at 8.5%. In the last decade alone, the Community of Madrid has lowered personal income taxes by 25% for the lowest incomes, and by 2.3% for the highest.

Madrid, unlike its regional counterparts, has also completely abolished wealth taxes: while Spain remains the only country in the EU that applies a wealth tax which is significantly higher than other countries such as Norway and Switzerland, the regional government of Madrid has recognised that it penalises investments and savings, and is confiscatory in nature. Additionally, the amount collected by the tax is negligible: in 2019, just 1.355 billion euros in wealth tax was collected in Spain in total, which is equivalent to 0.2% of public expenditure in that year. In lieu of its detrimental impact upon investments and savings, which are crucial to economic growth, Madrid has abolished wealth taxes.

Inheritance and gift taxes in Madrid are similarly discounted, up to 99% for descendants, ascendants and spouses, and between 10 and 15% for uncles, aunts, nephews, nieces and siblings. Per the regional government of Madrid, inheritance taxes are unjust: inheritance taxes involve a double taxation, since they involve the payment of taxes at the time of death for something that had already been taxed in the individual's lifetime. Notably, this discount has disproportionately benefitted those who receive inheritances below the average amount: since 2004, 82% of the taxpayers (approximately 900,000 people) who have benefitted from the tax discount have received an inheritance below the average, which in Madrid stands at 185,000 euros.

Property transfer tax and stamp duty are also discounted, but on a case-by-case basis. Crucially, the Community of Madrid is the only region of the Common Regime without its own taxes. In total, these tax cuts (since 2004) have culminated in more than 60.7 billion euros saved by residents, which represent an average of 17,620 euros per taxpayer. About 85% of the tax savings were for incomes below 60,000 euros, while 73% were for incomes below 33,000 euros. These liberal-oriented policies have translated in an increase in per capita income by more than 30 points, which is significantly higher than the national average, and instrumental to Madrid becoming the region with the highest income per capita despite it being the fourth region with the highest income per capita in 1980. Additionally, Madrid's cumulative growth of regional GDP between 2004 to 2020 (41%) is also significantly higher than the national average (30.5%), while its GDP grew by 6.5% in 2021 compared to the national average of 5.1%. Part of this growth is attributable to the contraction of the shadow economy in Madrid: since lower taxation disincentives tax fraud, Madrid has the smallest shadow economy of all the Autonomous Communities, with a percentage of 16.2% compared to the Spanish average of 23.1%. Madrid's continuous success in maintaining growth thus exemplifies the effects of lowering taxes on economic growth and job creation: lowering taxes incentives people to save, invest and engage in productive labour, thereby catalysing economic growth in the long term (see Pina, 2021 and Sanchez de la Cruz, 2021 for more information).

Pro-competition Reforms in Philippines

A properly functioning market economy is also one that is competitive. As such, the presence of monopolies or market dominance is a good cause for concern. What is less mentioned, however, is that market dominance is not always a result of market forces but may involve public sector firms too. Imposition of monopolies, whether public or private, generally diminishes incentives for innovation and cost-cutting, rewards politically connected 'cronies' at the public expense and imposes net losses on the public. Government regulations if too excessive and opaque, can often contribute to market dominance.

This focus upon clear and transparent government regulations is exemplified by the Foundation for Economic Freedom (FEF), a public advocacy organisation based in the Philippines, and their advocacy to amend the Public Service Act (PSA). The PSA, formally titled Commonwealth Act No.146, is a prominent example of a barrier to free and competitive markets embedded within regulations by the Philippine government that fosters monopolistic conditions (Alcantara et al., 2021). Such protectionist regulations serve as barriers to foreign direct investments, which are contributory to the Philippines consistently ranking last in the ASEAN region in terms of restrictiveness on foreign direct investments (Asian Development Bank, 2017). Specifically, the PSA limits foreign equity in the operation of a public utility to a maximum of 40% (Seventeenth Congress of the Republic of the Philippines, 2017). The PSA, however, fails to offer a definition of what constitutes a public utility: resultantly, this ambiguity has led to public utilities being interpreted to encompass public services, entailing that all public services such as telecommunications, transportation and shipping services were subjected to this restriction. The public service sector in the Philippines therefore became dominated by local monopolies and duopolies. Monopolistic conditions, however, are detrimental to long-term growth and societal welfare: per the Asian Development Bank, foreign investment limitations such the PSA hinder competition and development of public private partnership projects in most of the service sectors in the Philippines (Asian Development Bank, 2017), thereby offering firms little incentive to invest or engage in innovative practices in the absence of competitive market conditions. Reflectively, the quality of public utilities in the Philippines is often lacking: only 67% of Filipinos, for example, have access to the internet, with Philippines ranking 75th in terms of 4G availability and 85th on 4G speed per a 2018 study comparing 88 countries across neighbouring countries and the world (Kemp, 2020; Salikha, 2018). Additionally, Philippines is ranked 92nd in infrastructure and 101st in transport infrastructure across 140 countries: this translates to a high cost of logistics, which inflates the cost of food and other products (World Bank, 2019). The absence of an efficient mass transport system has also resulted in high costs of transportation: the vehicle operating cost and time cost spent by drivers and passengers on the road in Metro Manila was estimated at Php3.5 billion daily, or $72.17 million by the Japan International Cooperation Agency (JICA) (Rappler, 2020).

Cognisant of the significant impact the PSA exerted upon the Philippine economy, the FEF embarked upon an attempt to propose amendments to the PSA, such as to make it more flexible and consistent with global economic realities. Chiefly, FEF sought to amend the PSA to include a statuary definition of a public utility and differentiate between public utilities and services, thereby freeing sectors that do not fall under the definition of a public utility from the constitutionally mandated foreign equity restrictions. FEF, through collaborations and consultations with experts such as legal scholars and stakeholders from public service sectors, drafted a preliminary bill that was proposed to key legislators from the 17th Philippine Congress. While the bill was passed by the House and Representatives, the bill failed to pass in the Senate due to strong opposition presented by nationalist members of the Senate, who cited national security concerns and foreign domination of the economy by Chinese companies in their objection. Despite the setback, however, the FEF remained steadfast in their work, incorporating national security provisions such as the executive vetting of investments in critical infrastructure to protect the country from malign actors and limits on investments from State-Owned Enterprises (SOEs) into the bill in response to the aforementioned objections from the 17th Congress. Furthermore, the FEF coordinated with influential business groups and executive agencies for their vocal support of the bill, leading to the country's economic managers such as the Secretaries of the Department of Finance (DoF), the Department Trade and Industry (DTI) and the National Economic Development Authority (NEDA) actively and consistently calling for the enactment of the proposed amendments to the PSA (Arangkada Philippines, 2020; Vilanueva, 2021; Crismundo, 2021). FEF's rejuvenated effort to coordinate and coalesce support for their proposed amendments to the PSA from within the government and society itself culminated in the passing of the Amendments to the PSA on 15th December 2021 during the 18th Congress, with the bill eventually signed into law as Republic Act 11,659 on 21st March 2022 (Eighteenth Congress of the Republic of the Philippines, 2022).

While the effects of Republic Act 11,659 have yet to materialise in lieu of its recent passing, the amendment of the PSA will facilitate new opportunities and sustainable growth for Philippines in the long run by fostering competition in the public service sector and attract much-needed foreign direct investments to improve the access, quality and rates of public services for local businesses and individual consumers. Specifically, the amendments made to the PSA is projected by the Department of Trade and Industry (DTI) to bring in $100B in investments in telecommunications, transportation and logistics in by 2024 (Arcalas, 2022). Additionally, the inclusion of national security provisions will deter potential threats posed by foreign investors to national security, thereby ensuring that the Philippines will be less vulnerable to the domination of foreign interests from other countries.

Trade and Food Security in Indonesia

The freedom to trade and to agree voluntarily on prices and quantities and qualities of goods and services generates benefits, whether the parties doing the trading live in the same village, the same province, the same country, the same continent or the same world. Trade across national borders is in essence no different from trade within borders. Parties to voluntary agreements do so in anticipation of benefiting from them. The gains to people in poorer villages, provinces or nations tend to be far greater than those to people in wealthier villages, provinces or countries.

Indeed, the central role played by innovation is notably important in this role, because trade that introduces products of new technologies, or those new technologies themselves, has the same impact as innovations that were produced in the village, province or country. Importation of new technologies, such as pharmaceuticals that were developed in wealthy nations such as Germany, Japan or the UK, improves lives in poorer nations no less, and often much more, than in wealthier countries. 'Free trade' is not just a slogan, but a policy choice that has real impacts on the lives of ordinary people. An important case study worth reflecting on here is the issue of food security in Indonesia. Indonesia had a long history of mandated 'food self-sufficiency', which dramatically raised the cost of food for Indonesian people. The poor suffer more, because food makes up such a large percentage of their household budgets.

Since its independence in 1945, Indonesia's government has pursued a harmful policy of food self-sufficiency that imposes severe import restrictions, tariffs, price controls and barriers to entry: as of 2020, 466 non-tariff measures such as quantitative restrictions, technical barriers to trade, and sanitary and phytosanitary measure have been applied to goods in food and agriculture (Amanta & Wibisono, 2021). Such protectionist measures, however, have resulted in the formation of monopolies by state-owned enterprises, thereby increasing the cost of food and resulting in widespread malnutrition among Indonesia's low-income population. Statistically, these policies have led to a problem of significant food insecurity across Indonesia: 26 million people (or approximately a third of the population) lack the income to buy adequate food and an additional 68 million Indonesians are considered extremely vulnerable to food price increases (Amanta & Wibisono, 2021). In fact, it is estimated that removing non-tariff measures on rice and meat alone would lead to an overall reduction of the poverty rate by 2.8 percentage points (Amanta & Wibisono, 2021).

The problem of high prices arising from protectionist policies pursued by the Indonesian government is compounded by the productive inefficiency of domestic agricultural producers. In general, Indonesia's agriculture sector suffers from low productivity, high production costs, limited agricultural land, a lack of necessary infrastructure and climate change-related environmental risks, all of which significantly inhibit efficient production (Asian Development Bank, 2019). Despite these challenges in domestic production, however, the strong protectionist policies justified by nationalistic self-sufficiency goals that have resulted in food and agricultural products remaining among the most restricted and regulated import sectors, and food prices being artificially driven upwards in lieu of the absence of effective international competition (Andriamananjara et al., 2011; Munadi, 2019; Neilson, 2018). Indonesia's non-tariff measures on food imports alone have imposed an effective rate of protection of between 33 and 41% for agriculture products, which entail that domestic food producers can charge a premium of between 33 to 41% on their products because they are shielded from competition from cheaper imported products (Amanta & Wibisono, 2021; Marks, 2017). Notably, however, such policies are unsuccessful in their aim of self-sufficiency: Indonesia has been a net importer of agricultural products for most of the last decade, importing 6.2% of its rice, 28.4% of beef, 69.9% of sugar, 72.5% of soybeans, 93.7% of garlic and 100% of its wheat (World Food Programme, 2020).

Given the detrimental impacts of Indonesia's protectionist measures on societal well-being and its lack of success in promoting self-sufficiency, one organisation that prominently champions the removal of harmful trade barriers in Indonesia's food sector is the Center for Indonesian Policy Studies (CIPS). CIPS' primary campaign, called Hak MakMur, which means 'The Right to Eat Affordably' in Indonesian, focuses on the ways liberalising food trade can benefit low-income populations in Indonesia. CIPS has set out arguments in favour of unfettered trade through policy papers on topics including domestic farmers' income, reforms to reduce food prices through trade in rice, beef, sugar, corn and poultry and effects of trade restrictions on malnutrition and stunted growth among a third of all Indonesian five-year-olds (Atlas Network, 2020). Additionally, CIPS regularly releases a Monthly Food Price Index to show prices of staple foods in comparison to their prices in neighbouring countries: the translation of rigorous research into digestible products has allowed CIPS to increase public awareness on how trade barriers cause Indonesia's comparably high food prices relative to neighbouring countries. CIPS has also built a coalition of 11 organisations including think tanks, nutrition groups, local businesses in the food sector, networks of traditional market sellers and student groups to aid them in their advocacy, and has employed YouTube influencers to create entertaining and informative videos on the topic to boost public awareness. Such strategies have been so successful that one video drove a 400 percent increase in signatures for the campaign's online petition demanding free and open trade (Atlas Network, 2020).

CIPS' efforts have been met with considerable success: since the commencement of CIPS' Hak MakMur campaign, the Indonesian government has dropped food self-sufficiency from the government agenda, with a Director General within the Trade Ministry even asking for CIPS' policy papers to be made into briefs for the minister to help craft a trade-oriented agenda (Atlas Network, 2020). The campaign has further contributed to the reduction of import restrictions in beef, corn, rice and other food products, resulting in an estimated food cost savings of US$1.9 billion for Indonesian households between 2016 and 2019 (Atlas Network, 2020). Recently, the Indonesian parliament has passed into law the single largest set of policy reforms since 1945: while imports were only allowed when domestic supplies were insufficient previously, the new law drops import restrictions, penalties on imported commodities and arbitrary weight limits to support farmers, while allowing citizens to import livestock freely (Atlas Network, 2020).

This paradigm shift in attitude towards trade and imports, attributable to CIPS' constant advocacy, has been especially evident in recent years: in response to a surge in price of garlic and onion, the Indonesian Ministry of Trade temporarily liberalised garlic and onion imports by removing the requirements for Horticulture Import Recommendation Letter and Import License Letter in March 2020, which had previously served as significant barriers to imports (Center for Indonesian Policy Studies, 2020). Similarly, the Indonesian government cancelled its plan of imposing value-added tax on staple foods such as rice, corn, beef, fruits and vegetables in 2021, after staunch opposition from CIPS on the grounds that such a tax would have disproportionately burdened low-income households, whose expenditure is dominated by staple foods (Center for Indonesian Policy Studies, 2021). CIPS' advocacy for the acceptance of food imports, through its research and communication efforts to promote open food trade, has influenced the public discourse towards greater acknowledgement of the importance of food imports to food security, catalysing a shift in mindset critical for the herculean task that they have faced over the years (Center for Indonesian Policy Studies, 2020).

Tax and Migration Reforms in Lithuania

Free trade does not just include trade in goods and services, but also the free movement of factors of production, namely labour. Economic theory shows that when people are free to move to look for economic opportunities, there are significant efficiency gains to be reaped (Clemens, 2011). Receiving countries benefit from talent, and the economic potential of migrants is unlocked in the industries that they move into. In the short run, a flexible labour market also allows businesses to fill their labour needs and to respond to market conditions. There are thus long- and short-term benefits of having an open labour market, where the entry of migrants is enabled through clear, light and simple regulations.

Lithuania is a high-income developed nation in Eastern Europe but unfortunately one that has been encountering labour market shortages (ILO, 2022; Kalinkaitė-Matuliauskienė, 2021). This is on one hand a reflection of a larger demographic problem in the EU of an ageing population and the challenge of attracting skilled labour in the global race for talent. But in Lithuania specifically, it was found that, compared to its neighbours, they have one of the highest emigration rates and the lowest 'Migration Replacement Rate' (MRR), which is a measurement of how much emigrated locals are adequately replaced by migrant workers (Lithunianan Free Market Institute, 2018a). Put together, this means that Lithuania has had an acute difficulty of engaging foreign workers to compensate for its dearth of local labour, with attendant economic consequences and slower growth. It was found that since 2012, businesses have found it difficult to hire the many non-EU nationals who seek work in the EU, including seasonal workers and high-skilled talents. A range of regulations, such as annual entry quotas, application fees, labour market testing and labour market access requirements have raised the entry barriers of such workers in the Lithuanian labour market (Lithuanian Free Market Institute, 2018a). It has one of the strictest entry barriers in the region, with applications taking months longer, and residence permits having highly restrictive conditions on employment.

LFMI's advocacy on the issue, since the first article they published in October 2021 about the country's looming demographic problems and manpower crunches, has yielded some significant fruits. On 30th June 2022, the Lithuanian parliament adopted a law that liberalised labour migration of non-EU nationals and removed some restrictive regulations (see TRINITI, 2022; Deloitte, 2022).

The main changes include:

1. The time it takes non-EU workers to receive temporary residence permits was cut by one month (from two to one month for high-skilled workers, and from four to three months for all others).
2. Migrant workers will now be able to receive temporary resident permits while they are still abroad. Previously they had to be physically in Lithuania to apply for it.
3. To hire migrant workers, employers will have to submit information either about their qualifications or work experience. Previously both requirements were mandatory. If a labour migrant's wage is higher than the average wage, neither will be required any more. (LFMI has proposed to remove both requirements for all migrant workers.)
4. The reform eliminated so-called labour market tests for migrants applying for high-skilled positions. Previously, in order to hire a migrant worker, employers were required by law to register the vacancy with the Employment Service which in turn would make a public announcement of the vacancy in order to find a local worker. (LFMI has proposed to abolish labour market testing for all migrant workers regardless of their qualifications.)
5. Before the reform, whitelisted companies benefited from simplified procedures for employing migrant workers. This whitelisting has been eliminated, and simplified procedures will now apply to all companies.

Until the beginning of 2022, the only focus of Lithuania's labour migration policy had been to attract high value-added specialists and to simplify procedures only for this category of migrant workers. Following the public and policy debates initiated by LFMI, the government defined liberalisation of labour migration regulations for low and mid-skilled migrants as its key priority.

LFMI's work on labour migration restrictions is part of its long-running effort at promoting greater flexibility in the labour markets. Major research projects included lowering the requirements for employee dismissals and minimum wage statutes, some of which were due to European Union laws. Significantly, LFMI (2022a) also published the Employment Flexibility Index, which ranks countries accordingly and which is based on previously discontinued World Bank Data. Since its first edition in 2018 and after concerted efforts by LFMI, including media outreach, coalition building and policy advisory, there was a marked improvement in 2019, where Lithuania showed the biggest improvement in all of EU and OECD countries due to the reduction of redundancy costs (Lithuanian Free Market Institute, 2018b). LFMI has had a long track record of pushing for labour market reforms since the 1990s. Notably, in 1996, its analysts helped draft the country's new labour code, and in 1998, provided recommendations to streamline the complicated occupational licensing framework, a recommendation which was adopted in 2004.

In a further effort to boost Lithuania's economic competitiveness, LFMI has also championed the unique Estonian corporate tax model of fully retained profits. This is a model that Estonia adopted in 1999 and which actually originated from the recommendations by LFMI analysts at that time. With corporate taxes only being paid upon the distribution of profits, such a model incentivises the reinvestment of said profits, spurring capital accumulation (Masso & Meriküll, 2011). Certainly, Estonia's tax system is lauded as the most competitive in the world by the International Tax Competitiveness Index (Tax Foundation, 2021). Latvia emulated this system since 2018, and together, they are among the highest recipients of foreign direct investment in the Eastern and Central European Region.

Over the years LFMI has consistently made the case for low, simple and competitive taxation. Notably, they have repeatedly pushed for abolishing the road tax and numerous tax breaks, for opposing the real estate tax and for tying the size of levies and dues charged on government services to the costs of service provision. The official programs of the 1998 and 2000 government administrations endorsed almost all of the LFMI's proposed principles in regards to taxation (Lithuanian Free Market Institute, 2022b). Regarding the Estonian model, even though Lithuanian analysts from LFMI first proposed this approach, Lithuania itself did not fully implement it, and instead went for a 0% tax rate on reinvested profits from 1997 to 2022 (which still retains the need for tax accounting, as compared to the Estonian model). This zero tax rate on reinvested profits was then revoked 2002 upon Lithuania's accession to the European Union, and today, its effective tax rate stands at 27.7%, significantly higher than that of Estonia and Latvia. LFMI (2021a) has pointed out that since 2015, its labour productivity has been growing more slowly than real wages, which indicates that it is necessary to take measures for the country's economy to improve competitiveness. LFMI (2021b) has called for this Estonian model to come home to Lithuania, especially in the light of the post-COVID-19 economic challenges and since recently, Lithuania has had low net capital stock per employer by 2.7 times than the EU average. Their work on this project is ongoing, and is especially relevant in the light of current trends towards a global corporate tax minimum, a move which arguably reduces interjurisdictional tax competition.

Market Failure Theory

The chapter so far has presented the benefits of economic freedom, and some case studies of local actors pursuing said benefits through pro-market reforms. However, the reality is far more complex if one considers the theory of market failure, which is one, though not the only, criticism levelled against the market liberal position. Markets are not always efficient mechanisms to allocate resources. Markets are said to fail due to the presence of externalities (where spillover costs and benefits of individual transactions are not internalised), transactions cost, information gaps and asymmetries, public goods and a range of collective action problems (Bator, 1958; Stiglitz, 2000).

These failures of markets are to be understood in relation to the neoclassical paradigm of markets. In this paradigm, markets work efficiently because they fulfil certain conditions, such as the presence of perfect information, perfect competition, the absence of transactions costs and external costs, among others. Since real-world markets do not actually meet these conditions, failure is understandably commonplace. This neoclassical paradigm is an important normative benchmark around which the debate over markets has proceeded. On one hand, some pro-market economists believe that real-world markets do indeed come close to the neoclassical standard. Market failure theorists, however, condemn markets for not doing so, and hence call for the necessity of government intervention, such as taxes and subsidies (see Pigou, 1932). Whether this normative benchmark is appropriate is something to be considered shortly.

Market failure theory is worth considering in the context of development. Real-world markets do exhibit numerous imperfections, but when considering poor nations in a low state of development, such imperfections may indeed be exacerbated. First, given the low state of development in poor nations, there are great positive externalities to be reaped through state investments in merits goods like health care, transportation and infrastructure. Second, the dearth of indigenous capital and an entrepreneurial class may necessitate either the state or foreign direct investment, to pump capital into the local economy. Third, poor nations are typically characterised by weak governance: the rule of law may be absent, and the institutions of a market economy that are taken for granted are non-existent. The institutional environment for market exchanges is absent, and transactions cost are extremely high in a developing country context.

Perhaps the most significant market failure argument that may be applied in the context of development is that of 'coordination failure', which is a situation where various economic agents are unable to coordinate their actions with each other, leaving everyone in a sub-optimal outcome. In fact, the classical development economists (reviewed in Chap. 2) are very much operating within this perspective, where a coordination failure exists and which requires a 'big-push' intervention from the state to catalyse development. Development often requires the concerted action of different parties: the decision of some firms to invest depends on that of others, whether consumers spend may depend on jobs available, which in turn depends on industrial conditions, which may be connected to governmental decisions on infrastructure projects, and so on. The actions of various economic actors are complementary, and there could be failure for these necessary actions to be undertaken, which may end up in a collective failure. The apparent necessity of a 'big-push' by the state, to jumpstart the development process, seems sensible on this approach.

Economists working in this tradition typically believe that some form of state-led industrialisation plan is needed, lest developing countries find themselves stuck in a reliance on pre-industrial, agricultural types of production. Thus, some form of government intervention is simply needed in a development context. Rather than full-on central planning, strategic infrastructure investments or industrial policies may be required in developing nations' contexts.

Market Process Theory

That markets fail to achieve the standard of Pareto optimality in neoclassical economics is to be fully acknowledged. Externalities may at times be very significant, and arise from a myriad of private actions. One question though is whether or not corrective government action is able to restore the market to its ideal state, considering that state officials themselves suffer from a variety of problems of their own. It is often said that 'government failure' may at times outweigh 'market failure', in which case, an imperfect market equilibrium may be the best possible world on offer. A deeper problem with the standard market failure analysis is that it judges markets against an unrealistic standard, where any deviations from the ideal are considered a failure. This is a truism: it is not surprising that in the real world, for example, human beings often do not have all the information necessary to make the best decision possible, and often act in ways that are less than fully rational, as behavioural economists have rightly pointed out.

It is therefore important to critically reflect on the normative benchmark around which the state-market debate often revolves: neoclassical economics with its idealised conditions. Pro-market neoclassical economists (such as those from the Chicago School tradition) believe that markets really do approximate this standard, while market failure theorists criticise markets for failing to reach it. It is in this context that an alternative paradigm should be presented: market process theory. Market process theory is in turn derived most significantly from the work of the economist Israel Kirzner, who built on earlier contributions of Ludwig von Mises and F. A. Hayek.

According to market process theorists, markets are not a closed-ended system of equilibrium, where all individual preferences are given, and where actors simply maximise their utility within given constraints. Rather, markets are an open-ended *discovery process* where all actors, consumers and producers are constantly adjusting their plans and learning from new information (Kirzner, 1997a, 1997b. The market seldom reaches equilibrium, and it is the *process* by which markets equilibrate that should be prime focus of economic analysis. Accordingly, market process theorists believe that competition is the mechanism that drives this discovery process (Hayek, 1945, 2002); it is when competition occurs that trial-and-error learning ensues, and society better arrives at new and potentially better economic outcomes.

The implication of viewing markets this way is that the departures from neoclassical efficiency do not constitute the 'end of discussion'. Market imperfections are not the final word, but simply a starting point of analysis to consider alternative institutional arrangements and policies and their ability to close these gaps. The case for markets is not that it operates in a 'frictionless' way as depicted by models, but that is a robust system that minimises the knowledge and incentive problems which are inescapable in human societies (Pennington, 2011). It is *comparatively* superior to alternative institutional arrangements in dealing with the fact that human beings are primarily self-interested and are not omniscient.

Markets allow for economic coordination in the face of dispersed knowledge, complexity and human self-interest, and is thus the basis for any economy to achieve higher-order prosperity.

Thus, one can make the case for markets without necessarily resorting to neoclassical assumptions. In fact, it is important to clarify that neoclassical economics is not synonymous with neoliberal free market economics. The neoclassical paradigm may be used to both support and criticise market institutions. This insight is best demonstrated in the famous 'economic calculation debate' of the early twentieth century, which started when Ludwig von Mises (1922) argued that central planning would not be feasible since it lacked prices and profit-loss calculations necessary to calculate the value of scarce resources in their alternative uses. Karl Marx and Engels had initially argued that market economies relied on an 'anarchic' and uncoordinated approach to production, and that central planning would constitute scientific economic management:

> With the seizing of the means of production by society, production of commodities is done away with, and, simultaneously, the mastery of the product over the producer. Anarchy in social production is replaced by systematic, definite organization. The struggle for individual existence disappears. Then, for the first time, man, in a certain sense, is finally marked off from the rest of the animal kingdom, and emerges from mere animal conditions of existence into really human ones. The whole sphere of the conditions of life which environ man, and which have hitherto ruled man, now comes under the dominion and control of man, who for the first time becomes the real, conscious lord of nature, because he has now become master of his own social organization (Engels, 1880).

In the subsequent unfolding of the debate, market socialists, such as Oskar Lange and Abba Lerner, married the framework of neoclassical economics with their normative advocacy of central economic planning (see Lavoie, 1981 for a full review of these debates). They argued that if it was just a matter of getting the prices right, the problem was 'very simple', for 'the Central Planning Board has to fix prices and see to it that all managers of plants, industries, and resources do their accounting on the basis of the prices fixed by the Central Planning Board, and not tolerate any use of other accounting'. Any errors would be corrected by determining whether, at the end of the planning period, there was a 'surplus or deficit' of any commodity or factor of production (Lange & Taylor, 1952, pp. 80–81). Leonid Kantorovich (1965) added that in a socialist state 'the preparation of such a plan and its indices is an extremely complex task' and called for advanced mathematics, data collection, and calculation. Optimal indices would substitute for prices and could be calculated by sufficiently informed and skilled central planners, who would generate indices that would be equal to marginal costs. Such indices would then be fed into the central planning process, resulting in a variety of five-year plans.

The market socialist position demonstrates that neoclassical economics may also be employed towards a market-critical position (see Hodgson, 2000 for further examples). In fact, this market socialist position had caught the market liberals by surprise, and subsequently prompted market liberals in subsequent rounds of the debate, to clarify the need for the justification of market economics to rest on non-neoclassical grounds (Boettke et al., 2014). It is therefore important to separate the methodological toolkit with specific sets of policy conclusions.

Accordingly, the reason why market arrangements are deemed superior to planning alternatives, in our account, is not that it requires perfect information, but that *given the fact* that information is tacit, dispersed and often difficult to aggregate means that markets play an epistemic function and help coordinate human action. Markets of course still fail, and are imperfect, but at the very least, their competitive nature allows for experimental learning, as opposed to political decision-making, where the eventual singularity of outcomes means that there no learning can take place (DeCanio, 2014). In the absence of comparative learning, it is often impossible to determine whether a policy or course of action undertaken by the state, even in democratic contexts, was indeed the best possible one out of various alternatives—proper policy evaluation is impossible (DeCanio, 2021).

Market process theory is worth considering here because it highlights the relevance of institutions. In fact, in neoclassical economics, there are no institutions. In a frictionless world where all information is possessed and where individuals simply compute utility, there is no need to consider the wider environment of human action. Schools of thought which are wedded to the general equilibrium concept either use it as a way to describe how markets work (as some in the Chicago School tradition do), or as a benchmark with which to criticise market operations (market failure theorists), but both fail to consider the way institutions and practices emerge to cope with departures from perfection (see Boettke, 1997).

In fact, the actions of local actors documented in the case studies above make sense only in an open-ended world. Policy reformers play a valuable role precisely because the status quo is far from perfect. They notice gaps in the policy environment and work to improve social outcomes for all. Market process theory allows for institutional analysis and an appreciation for the role of institutional entrepreneurs, a theme that will be explored further in subsequent chapters.

Dependency Theory

A different and far more radical critique of markets comes from dependency theory. This perspective is worth considering since it constituted a leading paradigm in development studies in the late twentieth century. Most associated with Raul Prebisch Hans Singer, Andre Gunder Frank, dependency theory arose in a search to understand under-development in Latin America and also as a response towards modernisation theory, popular at the time (see previous chapter). One core tenet of dependency theory is that there exists an unequal power relationship between nations in the global capitalist system: the 'core' (or 'Metropolis'), typically Western capitalist nations, as opposed to the 'periphery' (or 'Satellite'), who occupy a subordinate position. This global inequality explains under-development. Nations in the periphery are trapped in a state of dependency vis-à-vis the core, and as such remain poor.

The Marxist underpinnings of dependency theory are clear. In the world of Adam Smith, there is a natural harmony of interests in free markets. Dependency theory challenges this directly and argues that the interests of the Western capitalist nations have historically been antithetical to the rest, who have been exploited. Colonialism is an obvious example where Western empires subjugated far-flung peoples. But even in post-war phase of decolonisation, 'neo-colonial' structures are said to persist. The following aspects help clarify. First, in the liberal world economic order where trade is the norm, Western nations often enjoy better terms of trade, usually due to their superior bargaining power. Trade is not 'win–win' as in the Smithian world, it creates winners and losers (Hickel, 2017; Pieterse, 2002). Aside from trade, poor nations are also locked in a state of dependency as recipients of foreign aid (Azam et al., 1999; Moyo, 2009). These aid programs come with strings attached, most infamously the 'structural adjustment programs' pushed by the International Monetary Fund, where loan recipients had to conform to the free market prescriptions of the lenders. Periphery nations are dependent as aid-recipients since debt is created and must be repaid.

A related third point is the influence of multi-national corporations (MNCs) especially in the last few decades. MNCs penetrate local markets, with negative ramifications. One clear example is that of resource extraction. Local industries are geared towards these dangerous activities which primarily benefit the multinationals, with safety, health and environmental consequences. A similar phenomenon is the rise of 'sweatshops', a product of MNC investment in poor nations in search of cheap labour (see Snyder, 2010 for an analysis of sweatshops' exploitative nature but also Powell & Zwolinski, 2012 for a rebuttal). To the extent that developing nations rely on these processes for growth, they become dependent on global capital. Domestic legislation becomes 'pro-business' and MNC friendly, neglecting local development.

Today, dependency theory is no longer a leading paradigm, and understandably so for several reasons. First, its strong opposition to capitalism is contradicted by the fact that numerous developing nations from the 'periphery', have themselves integrated into the global economy and experienced rapid developmental progress. As Chap. 1 has pointed out, global inequality has fallen (though in-country inequality has risen in various places), and a large middle class from previously 'periphery' nations has been formed. The anti-capitalist prescriptions of dependency theory, such as self-sufficiency and socialism, have themselves perpetuated exploitation and fostered immiseration. The dualistic portrayal of core vs periphery is also hard to sustain given the multi-layered interdependence of national economies; rich and poor nations are 'dependent' on each other in different ways. Second, market liberals also criticise dependency theory's weak explanation of under development. Exploitation has indeed been commonplace throughout history, and none of that can adequately account for the 'Great Enrichment' explained in the previous chapter. According to market liberals, it was the sudden shift towards entrepreneurial liberty and dignity in the 1800s that facilitated an explosion of wealth, and accounts for the head-start that the West enjoyed. This perspective is also quick to point out that capitalism is not synonymous with imperialism, contrary to Lenin's belief that one grew out of the other; Adam Smith envisioned progress by consent, and was a fierce critic of slavery, colonialism, and imperialism (Easterly, 2021).

Dependency theory, while having fallen out of favour, should not be totally dismissed, however. There are still some relevant insights we may draw for understanding present-day development studies (see Ghosh, 2019 for a recent analysis). In our opinion, the most valuable insight of dependency theory is to reveal the salience of power considerations in economics. This is once again a flaw of neoclassical economics, which ignores questions of power. Dependency helps shed light on how the exercise of power, whether through market concentration, political hegemony, ideology or the design of global governance, can 'distort' economic outcomes. Indeed, the way global institutions are structured sometimes do reflect the political interests, or dominance of the Western establishment. Scholars like Joseph Stiglitz have pointed this out amply. But one graphic example from recent history is illustrative: the recent coronavirus pandemic and the resulting global inequality in vaccine access. As of July 2022, rich countries have vaccinated more people than in poor ones, at a factor of five (Guardian, 2022). The problem also stems from the inequitable nature of global governance, particularly how rich nations and pharmaceutical companies prioritised their own interests rather than contribute to the public good of vaccine access. COVAX was designed to address this problem, but ultimately failed, in part due to 'vaccine nationalism', 'queue jumping by wealthy countries' and a preference for bilateral deals (Ashraf et al., 2021; Yamey et al., 2022). A recent report captures the collective tragedy best:

> Vaccine inequity is symptomatic of the failure of global governance of the pandemic. The haphazard way in which vaccines are currently distributed must be addressed as part of a global vaccine strategy that includes a system of intellectual-property management, manufacturing, and distribution that ensures that vaccines are made available equitably around the world. Vaccines against pandemic diseases, and the ability to manufacture them, must not be a sequestered asset that maximizes the return to pharmaceutical company executives and shareholders or increases the electability of politicians. They must be a global public good. (Hunter et al., 2022)

Understanding power inequality is one thing, trying to solve it is another problem altogether. Dependency theory, to the extent that it requires Marxist solutions, may ultimately not be tenable. However, it is important to note that dependency theory's insights need not necessitate the Marxist conclusions its early advocates propagated. In fact, many of the problems identified by dependency theorists may be rectified through *liberal reform* of global institutions. How might global institutions embrace greater democratic accountability and be more responsive to the voices of all nations is an ongoing question to explore further. Western nations that preach the virtues of liberal democracy and market capitalism should also 'walk the walk', and curb the harms they themselves impose through illiberal practices they are involved in. In the end, the challenges outlined here once again point to the merits of a bottom-up approach to change, where local actors are given centre stage, which this handbook has tried to outline.

Conclusion

Every society confronts a choice as to what mode of economic organisation to adopt, in order to manage the central economic problem of scarcity and to coordinate human action. Market-based organisation has historically been the superior option, given its ability to unleash human potential, create wealth and thus alleviate global poverty. Markets and market reforms, however, are expressed locally through the participation of local actors, which explain the sheer varieties of capitalist arrangements in the world. From India, to Spain, to Philippines and Indonesia, we have shown in this chapter actual cases where economic freedom is being achieved by local organisations and actors.

Markets, and the degree of economic freedom that a society should embrace, is understandably contested, and two leading positions in this regard are market failure theory and dependency theory. The first points to the way real-world markets deviate from the ideal conditions of efficiency, and the second illuminates the structural power imbalances that exist in global economic relations. These market-critical positions imply a range of policy conclusions, from targeted policy interventions by states, to large-scale overhaul of existing institutions, and even to radical Marxist programs.

A fruitful response to these criticisms may be found in market process theory, one which recognises the pitfalls of the neoclassical paradigm, and which is also sensitive to the institutional context of economic exchange. It is this institutional context that the subsequent chapters will more deeply explore, in order to paint the wider infrastructure necessary for successful market activity to take place.

Discussion Questions

1. What is 'economic freedom'?
2. What is the 'economic calculation problem', and how can this be solved?
3. How essential are market freedoms in achieving prosperity and progress?
4. Why do some market reforms succeed but others fail?
5. How useful is the neoclassical economics paradigm in understanding real-world economics and how does it differ from 'market process' theory?
6. What are some ways in which we may still apply dependency theory to analyse global inequality today?
7. What functions do local organisations and actors play in implementing policy reforms and achieving national development?
8. How may global governance be restructured in such a way as to embrace bottom-up forces?

References

Alcantara, K., Bernardo, R., Chikiamco, C., Clarete, R., de Dios, E., & Fabella, R. (2021). *Momen2m: More reforms for economic growth*. Foundation for Economic Freedom.

Amanta, F., & Wibisono, I. (2021). *Negative Effects of Non-Tariff Trade Barriers on the Welfare of Indonesians*. Center for Indonesian Policy Studies. https://www.cips-indonesia.org/publicati ons/negative-effects-of-non-tariff-trade-barriers-on-the-welfare-of-indonesians.

Andriamananjara, S., Dean, J. M., Ferrantino, M. J., Feinberg, R. M., Ludema, R. D., & Tsigas, M. E. (2011). The Effects of Non-Tariff Measures on Prices, Trade, and Welfare: CGE Implementation of Policy-Based Price Comparisons. *SSRN Electronic Journal*. https://doi.org/10.2139/ssrn.539705.

Arangkada Philippines. (2020). *Joint Statement of Support for Amending the Public Services Act*. The Arangkada Philippines Project. http://www.investphilippines.info/arangkada/wp-content/uploads/2020/03/Joint-Statement-of-Support-for-Amending-the-Public-Services-Act.pdf.

Arcalas, J. (2022). *New PSA to spur $100-billion investments–DTI chief*. BusinessMirror. https://businessmirror.com.ph/2022/03/22/new-psa-to-spur-100-billion-investments-dti-chief/.

Asian Development Bank. (2017, November 23). *Public-Private Partnership Monitor*. Asian Development Bank; Asian Development Bank. https://www.adb.org/publications/public-private-partnership-monitor.

Asian Development Bank. (2019, October 28). *Policies to Support Investment Requirements of Indonesia's Food and Agriculture Development during 2020–2045*. Asian Development Bank; Asian Development Bank. https://www.adb.org/publications/indonesia-food-agriculture-development-2020-2045.

Ashraf, M. A., Muhammad, A., & Shafiq, Y. (2021). The politics of Covid-19 vaccine distribution and recognition. *Public Health Reviews, 42*, 1604343. https://doi.org/10.3389/phrs.2021.1604343.

Atlas Network. (2020). *Center for Indonesian Policy Studies wins 2020 Templeton Freedom Award*. Atlas Network. https://www.atlasnetwork.org/articles/center-for-indonesian-policy-studies-wins-2020-templeton-freedom-award.

Atlas Network. (2021). *Centre for Civil Society wins the 2021 Templeton Freedom Award*. Atlas Network. https://www.atlasnetwork.org/articles/center-for-civil-society-wins-the-2021-templeton-freedom-award.

Azam, J. P., Devarajan, S., & O'Connell, S. A. (1999). Aid dependence reconsidered. *World Bank Publications 2144*, World Bank. https://doi.org/10.1596/1813-9450-2144.

Bator, F. M. (1958). The anatomy of market failure. *The Quarterly Journal of Economics, 72*(3), 351–379. https://doi.org/10.2307/1882231.

Bedi, J., & Narang, P. (2020). *Progress Report 2020: Implementing the Street Vendors Act*. Centre for Civil Society India. https://ccs.in/sites/default/files/2022-08/progress-report-2020-implementing-the-street-vendors-act.pdf.

Bedi, P. (2013). *Standing Committee Report Summary The Street Vendors (Protection of Livelihood and Regulation of Street Vending) Bill, 2012*. PRS Legislative Research. https://prsindia.org/files/bills_acts/bills_parliament/2012/SCR_summary-Street_Vendors_bill.pdf.

Berggren, N. (2003). The benefits of economic freedom: A survey. *The Independent Review, 8*(2), 193–211. https://www.independent.org/publications/tir/article.asp?id=48.

Bhowmik, S. K. (2003). National policy for street vendors. *Economic and Political Weekly, 38*(16). https://www.epw.in/journal/2003/16/commentary/national-policy-street-vendors.html.

Boettke, P. J. (1997). Where did economics go wrong? equilibrium as a flight from reality. *Critical Review, 11*(1), 11–64. https://doi.org/10.1080/08913819708443443.

Boettke, P. J., Coyne, C. J., & Leeson, P. T. (2014). Hayek versus the neoclassicists: Lessons from the socialist calculation debate. In R. Garrison & N. Barry (Eds.), *Elgar companion to Hayekian economics* (pp. 278–293). Edward Elgar Publishing.

Center for Indonesian Policy Studies. (2020). *Annual Report 2020*. Center for Indonesian Policy Studies. https://www.cips-indonesia.org/_files/ugd/c95e5d_d7fb1adb598548f5b86379824c7d8a0a.pdf.

Center for Indonesian Policy Studies. (2021). *Annual Report 2021*. Center for Indonesian Policy Studies. https://www.cips-indonesia.org/_files/ugd/c95e5d_9c4562ac24d548f5bbbe118447c04f91.pdf.

Clemens, M. A. (2011). Economics and emigration: Trillion-dollar bills on the sidewalk? *Journal of Economic Perspectives, 25*(3), 83–106. https://doi.org/10.1257/jep.25.3.83.

Crismundo, K. (2021). *NEDA, DTI chiefs laud PRRD's order to pass economic reform bills*. Philippine News Agency. https://www.pna.gov.ph/articles/1148368.

D'Emilio, J. (2007). Capitalism and Gay Identity. In R. Parker & P. Aggleton (Eds.), *Culture, Society and Sexuality* (pp. 266–274). Routledge.

DeCanio, S. (2014). Democracy, the market, and the logic of social choice. *American Journal of Political Science, 58*(3), 637–652. https://doi.org/10.1111/ajps.12072.

DeCanio, S. (2021). Efficiency, Legitimacy and the Administrative State. *Social Philosophy and Policy, 38*(1), 198–219. https://doi.org/10.1017/S0265052521000285.

Deloitte. (2022). *Immigration & Labour Law changes in Lithuania*. Deloitte. https://www2.deloitte.com/lt/en/pages/legal/articles/Immigration-Labour-Law-changes-in-Lithuania.html.

Easterly, W. (2021). Progress by consent: Adam Smith as development economist. *The Review of Austrian Economics, 34*(2), 179–201. https://doi.org/10.1007/s11138-019-00478-5.

Economist. (2021). *The world is entering a new era of big government*. The Economist Magazine. https://www.economist.com/leaders/2021/11/20/the-world-is-entering-a-new-era-of-big-government.

Eighteenth Congress of the Republic of the Philippines. (2022). *Republic Act No. 11659*. The Official Gazette, Philippines. https://www.officialgazette.gov.ph/downloads/2022/03mar/20220321-RA-11659.pdf.

Enache, C. (2021). *Regional Tax competition Is stopping Spain from becoming Europe's Tax Hell*. Tax Foundation. https://taxfoundation.org/tax-competition-spain-europes-tax-hell/.

Engels, F. (1880). *Socialism: Utopian and Scientific*, reprinted in 1970, Marx and Engels, Selected Works, Vol. 3. Progress Publishers.

Feldmann, M. (2019). Global varieties of capitalism. *World Politics, 71*(1), 162–196. https://doi.org/10.1017/S0043887118000230.

Fernandez-Lasquetty, J. (2022). *Key Facts and Figures on Madrid Taxation*.

Gartzke, E. (2007). The capitalist peace. *American Journal of Political Science, 51*(1), 166–191. https://doi.org/10.1111/j.1540-5907.2007.00244.x.

Ghosh, B. N. (2019). *Dependency theory revisited*. Routledge.

Guardian. (2022). *Covid vaccine figures lay bare global inequality as global target missed*. Guardian. www.theguardian.com/global-development/2022/jul/21/covid-vaccine-figures-lay-bare-global-inequality-as-global-target-missed.

Halliday, D., & Thrasher, J. (2020). *The ethics of capitalism*. Oxford University Press.

Hanke, S. H., & Walters, S. J. (1997). Economic freedom, prosperity, and equality: A survey. *Cato Journal, 17*(2), 117–146. https://www.cato.org/sites/cato.org/files/serials/files/cato-journal/1997/11/cj17n2-1.pdf.

Hayek, F. A. (1945). The use of knowledge in society. *The American Economic Review, 35*, 519–530.

Hayek, F. A. (2002). Competition as a discovery procedure. *Quarterly Journal of Austrian Economics, 5*(3), 9–23.

Hickel, J. (2017). *The divide: A brief guide to global inequality and its solutions*. Random House.

Hodgson, G. M. (2000). What is the essence of institutional economics? *Journal of Economic Issues, 34*(2), 317–329. https://doi.org/10.1080/00213624.2000.11506269.

Horwitz, S. (2015). *Hayek's modern family: Classical liberalism and the evolution of social institutions*. Palgrave Macmillan.

Hundt, D., & Uttam, J. (2017). *Varieties of capitalism in Asia: Beyond the developmental state*. Springer.

Hunter, D. J., Abdool Karim, S. S., Baden, L. R., Farrar, J. J., Hamel, M. B., Longo, D. L., & Rubin, E. J. (2022). Addressing vaccine inequity—Covid-19 vaccines as a global public good. *New England Journal of Medicine, 386*(12), 1176–1179. https://doi.org/10.1056/NEJMe2202547.

ILO. (2022). *About the ILO in Lithuania*. International Labour Organisation. https://www.ilo.org/budapest/countries-covered/lithuania/WCMS_476067/lang--en/index.htm.

Kalinkaitė-Matuliauskienė, V. (2021). *Lithuanian firms ask to allow immigration from "culturally proximate" countries*. Lithuanian National Television and Radio. https://www.lrt.lt/en/news-in-english/19/1541662/lithuanian-firms-ask-to-allow-immigration-from-culturally-proximate-countries.

Kantorovich, L. (1965). *The best use of economic resources*. Pergamon Press.

Kemp, S. (2020). *Digital 2020: The Philippines*. Data Reportal.https://datareportal.com/reports/digital-2020-philippines.

Kirzner, I. M. (1997a). Entrepreneurial discovery and the competitive market process: An Austrian approach. *Journal of Economic Literature, 35*(1), 60–85.

Kirzner, I. M. (1997b). *How Markets Work: Disequilibrium, Entrepreneurship and Discovery*. Institute for Economic Affairs. https://iea.org.uk/publications/research/how-markets-work-disequilibrium-entrepreneurship-and-discovery.

Lange, O., & Taylor, F. (1952). *On the economic theory of socialism*. University of Minnesota Press.

Lavoie, D. (1981). *Rivalry and central planning: A re-examination of the debate over economic calculation under socialism*. Mercatus Center.

Lithuanian Free Market Institute. (2018a). *Labour migration and flexibility of regulation for employing Non-EU Nationals*. Lithuanian Free Market Institute. https://www.llri.lt/wp-content/uploads/2018/06/Labour-Migration_3.pdf.

Lithuanian Free Market Institute. (2018b). *Employment Flexibility Index 2019 Shows the Biggest Leap for Lithuania\Lithuanian Free Market Institute*. https://en.llri.lt/news/economic-policy/employment-flexibility-index-2019-shows-the-biggest-leap-for-lithuania/lrinka.

Lithuanian Free Market Institute. (2021a). *Invest in Lithuania - proposals for the transformation of the Lithuanian economy*. Lithuanian Free Market Institute. https://www.llri.lt/wp-content/uploads/2021/02/2021-Vilties-bures.-Last-one-4.pdf.

Lithuanian Free Market Institute. (2021b). *Estonian Corporate Tax Model Should Return Home, to Lithuania*. Lithuanian Free Market Institute. https://en.llri.lt/news/estonian-corporate-tax-model-should-return-home-to-lithuania/lrinka.

Lithuanian Free Market Institute. (2022a). *Labour market research*. https://en.llri.lt/labour.

Lithuanian Free Market Institute. (2022b). *Works of LFMI*. Lithuanian Free Market Institute. https://en.llri.lt/lfmi/history-of-lfmi.

Marks, S. V. (2017). Non-tariff trade regulations in Indonesia: Nominal and effective rates of protection. *Bulletin of Indonesian Economic Studies, 53*(3), 333–357. https://doi.org/10.1080/00074918.2017.1298721.

Masso, J., & Meriküll, J. (2011). Macroeconomic effects of zero corporate income tax on retained earnings. *Baltic Journal of Economics, 11*(2), 81–99. https://doi.org/10.1080/1406099X.2011.10840502.

Mises, L. V. (1922). *Socialism: An economic and sociological analysis*. Gustav Fischer Verlag.

Miozzi, V. J., & Powell, B. (2022). Measuring economic freedom during the Covid-19 pandemic. *Journal of Institutional Economics, 19*(2), 229–250. https://doi.org/10.1017/S1744137422000376.

Moyo, D. (2009). *Dead aid: Why aid is not working and how there is a better way for Africa*. Macmillan.

Munadi, E. (2019). Indonesian non-tariff measures: Updates and insights. In T. T. D. Ha & S. Rosenow (Eds.), *Non-tariff measures in ASEAN-an update* (pp. 67–84). Economic Research Institute for ASEAN and East Asia (ERIA). https://www.eria.org/publications/non-tariff-measures--an-update/.

Narang, P., & Sharma, M. (2021). *Examining the Implementation of Street Vendors Act, 2014*. Centre for Civil Society India. https://ccs.in/sites/default/files/2022-12/examining_the_implementation_-_02.pdf.

Narang, P., & Sabharwal, V. (2019). *Do street vendors have a right to the city?* Innovative Governance of Large Urban Systems. Centre for Civil Society. https://iglus.org/wp-content/uploads/2019/10/Do-street-vendors-have-a-right-to-the-city-IGLUS.pdf.

Neilson, J. (2018). Feeding the bangsa: Food sovereignty and the state in Indonesia. In A. A. Patunru, M. Pangestu, & M. C. Basri (Eds.), *Indonesia in the new world: Globalisation, nationalism and sovereignty* (pp. 73–89). ISEAS Publishing.

Pennington, M. (2011). *Robust political economy.* Edward Elgar Publishing.

Pieterse, J. N. (2002). Global inequality: Bringing politics back in. *Third World Quarterly, 23*(6), 1023–1046. https://doi.org/10.1080/0143659022000036667.

Pigou, A. (1932). *The economics of welfare* (4th ed.). Macmillan.

Pina, J. (2021). *Spanish regions reduce taxation further in response to Fundalib Index.* Atlas Network. https://www.atlasnetwork.org/articles/spanish-regions-reduce-taxation-further-in-response-to-fundalib-index.

Powell, B., & Zwolinski, M. (2012). The ethical and economic case against sweatshop labor: A critical assessment. *Journal of Business Ethics, 107*(4), 449–472. https://doi.org/10.1007/S10551-011-1058-8.

Rappler. (2020). *Metro Manila's traffic problem explained.* Rappler. https://www.rappler.com/newsbreak/explainers/explanation-metro-manila-traffic-public-commute-problem/.

Salikha, A. (2018). *Latest: Southeast Asian 4G availability and speed rankings.* Seasia. https://seasia.co/2018/02/22/latest-southeast-asian-s-4g-availability-and-speed-rankings.

Sánchez de la Cruz, D. (2021). *Liberalismo a la madrileña.* Ediciones Deusto.

Sankrit, R. (2015). SEWA Bharat and Street Vendors in Delhi: Inclusive Cities Project.

Schmidtz, D., & Brennan, J. (2010). *A brief history of liberty.* Wiley-Blackwell.

Seventeenth Congress of the Republic of the Philippines. (2017). *An Act Further Amending Commonwealth Act No. 146 Otherwise Known as the Public Service Act, as Amended.* Senate of the Philippines. https://legacy.senate.gov.ph/lisdata/2525521749!.pdf.

Snyder, J. (2010). Exploitation and sweatshop labor: Perspectives and issues. *Business Ethics Quarterly, 20*(2), 187–213. https://doi.org/10.5840/beq201020215.

Stiglitz, J. E. (2000). The contributions of the economics of information to twentieth century economics. *The Quarterly Journal of Economics, 115*(4), 1441–1478. https://doi.org/10.1162/003355300555015.

Tax Foundation. (2021). *Estonia\International Tax Competitiveness Index.* Tax Foundation. https://tax-competition.org/estonia.

TRINITI. (2022). *Starting from 1 August, the legal situation of aliens in Lithuania is further improved.* TRINITI. https://triniti.eu/insights/starting-from-1-august-the-legal-situation-of-aliens-in-lithuania-is-further-improved/.

Villanueva, J. (2021). *Economic managers echo measures for PH recovery.* Philippine News Agency. https://www.pna.gov.ph/articles/1155156.

White, L. (2012). *The clash of economic ideas: The great policy debates and experiments of the last hundred years.* Cambridge University Press.

World Bank. (2019). *Creating markets in the Philippines.* World Bank. https://documents1.worldbank.org/curated/en/217141587025934915/pdf/Creating-Markets-in-the-Philippines-Unlocking-Private-Sector-Markets-to-Create-Better-Jobs-Country-Private-Sector-Diagnostic.pdf.

World Food Programme. (2020). *Indonesia—Covid-19: Economic and Food Security Implications.* World Food Programme. https://www.wfp.org/publications/covid-19-economic-and-food-security-implications-indonesia-4th-edition-december-2020.

Yamey, G., Garcia, P., Hassan, F., Mao, W., McDade, K. K., Pai, M., & Udayakumar, K. (2022). It is not too late to achieve global covid 19 vaccine equity. *Bmj, 376.* https://doi.org/10.1136/bmj-2022-070650.

Zwolinski, M. (2019). Libertarianism and the Welfare state. In J. Brennan, B. van der Vossen, & D. Schmidtz (Eds.), *The Routledge handbook of libertarianism* (pp. 323–341). Routledge.

Institutions and Market-Driven Development

4

Rise (or Resurgence) of Institutional Economics

The purpose of this chapter is to explain the institutional basis of market-based development. As previously established, markets are necessary for nations to experience the gains from trade and innovation, and thereby achieve economic progress. However, market exchange must be understood not from the perspective of neo-classical theory, but with regard to the institutional context within which human agency is embedded. Thus, the question of development may be understood with regard to a 'central institutional question': what are the rules and norms which facilitate economic exchange, development and progress? Our answer to this question is the liberal institutional package of private property rights and the rule of law, which will be further elucidated.

Accordingly, it is first necessary to introduce 'institutional economics', specifically how it differs from mainstream economics and its contributions to development studies. A distinguishing essence of institutional economics is its providing a richer conception of human action and how it focuses attention on the wider environment of decision-making (Hodgson, 2000, 2017). This in turn opens the door to consider non-economistic ingredients of successful development, such as the legal system, state capacity and cultural values, which the subsequent chapters will further unpack. Institutional economics is characterised by (though not exclusively defined by) a high degree of interdisciplinarity which is to be welcome in the study of development.

Institutional economics is a diverse, complex and well-established tradition, and the full scope of which cannot be adequately covered in this volume. Interested readers should consult the relevant literatures to track and evaluate the development of institutionalism in the history of economic thought (Ménard & Shirley, 2022; Hodgson, 2004). The purposes of this chapter are to highlight some of its key concepts and their relevance for understanding development.

© The Author(s), under exclusive license to Springer Nature Singapore Pte Ltd. 2023   89
B. Cheang and T. G. Palmer, *Institutions and Economic Development*,
Classroom Companion: Economics, https://doi.org/10.1007/978-981-99-0844-8_4

Viewing development through the lens of institutionalism is not 'new'. Classical thinkers of the past have always sought to consider the institutions that give rise to the wealth of nations, or the absence thereof. However, it was in the late twentieth century that there was a rise (or one might argue resurgence) of institutionalist thinking in not just development, but economics widely understood, in the form of 'New Institutional Economics' (NIE). There are generally three branches of NIE, laid out in Table 4.1.

NIE is a branch of economic thought that can be understood with reference to several core concepts: transactions costs, property rights and contracts, which were thought to have been undertheorised in mainstream economic thinking (Menard & Shirley, 2014). Ronald Coase's groundbreaking inquiry pointed attention to the nature and implications of transactions costs, which are impediments to market exchanges that prevent the gains of which from being realised in the first place;

Table 4.1 Branches of new institutional economics

Branch	Brief description
Oliver Williamson's Transactions Cost Economics	Oliver Williamson was an early pioneer in NIE who extended Ronald Coase's insights on transactions costs to a variety of applications. Most of these applications focus on the nature of firms and the mechanisms used to overcome coordination and information problems
Douglass North's Historical Institutionalism and Development Economics	Douglass North focused on the institutions that contribute to economic development and explored them through a historical lens. The institutions that North explored generally are property rights institutions and those that facilitate a dispersion of political power. This was motivated by a desire to fill the gap in neoclassical economics which ostensibly neglected institutions In later works, North also identified the importance of values and beliefs in trapping nations in a path-dependent state of under-development
Ostrom's Bloomington School of Political Economy	Elinor Ostrom's work was focused on the management of common-pool resources. Her extensive fieldwork found that aside from state or private management, local communities could devise rules to govern resource use and overcome collective action problems While her work was not explicitly focused on development issues, her vision of polycentricity and self-governance, however, has far-reaching implications on political theory and the politics of development

Source Ménard and Shirley (2022)

these may be logistical, arising from a lack of information or from a lack of trust, etc. It is due to the presence of transactions costs that firms exist and in fact, give rise to a range of devices that facilitate market exchange (Coase, 1998). Among the many institutions that arise to cope with such costs include property rights, which concern the de facto and de jure rules that govern resource use, and (relatedly) contracts, which are agreements that aim to transfer and specify these rights between parties.

The basic premise of this line of thinking is that contrary to textbook models of economics which are 'frictionless', the real world of transactions costs means that there are various impediments to market exchange, which have consequences on a nation's prospects of achieving economic progress and other positive outcomes. From a development context, one must examine the institutional environment and ascertain how well it overcomes these impediments (Shirley, 2005). What are the rules and norms that govern mutual interactions, resource use and thereby foster wealth-creating exchange? Seen this way, one would be interested in the political system, the economic institutions, the cultural environment and more, since they all have implications on development outcomes.

New or Not?

It is worth considering whether this approach to thinking about economics is necessarily 'new'. Certainly, NIE scholars believe so, in terms of how they depart from neoclassical economics. Neoclassical economics is one which has as its centre *homo economicus*, a version of man as a rational utility maximiser, who possesses all available information and whose preferences are given. Such an economic agent makes maximising conditions, and markets generally operate in equilibrium. Such a picture helps us see why institutions have no place: it is a frictionless world in which the need for institutions is made irrelevant. Additionally, the key role of entrepreneurs, stressed by the market process theory of the previous chapter, is also absent.

However, it should be seriously clarified that the reality is far more complex. There are internal differences between NIE scholars; for example, Oliver Williamson was more wedded to the standard conception while Douglass North and Coase developed concerns about it (Hodgson, 2014). It should also be crucially noted, as pointed out by Hodgson (1998) that early work in NIE explained the emergence of institutions with reference to this very same model of rational man, through methodologically individualist analyses. As such, the theories of NIE should also be situated within a larger appreciation for a longer school of institutionalism that preceded it, which features the likes of Thorstein Veblen, John Commons, Wesley Mitchell, John Kenneth Galbraith, Gunnar Myrdal and most recently, Geoffrey Hodgson.

Their insights are varied, but it is safe to say that one of its defining characteristics is its more culturally-situated model of man as a *habit-following* creature. Perhaps the most famous example of this reasoning is by Galbraith (1958) who explored the powerful influences of the advertising industry and thereby challenging the naïve assumptions of given preferences. Taking this different conception of man also allows social scientists to admit that power plays a big role in shaping economic outcomes, a variable that the economism of mainstream thinking is blind to (Ozanne, 2016). Of course, this does not mean that individuals are merely 'slaves' to their environment with no autonomy of their own (pure determinism), but that in a mutually constitutive fashion, both individuals and their institutional environments shape each other (Commons, 1934; Hodgson, 1998). Such a two-way understanding of agency and structure is also connected to an evolutionary view of the market where actors learn, respond to external stimuli and themselves shape the environment, rather than circulating in a closed-ended loop (Alchian, 1950; Nelson & Winter, 1982, 2002; Witt, 2016).

Therefore, it may be more accurate to depict institutionalism not as a 'new' contribution to economics, but one which refined and extended an older tradition. Institutionalist insights, however, as the next section will show, were not always embraced by the development community. In that sense, institutionalism may be 'new' to the extent that the development community incorporated these insights in their models and policymaking.

While it is not the scope of this volume to develop a new theory of institutionalism, the approach taken here is one that recognises the culturally-situated nature of man, the importance of learning processes in economic exchange and in people's attempts to shape their institutional environment. The specific scholars that best exemplify our position are Douglass North, F.A. Hayek and Elinor Ostrom, all of whom—though to varying degrees—admit a role for social structures in their analyses, moderating the excesses of neoclassical economics and strict methodological individualism.[1]

There are specific ways in which these scholars are relevant to our analysis. First, economic actors should be seen not as rational utility maximisers, but as fallible individuals who do not always possess the highest virtue, knowledge or capabilities. The beliefs, values and mental models that people hold affect their actions and may themselves be in error and will finally have implications on development outcomes (Denzau & North 2000). Nonetheless, individuals engage in evolutionary learning and in that process *discover* opportunities for not only economic profit, but socio-cultural change (Hayek, 2002; Horwitz, 2015). Individuals are both a product of social structures but often also change these structures.

Market institutions therefore are systems of polycentricity which allow for local knowledge to be used and for local communities to participate in social

---

[1] It should be acknowledged that F.A. Hayek is not typically considered an NIE economist. That said, Hayek's scholarship has extensively explored the political infrastructure that undergird a liberal social order, especially his works on constitutionalism and the rule of law. In that way, Hayek's insights are relevant in highlighting the importance of *liberal institutions* in a healthy social order. Additionally, Hayek's social ontology transcends strict methodological individualism; much of his writings acknowledge preference endogeneity and situate individuals within larger social structures (see Lewis, 2014; Dold & Lewis, 2022).

change (Aligica & Tarko, 2012; Ostrom, 2010). This market process, institution-alist conception means that institutions are not given but are themselves shaped endogenously. The institutions that people live under are not static but are in con-stant flux due to the entrepreneurial actions of change agents. Accordingly, the institutions of property rights and rule of law which this chapter will explore fur-ther need to be shaped by local agents if they are to be successfully adopted, and which will thus take different flavours according to local cultural patterns.

Defining Institutions

With this conception, institutions may now be more accurately defined. Douglass North's (1990) classic definition forms a useful starting point: 'institutions are the rules of the game in a society which define the framework within which human interaction takes place'. This definition is admittedly imperfect and sub-ject to disputation by numerous institutional economists over the years. However, it is helpful in highlighting the *enduring, relatively persistent* quality of institutions and how human behaviour is shaped by them.

Accordingly, institutions may first be understood in terms of 'formal institu-tions', which are the rules in society which are codified through official, legal and political means. A political constitution under a presidential regime which states the conditions and frequency of presidential elections is an example of a formal institution. That constitution is encoded in legislation, and it shapes the expec-tations of citizens and political actors. Such legislation is found within a legal system, which provides legal means to seek address, resolve disputes and govern human conduct. The nature of such political constitutions and legal institutions shapes economic conduct: contracts, courts and financial regulations are examples of economic institutions. Ultimately, there are two key characteristics of formal institutions: first, the rules that they embody are made explicit, such as through written form, and second, formal institutions are enforced through channels that are widely accepted as official (Baland et al., 2020).

The Northian definition of institutions has also included informal institutions. Unlike formal institutions which are codified in some form of official writing, informal institutions resemble routines or unwritten ways of doing things that are learned through lived experiences rather than through abstract knowledge acquisi-tion (Nelson & Winter, 1982). They may not be written down in legal codes, but that does not mean that they cannot be understood, followed or even described (Eggertsson, 1990; Voigt, 2019).

Even though informal institutions are not formally codified in law, they nonethe-less influence behaviour. Customary law is not generally found in legislation, but that makes it no less law, in the sense that people will act on it, will guide their behaviour by it and will sanction those who don't. A wider understanding of law was offered by Lon Fuller (1965), who defined law as 'the enterprise of subject-ing human conduct to the governance of rules'. Unlike formal institutions, which are enforced by the state over a geographical territory, informal institutions are usually 'enforced' through social pressure, sanction or even physical force. They may sometimes be more 'liberal' than formal state-enforced law, and sometimes less so. One of us was recently in Cameroon working with local organisations on women's economic empowerment; although the formal legal codes did not formally entrench patriarchal power, widespread custom, especially in rural areas, considers a husband 'the chief of the family', meaning that inheritance rights for widows, among other rights, are severely attenuated.

The inclusion of informal institutions is crucially connected to a paring away of the thick rationality of conventional economics. As compared to some other institutionalists, North believed that norms, values and 'mental models' shape behaviour too. Simply put, there are unwritten rules, customs and social norms that are deemed legitimate by individuals, and thus shape their behaviour. Crucially, this Northian embrace of norms is also echoed in Ostromian institutionalism, where norms and the social enforcement of which matter for the management of common-pool resources (Ostrom, 2014). If one were to move in such a direction of analysis, the entire concept of 'institutions as rules' may itself be abandoned, if not severely attacked, as Deirdre McCloskey (2022) has done in her elevation of rhetoric and discourse as the chief ingredients of social change (as the next chapter will explain).

Moving in such a direction means that one is going towards the direction of 'old institutional economics', which is grounded on a *habit-following* conception of man. Such a direction involves taking into greater account the roles of values, culture and informal norms. While formal institutions may be understood by those who read the language, informal institutions are often *unique to particular social contexts and sets of experiences.* Learning Italian does not, by itself, help one to understand the rules of queuing in Italy, just as learning to read is not as helpful to learning how to ride a bicycle as is actually getting on and trying … and falling off and trying again. Additionally, given that informal rules are characteristically not spelled out formally, the practice of informal institutions is generally more flexible. Consider the interesting informal norms and conventions governing escalator etiquettes, something that an uninformed traveller might be confused by in a new country!

Central Institutional Question and Liberal Political Economy

The study of development may accordingly be understood with reference to the 'central institutional question': what are the rules and norms in society which facilitate economic progress?

Recognising that institutions matter and defining what they are is one thing, specifying the actual institutions that lead to development is another matter. To answer the central institutional question is a task that is inescapably normative; the type of institutions that one advocates cannot be divorced from specific value-commitments, whether principles of justice, liberty or equity. Accordingly, the answer to the central institutional question that this chapter will proceed to explain is the institutional package espoused by liberal political economy: private property rights protections and the rule of law. It must also be pointed out that this liberal institutional package is not a product of a narrow school of thought, but in fact widely acknowledged today by numerous development practitioners and organisations, many of whom may not necessarily label themselves as 'liberal' (see Rodrik et al., 2004; Acemoglu et al., 2005 and Prado & Trebilcock, 2011, 2021).

Despite continued debate over the precise range and nature of the institutions that are necessary for development, most scholars accept that such institutions should at the minimum lower transactions costs and thus facilitate trade, wealth creation, and enterprise. Pro-growth institutions, as famously expressed by Daron Acemoglu and James Robinson (2012), should be inclusive as opposed to extractive. Inclusive institutions are institutions that allow and encourage participation by a broad swathe of society in a range of activities, economic or otherwise, and which allow them to make use of their talents and skills in pursuit of their own goals. Inclusive economic institutions include an unbiased system of law that secures property rights for all and the provision of public services on an equal basis, notably including access to the judicial system, thereby providing a level playing field on which people can exchange and contract. Inclusive institutions also permit the entry of new businesses, without favouring established and well-connected enterprises, promoting free choice and competition. In contrast, extractive institutions extract incomes and wealth from one subset of society to benefit a different subset, thus benefitting one group or specific elites at the expense of others (Acemoglu & Robinson, 2012) (Table 4.2).

At the heart of this inclusive institutional arrangement is a legal system that protects persons and property, and in which social order is law-governed (rule of law), rather than based on the arbitrary exercise of power. Those conditions generally, though not perfectly, translate into an institutional arrangement centred around liberal democracy and open and contestable markets. Notably, according to

Table 4.2 Inclusive and extractive institutions

	Inclusive	Extractive
Economic	• Property rights protections • Rule of law and contract enforcement • Provision of public services • General freedom of entry and exit into various market arenas	• Absence of secure and effective protections of property rights • Absence of rule of law • Absence of public provision • High levels of restrictions into industries and sectors in market
Political	• Effective central political authority and state capacity • Political mechanisms that facilitate pluralism, i.e. democratic voting, checks and balances, separation of powers, civil rights and liberties	• Weak or absence of central political authority and state capacity • Lack of pluralism in political system, through elite-based arrangements such as authoritarianism, totalitarianism and feudalism

Source Acemoglu and Robinson (2012)

this view, inclusive economic institutions are embedded within inclusive political institutions. These include an effective central state, and one which rests on political pluralism and the limitation of arbitrary power. Sound economic management, in other words, rests on good governance.

Property Rights

One institution pivotal to economic development, and indeed the heart of any functioning economy, is property, which is often taken for granted in prosperous countries. Today, a large percentage of humanity live under governments that generally protect property. What does that mean? Having property rights means having the right to use an asset in ways that one chooses, so long as that use does not infringe on the equal rights of others, and the right to transfer to others assets, on terms that are mutually agreeable. The right to use assets and the right to transfer said assets are two components of a property right.

While this definition may seem straightforward, the reality is far more complex. Property rights are perceived most to be codified in formal law and enforced by state institutions (see Brennan & Buchanan, 1985; Voigt, 2008, 2019). Such rights may be termed 'legal property rights'. Formal law makes clear the ownership of assets, which are typically classified as either state-run or privately-owned. In most capitalist economies, private ownership of the means of production dominates, though most states still retain ownership of certain sectors, either for strategic, security or equity reasons.

However, formal law may not always align with the informal reality on the ground. This disjuncture can be understood on two levels. First, legal property rights may not always be enforced, either because of high costs of enforcement or because of the unclear or disputed nature of the law itself. Importantly, this problem can afflict both state and private assets.

The second aspect is this: the function of property rights may at times be filled through informal mechanisms outside of the formal sector (see Ellickson, 1994; Ostrom, 1990; Greif, 2006). Throughout history, human beings have devised ways to enforce property rights on a personalistic basis, such as the simple gesture of a handshake, or through the reliance of reputation. Additionally, there are also semi-formal networks which provide property rights enforcements in a club-good fashion. This is best demonstrated in the works of institutional economist Avner Greif (1993, 2006), who documented how various institutions, such as guilds, networks, associations and other community-centric forms of enforcement, emerged to facilitate trade in the medieval world. While Greif's work focused on trade between homogenous groups, others have also shown the possibility of informal mechanisms to enforce rights across and between heterogeneous groups (Clay, 1997; Leeson, 2006). Simultaneously, it should be noted that in the absence of legal property rights, the private governance that steps in to fill the gap may not always have positive outcomes, due to the potential for private extortion and exploitation of citizens, as Shelby Grossman (2021) has shown in her work on informal governance in Nigeria.

The formal-informal disjuncture means that one must transcend the simple dichotomy of state versus private property rights (see Ostrom's, 2010 Nobel Lecture). As Elinor Ostrom (1990) has shown, 'tragedy of the commons' problems can be avoided endogenously *from within* the community, where individuals within such communities are able to communicate, monitor and enforce its internal rules and thereby police behaviour and sanction misconduct. Thus, her work suggests the potential for self-governance (Ostrom et al., 1992), a theme which will be revisited in Chapter 6. It must be acknowledged of course that the possibility of such self-governance is conditional, and in fact, Ostrom (2015) herself laid out 'design principles' characterising successful cases.

It is entirely possible for communal enforcement to ultimately fail, leaving us with the case of 'open access' resources. In such cases, the enforcement of property rights is either non-existent or too costly, resulting in the inability to limit access, free-riding and conflicts over resource use (Araral, 2014; Libecap, 2009). The best example of such a case would be the challenge of climate change, which may be modelled as a 'global commons' (see Soroos, 2005 for an overview). The high transactions cost of facilitating agreements, the transboundary nature of emissions pollution and unclear property rights mean that it remains a most difficult collective action problem with no easy solutions. That said, Ostrom (2009) herself favoured a polycentric approach to global climate governance. Scholars inspired by her approach have since recommended other 'partial' solutions to the challenge of mitigating or adapting to climate change (see Cai et al., 2022, Chap. 6 for a recent survey).

Table 4.3 Forms of property rights

Type of property rights	Description
Private	In this case, private individuals, organisations and firms have the exclusive rights to use and transfer assets. Market-oriented economies generally see private agents owning a large share of the means of production.
State	Government agencies and representatives possess the rights to use and transfer assets. Hybrid economies exhibit higher state ownership of the means of production.
Communal	The rights to use and transfer assets are not held by state agents or by private agents, but by a community at large, who sometimes manage to devise informal mechanisms to govern resource use. Even though rights are not held privately or by government, informal mechanisms still exist to potentially exclude entrants.
Open access	In this case, resources are accessible to all, and no exclusion is possible, unlike in the above three scenarios. Parties are unable to govern resource use as it may be too costly to do so. 'Tragedy of the commons' problems are likely to ensue.

In the end, it is important to remember that property rights have various forms and as this section has shown, may be private, state, communal or simply 'open access' in nature (see Table 4.3). From the perspective of development, nations should avoid the last case of 'open access', as the absence of enforceable rules on the use of property means that resources may not be conserved and used to their full value. Common-pool resources may well be managed well through Ostromian solutions (communal property rights), but this is potentially difficult to exist on a large scale where a mass of impersonal interactions is to be sustained. Thus, from a development perspective, the state has an important role to play, either in managing productive assets on its own, or in crafting a framework for private agents to do so. Regardless of the precise form, we now turn to why the *functions* that property rights plays are important for the development context.

Why Property Rights?

In the context of economic development, property rights enable individuals and groups to reap the gains from trade, innovation and entrepreneurship. If property rights are absent or not well-enforced, the costs of mutually beneficial economic exchange will be raised and, as a consequence, engaging in trade is likely to be less profitable (Coase, 1992). 'Spot transactions', in which goods are exchanged immediately, are likely to dominate, and long-term transactions, in which promises are made to deliver goods later, are made much less likely, with important consequences for investment and other forms of long-term planning. In a society with insecure property rights, people are forced to invest more in private security, which shifts resources that could have been allocated to production instead. When property rights are secured, in contrast, resource owners are provided with secure foundations upon which to invest in increasing the long-term value of their property, to do business with others, to share knowledge and to innovate (North, 1990; Besley & Ghatak, 2010). Countries that have strong reputations for the protection of property tend to see more investment, both foreign and domestic (Johnson et al., 2002).

Crucially, strong property rights protections, including the right to sell and to receive the capitalised value of the asset, mean that owners act as stewards to increase the value of the stream of services their assets generate, the present-value of which is reflected in the value of the asset. Restrictions on the property rights to sell or transfer assets tend to reduce the incentive to increase that stream of services, with negative consequences for the entire economic order. At the extreme, owners are incentivised to consume the value entirely. Moreover, allowing free transfer of assets means that those who have the knowledge, skills and plans to use assets to generate more value have the incentive to purchase those assets from others and to put them to better use, thereby creating more value.

For a variety of reasons, nations may be stuck with poor institutions and thus will be unable to reap the benefits of economic freedom or enjoy the gains from trade and innovation. One way to 'circumvent' this problem is to simply allow people who live under sub-optimal institutions to move—via free immigration—to better countries with better institutions (see Nowrasteh & Powell, 2020), where they are able to multiply—often quite dramatically—their productive abilities. The relaxation of existing immigration controls would unlock human potential, allowing people to create far greater economic value for themselves and others, including for the people of their host societies, who gain from those talents as well.

The more difficult approach is for local actors to pursue institutional reforms to formally establish, delineate and enforce property rights. Of course, the previous section has established that property rights need not be formal and may in fact be 'emergent phenomena' (Chap. 6 will further explain 'private governance'). That said, it is unrealistic to expect property rights to be fully self-sustaining in the absence of a central state. The relative advantage of formal property rights is that they are impersonal, which is instrumental for facilitating the sort of exchange and relationships that characterise modern society, which Hayek referred to as the 'Great Society' (North et al., 2009). Formal property rights are also clearly codified and allow for stable expectations and third-party enforcement, typically the state. The challenge in development therefore is how to improve property rights protections in the formal sphere and increase public support for the values that undergird such rights.

Institutional reforms to formalise property rights are precisely what the economist Hernando de Soto (2011) famously documented in Peru, where he explained how poverty resulted from 'dead capital'. According to him, 'what the poor lack is easy access to the property mechanisms that could legally fix the economic potential of their assets so that they could be used to produce, secure, or guarantee greater value in the expanded market' (de Soto, 2001). The reason why reforming such institutions is difficult is because bad institutions may be a historical inheritance; vested interests block reforms, or there are norms or belief systems that resist change (Acemoglu & Robinson, 2000; Engerman & Sokoloff, 2002; North, 2010).

Such an institutional impasse may be overcome through institutional entrepreneurship, where local organisations spot opportunities to change mindsets, and elicit the support of political elites in a positive direction. Improving the legal protection of property rights is difficult, but the following case study showcased suggests that it is possible.

An organisation that champions equal property rights as an avenue for economic growth is the Foundation for Economic Freedom (FEF) in the Philippines. Since 2005, the FEF has been dedicated to working on various policy reforms and projects focused upon property rights: in 2005, around half of the 24 million land parcels in the Philippines were untitled, thereby posing an impediment to economic development (Chikiamco, 2014). With its sustained focus on promoting respect for well-defined and legally secure property rights in the Philippines, FEF and the advocacy coalition it formed successfully passed into law a policy reform (RA 10,023, Residential Free Patent Act) which allowed residential lands to be titled administratively. That reform eased the process whereby landowners could

obtain formal recognition of their claims over land: previously, landowners had
to go to court to establish their claims, rendering the process tedious and expen-
sive. Residential titles issued by the government significantly increased from an
average of 4,000 titles to an average of 57,000 patents annually (Bernardo et al.,
2019). Crucially, the reform, according to records on land transactions from the
Philippine Land Registration Authority, has promoted the use of residential titles
by landowners for transactions such as sale and mortgage, thereby resolving the
problem of dead capital identified and described by Hernando de Soto.

The FEF's success in championing formal recognition of property has not been
limited to residential property. Between 2015 and 2019, the FEF focused its efforts
on the removal of restrictions on agricultural patents, which culminated in the
passing of a law (RA 11,231, Agricultural Free Patent Reform Act) by Congress
and signed by President Rodrigo Duterte on 22 February 2019 (Nicolas, 2019).
Agricultural patents, which comprised around 90% of titles issued to agricultural
lands, restricted patent holders from selling, dividing or combining parcels, as well
as from using them for collateral for loans to improve the productive capacity of
the land. The Rural Agricultural Patents placed a five-year restriction on sale and
mortgage of the land and granted owners a five-year right to repurchase the land
after sale, thus reducing the price purchasers would pay to acquire such uncertain
title. Moreover, such titles could not be acquired by corporations, meaning that
banks, which are legal corporations, could not accept the titles for collateral. In
a 2017 survey conducted by FEF, a majority of rural banks did not accept agricultural patents as collateral because of those and other encumbrances, including
difficulty of foreclosure, non-acceptance by the Land Bank of the Philippines for
purposes of rediscounting and low marketability after the property was foreclosed
(Bernardo et al., 2019). The minority that accepted agricultural patents as collateral only did so upon expiry of the five-year restriction on sale and mortgage, with
additional requirements and at lower loan value. As Representative Joey Salceda,
Former Member of the Philippines House of Representatives, noted, the restrictions upon agricultural patents presented 'poor farmers limited options to obtain
funds to modernize, hike farm productivity and investing in their improvement'.

In early 2019, the FEF further succeeded in advocating for the passage of a law
(RA 11,573, Act Simplifying Land Titling) which simplified and facilitated the
process of titling for all lands. Specifically, the law abolished the period limitation
that had previously been imposed upon agricultural landowners and enabled them
to title their lands easily through an administrative process. What is significant
to note is that under the old law, the period of possession was 77 years, and a
certification from the Secretary of Natural Resources was needed, to prove that
the land was alienable and disposable. Under a new streamlined process, thanks to
FEF's efforts, the period of possession is now reduced to 20 years, with no time
limit imposed, and a simple certification by a geodetic engineer would suffice.
Additionally, the law allowed landowners with tax declarations to file for a judicial
titling in a simplified and easier process, thereby easing the previously complex
process to obtain formal property rights (Angara, 2021).

Rule of Law

Closely related to property rights protections is a system that respects the rule of law. While that term is very much contested, the rule of law is generally understood to refer to a legal system where the rules in society apply to all; the rules are general, predictable and stable. There are two components to the rule of law. First, there must be a degree of impersonality in the formulation and enforcement of law, such that people are not treated arbitrarily by the state, and also a sustained adherence to law over time despite turnover in government officials (Weingast, 2009).

The promulgation and enforcement of a stable and secure rule of law are crucial for economic development because of the way it reduces transaction costs and enables people to make long-term plans. An all-encompassing and universal rule of law is crucial in its ability to generate predictable and stable expectations of the actions of individuals. Rule of law, when enforced equitably, ascertains that social actors from both the state and the population conform to a pre-defined set of the rules. Officials are also guided by the rules, not by whim or personal interest, region, class, caste, ethnicity, religion or other biases of decision-making, and the rules will be internalised by most of the population. This produces a stable environment in which exchange, enterprise and innovation can flourish. It is only when the rule of law is enforced and promulgated in such a manner that individuals are certain that they will be able to reap the fruits of their productive inputs: the rule of law is crucial in incentivising the commitment of resources by private individuals to growth and investment, thereby allowing for long-term economic growth and development.[2]

Successful development thus has its roots in a sound legal system. The importance of law has been internalised by much of the development community, including the World Bank (Krever, 2011). That is reflected by the World Governance Indicators project launched since 2002, which operationalises the concept of the rule of law based on six components:

1. Voice and Accountability
2. Political Stability and Absence of Violence/Terrorism
3. Government Effectiveness
4. Regulatory Quality
5. Rule of Law
6. Control of Corruption.

With data involving 200 countries, that indicator incorporates several hundred variables that measure the quality of governance, including both subjective perceptions and objective measurements (Hamilton & Hammer, 2018; Kaufmann et al., 2004).

---

[2] Krever (2011). The Legal Turn in Late Development Theory: The Rule of Law and the World Bank's Development Model. Harv. Int'l LJ, 52, p. 312.

The empirical data shows a strong association between 'good governance' and successful development. The rule of law is essential in the provision of an environment conducive for economic activities and a crucial precondition for private individuals to contribute to economic development by confidently engaging in economic activities.

Knowing what institutions matter and actually achieving change is a different story altogether. Many countries remain stuck in under-development due to poor governance, with little progress in institutional developments. There are numerous reasons for such institutional stasis, including cultural and historical constraints, as well as political vested interests (see Eggertsson, 2005 for a deep discussion). The importance of culture and history thus necessitates not just reforms in formal institutions, but also in a nation's climate of ideas, values and cultural heritage, as the next chapter will clarify. A common reason for path dependency in a nation's institutional trajectory is also the existence of vested interests who resist change, since there are political elites who benefit from existing bad institutions (Kaufmann, 2003; Acemoglu & Robinson, 2000).

Reforms, both at the policy level and at the institutional level, are best pursued in a gradualist manner and driven by local actors. As shown through some of the case studies above, when local actors are empowered to make the case for market freedoms, change tends to be more sustainable, though never guaranteed. One interesting case study here are rule of law reforms pursued by a local organisation in Malaysia, the Institute for Democracy and Economic Affairs (IDEAS).

The Democracy and Governance unit of IDEAs carries out research and advocacy in the areas of transparent and accountable governance, with the aim of strengthening democratic institutions and promoting a multiracial Malaysian identity (Institute for Democracy and Economic Affairs, 2022). One prominent project that IDEAs has focused upon is its advocacy for increased budget transparency of the Malaysian government: budget transparency, as identified by IDEAs, is associated with better performance, accountability, and public and market confidence. Presented annually to the legislatures, the budget is the government's proposal to raise revenues through taxation and other measures for the upcoming fiscal year, and outlines ways in which this revenue will be spent for various purposes such as building and maintaining public infrastructure, as well as providing security and education purposes. The budget hence reflects the government's strategy and its ability to allocate scare resources for sound use (Sri Murniati, 2016).

Transparent budgets are therefore especially crucial to allow members of civic society to evaluate the government's strategy and commitments, thereby allowing them to hold the government accountable, a crucial aspect of the rule of law in states. The Malaysian government, however, consistently fails to disclose budgets in a timely and transparent fashion: the Open Budget Index, which is produced by the International Budget Partnership and evaluates the quality of budget documents produced by governments in the world in accordance with international standards produced by organisations such as the Organisation of Economic Cooperation and Development (OECD) and the International Monetary Fund (IMF), for example, consistently scores Malaysia low in its rankings. In 2021, Malaysia obtained a score of 47 out of 100, low in comparison with its regional neighbours Philippines (76), Indonesia (70) and Thailand (61) (Institute for Democracy and Economic Affairs, 2021). Similarly, Malaysia was ranked 49 out of 102 countries in 2015, 60 out of 100 countries in 2012 and 55 out of 99 countries in 2010 (Sri Murniati, 2016). Malaysia's consistent low ranking in the Open Budget Index is reflective of the failure of the Malaysian government to provide the public with adequate information on its budget: specifically, the 2015 Open Budget Index for Malaysia noted that the Malaysian government publishes only five out of eight necessary budget documents annually. Some of these documents, however, fail to provide key information necessary for meaningful evaluation by everyday citizens: for example, limited information on extra-budgetary funds, contingent liabilities and future liabilities is provided, thereby debilitating the ability of Malaysians to hold their government sufficiently accountable (Sri Murniati, 2016).

IDEAS has thus embarked upon a mission to rectify this problem of insufficient transparency by the Malaysian government through the publication of research papers, social outreach programmes, advocacy for reforms and cooperation with government agencies. One prominent initiative by the organisation is the consistent tracking of the Malaysian government's position in the Open Budget Index: in lieu of the possibility of reforms arising from the 2018 elections and the subsequent change of government, IDEAS heightened its advocacy with the formulation of MyOBI. MyOBI, an initiative to create greater demand for accountability at the state level, is a questionnaire based on the subnational budget transparency evaluation devised by the International Budget Partnership to gauge the level of budget transparency at the state level (Yusuf et al., 2022). Key insights from the results of MyOBI, such as that state governments do not disclose vital budget information to the public adequately, were published reports, alongside recommendations to improve the public availability of financial documents by the Malaysian government (Yusuf et al., 2022).

IDEAS' consistent effort to promote increased government transparency has borne significant fruit: in 2021, the Malaysian Ministry of Finance released its first ever Pre-Budget Statement (PBS) and announced a plan to release a consultation paper on the Fiscal Responsibility Act (FRA), which will provide a clear strategic direction of Malaysia's fiscal plans in the future. Today, more and more of the Malaysian government's budgets are put online for public review (see Institute for Democracy and Economic Affairs, 2020). One of the eight key budget-related documents in the Open Budget Index, the PBS, provides an update on the progress of the budget implementation, including the implementation of stimulus packages, progress of revenue collection and expenditure, and revised growth rate (Institute for Democracy and Economic Affairs, 2021). Additionally, the PBS provides the growth forecast and priorities of the 2022 budget, thereby increasing the transparency of the Malaysian budget to its citizens. Despite its success in effecting reform, however, IDEAS is continuing its advocacy for even greater degrees of public accountability: IDEAS has called for the provision of more information in the 2022 budget, as well as projections of revenue, expenditure and debt levels for the next two to three years, and welcomed the plan for the Malaysian government to review its public spending in a transparent and timely manner (Institute for Democracy and Economic Affairs, 2021).

Neglect of Institutions

Classical economics, from Adam Smith to Jean-Baptiste Say, David Ricardo and Karl Marx, approached the study of economics as part of a broader inquiry about society. The contributions of such intellectuals were fundamentally interdisciplinary and combined insights from history, politics, sociology, law, psychology and moral philosophy to inform insights about social interaction. Adam Smith's 1776 book, *An Inquiry into the Nature and Causes of the Wealth of Nations*, drew on his moral thought to *redefine* both *the nation* and *the wealth of nations* as what 'any man' might procure, rather than only the powerful and influential in the state: 'That state is properly opulent in which opulence is easily come at, or in which a little labour, properly and judiciously employed, is capable of procuring any man a great abundance of all the necessaries and conveniencies of life' (Smith, 1982). Smith provided an institutionalist account: economic development was the result of expanding the division of labour within society, which could only be attained when certain political, legal and economic institutions and practices, such as well-defined and legally secure property rights, monetisation of exchange, and reduction or elimination of trade restrictions. Those institutions allowed for the expansion of the market, which was pivotal for the development of specialised production and exchange. Extending the range of trade was central to increasing output, and thus consumption, or, as Smith put it, 'the division of labour is limited by the extent of the market' (Smith, 1976a, b, I).

The institutionalism of the classical era, however, was lost as economic thought evolved. Specifically, the rise of formalism, positivism and thus academic hyper-specialisation stamped its imprint on social science during the twentieth century (see Boettke, 1997). Formalism started to take hold in the discipline of economics, which entailed the increasing use of mathematical techniques to model economic behaviour. Mathematics would reduce ambiguity in ways that narratives might not be able to (see Samuelson, 1952). That hope was based on the deeper belief that economic activity may be quantified and understood in a uniform, rational and law-like manner, just as physical scientists approach the natural world. One implication of this positivist trend was the elimination of ideas, values and institutions from economic analysis. Granted, institutional theories did exist in economics in the early twentieth century, but that 'old institutionalism' came to be displaced as the economic discipline shifted towards formal techniques and mathematical approaches (Hodgson, 1998). As a result, mainstream economics became focused on a narrowly defined aspect of economic activity centred around maximising behaviour, equilibrium analyses, and the use of quantitative methods and formal modelling (Alvey, 1999; Coase, 1998; Friedman, 1953). Such an approach is not wrong, but it is limited in scope and it limits our ability to explain many complexities and nuances of social life. It also overlooks important dimensions of economic development, with regard to both its nature and its causes.

There is also an ideological dimension to the omission of institutions in twentieth-century intellectual thought. Due to the appeal to many intellectuals of comprehensive and centralised economic planning, as represented by the Soviet Union and other states, and the attraction of Keynesian macroeconomic management of aggregate demand in the Western world, the normally lawful operations of the institutions of markets, Adam Smith's 'simple system of natural liberty', in which 'The sovereign is completely discharged from a duty, in the attempting to perform which he must always be exposed to innumerable delusions, and for the proper performance of which no human wisdom or knowledge could ever be sufficient; the duty of superintending the industry of private people, and of directing it towards the employments most suitable to the interest of the society' (Smith, 1976a, b, II), were seen as outmoded. As explained by Peter Boettke (1994), 'the focus of developmental economics shifted away from designing appropriate institutional structure of governance to the necessary activities that government must undertake'.

The neglect of the interaction of institutions and behaviour in much of the early development literature is not merely a matter of esoteric interest but has had real-world implications. Those implications should be understood with reference to two dominant approaches to development in the twentieth century: foreign aid and the Washington Consensus. Both those sets of policies have received strong criticism from various quarters, and the problems they have revealed can be drawn on to elucidate the importance of institutions.

Failure of Washington Consensus

The late twentieth century saw the intellectual pendulum swing from central planning towards market coordination of economic activity, usually labelled 'capitalism', although the focus implicit in the term on 'capital', rather than on voluntary and decentralised coordination, is in our opinions misleading. Various nations, especially those emerging from the shadows of Soviet socialism, started to embrace the institutions of economic liberalism described above. Global organisations advocated a set of policy reforms that came to be known as 'the Washington Consensus'. That Consensus comprised of ten policy recommendations that were grouped under four broad categories: macroeconomic stabilisation (fiscal discipline, tax reforms, and reductions in public expenditures); liberalisation (open trade and reduction in state intervention); privatisation; and policies to attract foreign direct investment (FDI) and to stimulate private entrepreneurship (reduction of tax burdens, availability of credit for private investors and fostering of competition within sectors) (see Williamson, 2005).

Criticisms followed and persist to the present day. Critics of both the embrace of markets and the Washington Consensus (which policies do not always coincide) alleged that they led to greater inequality, the emergence of oligarchs in former Soviet states (which suggest a failure of transition), as well as successive economic crises in newly liberalised countries in the 1990s (Rodrik, 2006; Stiglitz, 2002). Perhaps the leading critic of Washington Consensus is Joseph Stiglitz, who has criticised the 'narrow' preoccupation of this approach on neoliberal policies such as privatisation, liberalisation and small government (Stiglitz, 2005). Even the World Bank and the International Monetary Fund (IMF) note in separate reports that growth in the 1990s was disappointing, with results being mixed, despite developing countries largely abiding to the policy prescriptions delineated in the Washington Consensus (World Bank, 2005; Belaisch et al., 2005).

It should be stated at this point that the final verdict on Washington Consensus is not yet out. Very much may depend on the timeframe of evaluation. The development economist William Easterly (2019) recently showed that even though the 1980s and 1990s may have been 'lost decades', recent periods into the 2000s witnessed more positive economic effects. The 'neoliberal' economic policies, so widely criticised by some, may simply have needed more time to work its positive effects. A set of recent studies with more ambitious causal claims also echo that positive perspective: examinations of economic performance show that countries that adopted the market reforms had at least 5 to 16% higher incomes compared to those that did not (Grier & Grier, 2021; Marazzo & Terzi, 2017). At the same time, when Latin American countries adopted left-wing populism, as in Venezuela, Nicaragua and Bolivia, they were 20% poor than they otherwise would be, as measured against a plausible counterfactual (Absher et al., 2020).

Washington Consensus-type policies typically failed to address governance problems in developing countries, which may go a long way towards explaining disappointing results. In other words, before 'getting the prices' right, one must first 'get the institutions right' (Boettke et al., 2005). A major problem with the Consensus was its lack of emphasis on institutional reform. Market-based policies were pursued without first attending to the necessary legal, judicial, financial and political institutions needed to make them work. The failure of transition in Russia, for example, may be traced to the lack of property rights protections and the absence of a cultural heritage supportive of liberal values, such as probity, respect for entrepreneurship and profits earned through exchange, and understanding of the role of abstract rules, rather than exertions of state power, in achieving social order. Of great significance, markets require supervisory institutions, such as an independent judiciary, and in their absence, it is unsurprising that many of these reform efforts were mired in political corruption.

Problems of pacing and sequencing frustrate reform efforts. Washington Consensus policies, which encouraged both fiscal restraint and monetary stabilisation along with economic freedom and private enterprise, were not wrong, but were implemented too quickly and from the top, generally through agreements with global institutions such as the International Monetary Fund and the World Bank with decision-makers in central governments. These were implemented without local consultation, participation and knowledge. Leading critics of 'neoliberalism' have written about how, in tandem with the advocacy of such global organisations, and influenced by Western expert advisors, various governments forced through what was essentially an elitist project (Babb & Kentikelenis, 2018; Klein, 2007). One such argument is made by Quinn Slobodian (2020), who has claimed that neoliberal thinkers—'globalists'—laid the foundations of a global liberal order that suppressed local democracy and governance. A similar point is made by Jason Hickel (2016), who claims that 'neoliberalism' eventually undermines 'national sovereignty, to the point where the parliaments of putatively independent nations no longer have power over their own policy decisions, but are governed instead by foreign banks, the US Treasury, trade agreements, and undemocratic international institutions, all of which exercise a kind of invisible, remote-control power'.

While those critics, in our opinion, err in their denunciation of markets, there is a grain of truth in their argument, which is that much of the attempts at market reform during the late twentieth century were driven by global organisations, whose experts and advisors were almost invariably outsiders who lacked the knowledge, as well as the incentives, to interact with local institutions and practices in low-income countries in ways that would promote widespread enrichment and development. Markets and the institutions that make them possible and which regulate the behaviour of market participants are essential for development and, in line with the same reasons that favour the spontaneous ordering processes of markets over centralised control, they tend to function much better when they emerge on the basis of local participation, drawing on local knowledge and support. The case studies in this handbook suggest that it is very much possible for economic freedom to be fostered from the ground up.

There is a close alignment between institutions and culture, which the next chapter will focus on. Market institutions also need to cohere with a supportive cultural environment, without which they may be nothing more than exogenous impositions (Boettke et al., 2008). One reason why it has been difficult to 'get the institutions' right in many developing countries, including in the former USSR state abovementioned, is that there was a lack of cultural appreciation of liberal values. In the contemporary era, many efforts of foreign powers to engage in nation-building in the developing world and implement democratic reforms have also backfired, because they lacked local participation and cultural alignment (Coyne, 2008). So in addition to getting the policies and institutions right, nations will need to get the culture right, which, as the next chapter will show, is easier said than done.

Failure of Foreign Aid

The neglect of institutions and governance has had a similarly negative impact on the outcomes of foreign aid policies, which in recent decades were often executed in the light of the Washington Consensus. Despite the enormous flow of development aid to low-income countries during the post-war era, many of these countries have seen their real per capita incomes stagnate or even decline. Studies of the effect of development aid on economic growth, such as that conducted by Tomi Ovaska (2003) for the years 1975–98, report that a 1 percent increase in aid as a percent of GDP actually decreased annual real GDP per capita growth by 3.65%.

Academic research on the efficacy of foreign aid on promoting development is quite polarised. Some thinkers have called for drastic increases of aid to fund a 'big–push' investment so that poor countries can escape the poverty trap and reform economic, political and social institutions for the better (Sachs, 2014; Sachs et al., 2014). Others are sceptical that increased aid for economic development and reforms can help in creating functional institutions. The latter generally argue that the provision of foreign aid is made without regard to incentives and allocation: for aid to be effective, recipients of aid must have the incentive to use the aid specifically for economic development and institutional reform (Easterly, 2010). Additionally, aid organisations and global elites lack the necessary knowledge to administer development programs efficiently.

Effective allocation and use of foreign aid require strong and well-functioning institutions. Aid, however, is, unsurprisingly, typically given to countries with poor or failing institutions: since those countries are often the poorest, they often receive the greatest amounts of foreign aid (Coyne & Ryan, 2009; De la Croix & Delavallade, 2014). While that has sometimes been justified by the argument that it is precisely such countries that need aid the most to strengthen their political institutions, the provision of aid generally gives such governments little incentive to reform. In fact, it frequently has the effect of insulating them from the preferences and interests of their own citizens and widens the 'democracy deficit', as they are more attuned to respond to foreign donor organisations than to their own citizens. Such governments tend to face few constraints on their behaviour and have little reason to establish mechanisms of accountability or to open to popular participation their political institutions, since doing so would reduce their hold on power. As a result, it is unlikely, as reflected in empirical literature, that foreign aid can effectively stimulate or incentivise institutional reforms (Djankov et al., 2006; Easterly, 2003).

Such aid can also contribute to internal conflict through the politicisation of daily life. According to a survey by François Bourguignon and Jan Willem Gunning (2020), one mechanism that explains this is when aid, delivered to oppressive regimes, directly finances the activities of the ruling elite, notably including repression and defence against coups or secession attempts. The provision of external aid to recipient governments reduces their reliance on domestic taxation and thus reduces both their accountability to taxpayers and their attunement to the impact on productive activities of their policies. They tend to be more attentive to well-connected interests than to a wide tax base. The lack of a wide tax base tends to reduce citizen attentiveness to parliamentary and other representative governing bodies.

Aid undermines political institutions and makes collective action difficult. Governments are thus more likely to pursue their own objectives, rather than to take the interest of their own citizens into account: consequently, and again unsurprisingly, foreign aid generally benefits the recipient governments and the interest groups they represent at the expense of the public welfare. The protracted durability of regimes buttressed by aid, compounded by their reduced accountability to society, can increase the incentives for governments to engage in rent-seeking, or the use of political processes to extract resources from others, thus enabling governments and those close to power to capture further wealth and privilege without any reciprocal contribution of productivity or to the public weal (Bourguignon & Gunning, 2020; Moyo, 2009).

Elite capture of aid, i.e. retention and direction of aid monies into the pockets of the politically connected, to fund their own consumption, is a highly likely outcome: resultantly, aid ultimately undermines institutional quality and enriches a ruling elite who are both oppressive and corrupt and who have little or no incentive to engage in net wealth-generating economic activity or to create the reliable institutional frameworks for their citizens to do so.

It is important to clarify, however, that aid is not to be wholly dismissed. Aid, understandably, can produce positive outcomes in limited and modest cases, such as in the well-known case of the distribution of insecticide-treated mosquito bed nets in Africa. Aid is understandably able to achieve specific and technically limited objectives (building schools, giving nets, feeding people, etc.) but struggles to overcome the *structural* bases of under-development (Skarbek & Leeson, 2009). Additionally, aid may also come from private philanthropic organisations, which may be more attuned to local institutions and less inefficient than government-to-government aid. Studies that point to positive effects of aid show that these benefits are possible in the presence of good policies (Burnside & Dollar, 2000). Herein lies the problem. If under-development indeed stems from poor governance, then that is the root problem that must be tackled, and aid, however beneficial in limited cases, is *at best* a band-aid, or a temporary amelioration.

Conclusion

Markets are essential for human progress, but need to be established upon an institutional foundation. The failure to do so may mean that the benefits of markets, explained in an earlier chapter, cannot be reaped. In fact, many market reforms of the 1990s in Eastern Europe met a dead end due to a lack of these institutional pillars that make market economies work. If poor nations have bad governance, then foreign aid programs may also prolong poverty since they do nothing to change the institutional status quo. The consensus today is that property rights protections and the rule of law are the key institutions of market economies, but actually achieving this is easier said than done.

Today, we know a lot about the importance of markets and institutions, but less so about the actual steps to take to implement them. This is why, as has been stressed, local actors within countries play a very important role in sequencing, structuring and pursuing reforms. As documented in this chapter, the efforts by local organisations to improve formal property protections and improve rule of law are praiseworthy and provide the contextual knowledge that so often is missing in top-down reforms pursued by global organisations. In the next chapter, we also turn to the importance of cultural values and how they interact with institutions to produce development outcomes.

Discussion Questions

1. What are 'institutions' as defined by economists?
2. What are the differences between formal and informal institutions and how does this matter for development?
3. What lessons can we draw from Washington Consensus policies?
4. Do foreign aid programs help or hurt, and how do institutions matter for the design of aid programs?
5. How did the institution of private property emerge in history and how might this be established today?
6. What are the challenges faced in the implementation of the rule of law in developing countries?
7. To what extent are governance problems in developing nations a function of political interests, or historical legacies, or international exploitation?

References

Absher, S., Grier, K., & Grier, R. (2020). The economic consequences of durable left-populist regimes in Latin America. *Journal of Economic Behavior & Organization, 177*, 787–817. https://doi.org/10.1016/j.jebo.2020.07.001.

Acemoglu, D., & Robinson, J. A. (2012). *Why nations fail: The origins of power, prosperity, and poverty.* Crown Business.

Acemoglu, D., Johnson, S., & Robinson, J. A. (2005). Institutions as a Fundamental Cause of Long-Run Growth. In P. Aghion & S. N. Durlauf (Eds.), *Handbook of Economic Growth* (Vol I) (pp. 385–472). Elsevier.

Acemoglu, D., & Robinson, J. A. (2000). Political losers as a barrier to economic development. *American Economic Review, 90*(2), 126–130. https://doi.org/10.1257/aer.90.2.126.

Alchian, A. A. (1950). Uncertainty, evolution, and economic theory. *Journal of Political Economy, 58*(3), 211–221. https://doi.org/10.1086/256940.

Aligica, P. D., & Tarko, V. (2012). Polycentricity: From Polanyi to Ostrom, and beyond. *Governance, 25*(2), 237–262. https://doi.org/10.1111/j.1468-0491.2011.01550.x.

Alvey, J. E. (1999). A short history of economics as a moral science. *Journal of Markets & Morality, 2*(1), 53–73.

Angara, S. (2021). *A simpler land titling system.* BusinessMirror. https://businessmirror.com.ph/2021/08/26/a-simpler-land-titling-system/.

Araral, E. (2014). Ostrom, Hardin and the commons: A critical appreciation and a revisionist view. *Environmental Science & Policy, 36*, 11–23. https://doi.org/10.1016/j.envsci.2013.07.011.

Babb, S., & Kentikelenis, A. (2018). International Financial Institutions as Agents of Neoliberalism. In D. Cahill, M. Cooper, & M. Konings (Eds.), *The SAGE Handbook of Neoliberalism* (pp. 16–27). SAGE.

Baland, J. M., Bourguignon, F., Platteau, J. P., & Verdier, T. (2020). Economic Development Institutions: An Introduction. In J. M. Baland (Ed.), *The Handbook of Economic Development and Institutions* (pp. 1–22). Princeton University Press.

Belaisch, A. A., Collyns, C., De Masi, P., Meredith, G. M., Singh, A., Krieger, R., & Rennhack, R. (2005). *Stabilization and Reform in Latin America: A Macroeconomic Perspective of the Experience since the 1990s*. International Monetary Fund.

Bernardo, R., Chikiamco, C., de Dios, E., Fabella, R., & Paderanga Jr., C. (2019). *Momentum: Economic Reforms for Sustaining Growth*. Foundation for Economic Freedom.

Besley, T., & Ghatak, M. (2010). Property Rights and Economic Development. In D. Rodrik (Ed.), *Handbook of Development Economics* (pp. 4525–4595). Elsevier.

Boettke, P. J. (1994). The political infrastructure of economic development. *Human Systems Management, 13*(2), 89–100.

Boettke, P. J. (1997). Where did economics go wrong? Modern economics as a flight from reality. *Critical Review, 11*(1), 11–64. https://doi.org/10.1080/08913819708443443.

Boettke, P. J., Coyne, C. J., Leeson, P. T., & Sautet, F. (2005). The new comparative political economy. *The Review of Austrian Economics, 18*(3), 281–304. https://doi.org/10.1007/s11138-005-3113-0.

Boettke, P. J., Coyne, C. J., & Leeson, P. T. (2008). Institutional Stickiness and the New Development Economics. *American Journal of Economics and Sociology, 67*(2), 331–358. https://doi.org/10.1111/j.1536-7150.2008.00573.x.

Bourguignon, F., & Gunning, J. W. (2020). Foreign Aid and Governance. In J.-M. Baland, F. Bourguignon, J.-P. Platteau, & T. Verdier (Eds.), *The Handbook of Economic Development and Institutions* (pp. 308–356). Princeton University Press.

Brennan, G., & Buchanan, J. M. (1985). *The reason of rules: constitutional political economy*. Cambridge University Press.

Burnside, C., & Dollar, D. (2000). Aid, policies, and growth. *American Economic Review, 90*(4), 847–868. https://doi.org/10.1257/aer.90.4.847.

Cai, M., Murtazashvili, I., Brick Murtazashvili, J., & Salahodjaev, R. (2022). *Toward a Political Economy of the Commons: Simple Rules for Sustainability*. Edward Elgar Publishing.

Chikiamco, C. (2014). *One sure way to jump-start the economy: Free the land market*. Foundation for Economic Freedom. https://www.fef.org.ph/calixto-chikiamco/one-sure-way-to-jump-start-the-economy-free-the-land-market/.

Clay, K. (1997). Trade without law: Private-order institutions in Mexican California. *The Journal of Law, Economics, and Organization, 13*(1), 202–231.

Coase, R. (1992). The Economic Structure of Production. *American Economic Review, 82*(3), 713–719.

Coase, R. (1998). The New Institutional Economics. *American Economic Review, 88*(2), 72–74.

Commons, J. R. (1934). Institutional Economics. University of Wisconsin Press.

Coyne, C. J., & Ryan, M. (2009). With Friends Like These, Who Needs Enemies? Aiding the World's Worst Dictators. *The Independent Review, 14*(1), 26–44.

Coyne, C. J. (2008). *After war: The political economy of exporting democracy*. Stanford University Press.

De la Croix, D., & Delavallade, C. (2014). Why corrupt governments may receive more foreign aid. *Oxford Economic Papers, 66*(1), 51–66. https://doi.org/10.1093/oep/gpt004.

de Soto, H. (2001). *The Mystery of Capital: Why Capitalism Triumphs in the West and Fails Everywhere Else*. Black Swan.

de Soto, H. (2011). This land is your land: A conversation with Hernando de Soto. *World Policy Journal, 28*(2), 35–40. https://muse.jhu.edu/article/450602/pdf.

Denzau, A., & North, D. (1994). Shared Mental Models: Ideologies and Institutions. *Kyklos, 47*(1), 3–31. https://doi.org/10.1111/j.1467-6435.1994.tb02246.x.

Djankov, S., Montalvo, J. G., & Reynal-Querol, M. (2006). Does Foreign Aid Help? *Cato Journal, 26*(1), 1–28. https://www.cato.org/sites/cato.org/files/serials/files/cato-journal/2006/1/cj26n1-1.pdf.

Dold, M., & Lewis, P. (2022). F.A. Hayek on the political economy of endogenous preferences: An historical overview and contemporary assessment. *Journal of Economic Behavior & Organization, 196*, 104–119. https://doi.org/10.1016/j.jebo.2022.01.019.

Easterly, W. (2003). Can Foreign Aid Buy Growth? *The Journal of Economic Perspectives, 17*(3), 23–48. https://doi.org/10.1257/089533003769204344.

Easterly, W. (2010). The cartel of good intentions: The problem of bureaucracy in foreign aid. *The Journal of Policy Reform, 5*(4), 223–250. https://doi.org/10.1080/1384128032000096823.

Easterly, W. (2019). In Search of Reforms for Growth: New Stylized Facts on Policy and Growth Outcomes. *National Bureau of Economic Research.* https://doi.org/10.3386/w26318.

Eggertsson, T. (1990). *Economic Behavior and Institutions.* Cambridge University Press.

Eggertsson, T. (2005). *Imperfect Institutions: Possibilities and Limits of Reform.* University of Michigan Press.

Ellickson, R. (1994) *Order without Law: How Neighbors Settle Disputes.* Harvard University Press.

Engerman, S. L., & Sokoloff, K. L. (2002). Factor Endowments, Inequality, and Paths of Development among New World Economies. *Economía, 3*(1), 41–109. https://muse.jhu.edu/article/10626.

Friedman, M. (1953). *Essays in Positive Economics.* University of Chicago Press.

Fuller, L. (1965). *The Morality of Law.* Yale University Press.

Galbraith, J. K. (1958). *The affluent society.* Houghton Mifflin Harcourt.

Greif, A. (1993). Contract enforceability and economic institutions in early trade: The Maghribi traders' coalition. *American Economic Review, 83*(3), 525–548.

Greif, A. (2006). *Institutions and the path to the modern economy: Lessons from medieval trade.* Cambridge University Press.

Grier, K. B., & Grier, R. M. (2021). The Washington consensus works: Causal effects of reform, 1970–2015. *Journal of Comparative Economics, 49*(1), 59–72. https://doi.org/10.1016/j.jce.2020.09.001.

Grossman, S. (2021). *The Politics of Order in Informal Markets: How the State Shapes Private Governance.* Cambridge University Press.

Hamilton, A. J., & Hammer, C. (2018). Can we measure the power of the grabbing hand? A Comparative Analysis of Different Indicators of Corruption. *World Bank Policy Research Working Paper No. 8299.* World Bank. https://papers.ssrn.com/sol3/papers.cfm?abstract_id=3099206.

Hayek, F. A. (2002). Competition as a discovery procedure. *Quarterly Journal of Austrian Economics, 5*(3), 9–23.

Hickel, J. (2016). Neoliberalism and the End of Democracy. In S. B. Springer & J. MacLeavy (Eds.), *Handbook of Neoliberalism* (pp. 142–152). Routledge.

Hodgson, G. (1998). The approach of institutional economics. *Journal of Economic Literature, 36*(1), 166–192.

Hodgson, G. (2000). What is the essence of institutional economics? *Journal of Economic Issues, 34*(2), 317–329. https://doi.org/10.1080/00213624.2000.11506269.

Hodgson, G. (2004). *The evolution of institutional economics.* Routledge.

Hodgson, G. (2014). On fuzzy frontiers and fragmented foundations: Some reflections on the original and new institutional economics. *Journal of Institutional Economics, 10*(4), 591–611. https://doi.org/10.1017/S1744137414000307.

Hodgson, G. (2017). Institutional economics. In L. Fischer, J. Hasell, J. C. Proctor, D. Uwakwe, Z. W. Perkins, & C. Watson (Eds.), *Rethinking Economics* (pp. 45–59). Routledge.

Horwitz, S. (2015). *Hayek's Modern Family: Classical liberalism and the evolution of social institutions.* Palgrave Macmillan.

Institute for Democracy and Economic Affairs. (2021). *IDEAS congratulates the Ministry of Finance on the release of its Pre-Budget Statement.* Institute for Democracy and Economic Affairs. https://www.ideas.org.my/ideas-congratulates-the-ministry-of-finance-on-the-release-of-its-pre-budget-statement/.

Institute for Democracy and Economic Affairs. (2020). *Open Budget: Why is budget transparency important?* Institute for Democracy and Economic Affairs. https://www.ideas.org.my/open-budget-why-is-budget-transparency-important/.

Institute for Democracy and Economic Affairs. (2022). *Democracy and Governance*. Institute for Democracy and Economic Affairs. https://www.ideas.org.my/democracy-and-governance.

Johnson, S., McMillan, J., & Woodruff, C. (2002). Property rights and finance. *American Economic Review, 92*(5), 1335–1356. https://doi.org/10.1257/000282802762024539.

Kaufmann, D. (2003). Rethinking Governance: Empirical Lessons Challenge Orthodoxy. *Social Science Research Network*. http://dx.doi.org/10.2139/ssrn.386904.

Kaufmann, D., Kraay, A., & Mastruzzi, M. (2004). Governance Matters III: Governance Indicators for 1996, 1998, 2000, and 2002. *The World Bank Economic Review, 18*(2), 253–287.

Klein, N. (2007). *The Shock Doctrine: The Rise of Disaster Capitalism*. Knopf .

Krever, T. (2011). The Legal Turn in Late Development Theory: The Rule of Law and the World Bank's Development Model. *Harvard International Law Journal, 52*(1), 288–319. https://harvardilj.org/wp-content/uploads/sites/15/2011/02/HILJ_52-1_Krever1.pdf.

Leeson, P. T. (2006). Cooperation and Conflict: Evidence on Self-Enforcing Arrangements and Heterogeneous Groups. *American Journal of Economics and Sociology, 65*(4), 891–907. https://doi.org/10.1111/j.1536-7150.2006.00480.x.

Lewis, P. (2014). Hayek: From economics as equilibrium analysis to economics as social theory. In R. Garrison & N. Barry (Eds.), *Elgar Companion to Hayekian Economics* (pp. 195–223). Edward Elgar Publishing.

Libecap, G. D. (2009). The tragedy of the commons: Property rights and markets as solutions to resource and environmental problems. *Australian Journal of Agricultural and Resource Economics, 53*(1), 129–144.

Marazzo, M., & Terzi, A. (2017). Structural Reform Waves and Economic Growth. *ECB Working Paper No. 2111*. Social Science Research Network. https://doi.org/10.2139/ssrn.3071545.

McCloskey, D. N. (2022). *Beyond Positivism, Behaviorism, and Neoinstitutionalism in Economics*. University of Chicago Press.

Ménard, C., & Shirley, M. M. (2022). *Advanced introduction to new institutional economics*. Edward Elgar Publishing.

Ménard, C., & Shirley, M. M. (2014). The future of new institutional economics: From early intuitions to a new paradigm? *Journal of Institutional Economics, 10*(4), 541–565. https://doi.org/10.1017/S174413741400006X.

Moyo, D. (2009). *Dead aid: Why aid is not working and how there is a better way for Africa*. Macmillan.

Murniati, S. (2016). *How can Malaysia's Budget Documents be Improved?*. Institute for Democracy and Economic Affairs. https://www.ideas.org.my/publications-item/policy-paper-no-27-how-can-malaysias-budget-documents-be-improved/.

Nelson, R. R., & Winter, S. (1982). *An Evolutionary Theory of Economic Change*. Yale University Press.

Nelson, R. R., & Winter, S. (2002). Evolutionary theorizing in economics. *Journal of Economic Perspectives, 16*(2), 23–46. https://doi.org/10.1257/0895330027247.

Nicolas, B. (2019). *Government eases restrictions on agricultural free patents*. BusinessMirror. https://businessmirror.com.ph/2019/03/14/government-eases-restrictions-on-agricultural-free-patents/.

North, D. C. (1990). *Institutions, institutional change and economic performance*. Cambridge University Press.

North, D. C. (2010). *Understanding the Process of Economic Change*. Princeton University Press.

Nowrasteh, A., & Powell, B. (2020). *Wretched Refuse?: The Political Economy of Immigration and Institutions*. Cambridge University Press.

Ostrom, E. (1990). *Governing the Commons*. Cambridge University Press.

Ostrom, E. (2009). *A Polycentric Approach for Coping with Climate Change*. World Bank Policy Research Working Paper.

Ostrom, E. (2010). Beyond markets and states: Polycentric governance of complex economic systems. *American Economic Review, 100*(3), 641–672. https://doi.org/10.1257/aer.100.3.641.

Ostrom, E. (2014). Do institutions for collective action evolve? *Journal of Bioeconomics, 16*(1), 3–30. https://doi.org/10.1007/s10818-013-9154-8.

Ostrom, E. (2015). Design principles of robust property-rights institutions: what have we learned. In D. Cole & M. McGinnis (Eds.), *Elinor Ostrom and the Bloomington School of Political Economy.* Lexington Books.

Ostrom, E., Walker, J., & Gardner, R. (1992). Covenants with and without a sword: Self-governance is possible. *American Political Science Review, 86*(2), 404–417. https://doi.org/10. 2307/1964229.

Ovaska, T. (2003). The Failure of Development Aid. *Cato Journal, 23*(2), 175–188. https://www. cato.org/sites/cato.org/files/serials/files/cato-journal/2003/11/cj23n2-2.pdf.

Ozanne, A. (2016). Power and neoclassical economics: a return to political economy in the teaching of economics. Palgrave Macmillan.

Prado, M. M., & Trebilcock, M. J. (2011). *What makes poor countries poor?: institutional determinants of development.* Edward Elgar Publishing.

Prado, M. M., & Trebilcock, M. J. (2021). *Advanced introduction to law and development.* Edward Elgar Publishing.

Rodrik, D. (2006). Goodbye Washington consensus, hello Washington confusion? A review of the World Bank's economic growth in the 1990s: Learning from a decade of reform. *Journal of Economic Literature, 44*(4), 973–987. https://doi.org/10.1257/jel.44.4.973.

Rodrik, D., Subramanian, A., & Trebbi, F. (2004). Institutions rule: The primacy of institutions over geography and integration in economic development. *Journal of Economic Growth, 9*(2), 131–165. https://doi.org/10.1023/B:JOEG.0000031425.72248.85.

Sachs, J. (2014). The case for aid. *Foreign policy.* https://foreignpolicy.com/2014/01/21/the-case-for-aid/.

Sachs, J., McArthur, J. W., Schmidt-Traub, G., Kruk, M., Bahadur, C., Faye, M., & McCord, G. (2014). Ending Africa's poverty trap. *Brookings papers on economic activity, 35*(1), 117–240. Brookings Institution. https://www.brookings.edu/wp-content/uploads/2004/01/2004a_bpea_s achs.pdf.

Samuelson, P. (1952). Economic theory and mathematics–An appraisal. *American Economic Review, 42*(2), 56–66.

Shirley, M. M. (2005). Institutions and development. In C. Menard & M. Shirley (Eds.), *Handbook of new institutional economics* (pp. 611–638). Springer.

Skarbek, D., & Leeson, P. T. (2009). What Can Aid Do? *Cato Journal, 29*(3), 391–397. https:// www.cato.org/sites/cato.org/files/serials/files/cato-journal/2009/11/cj29n3-2.pdf.

Slobodian, Q. (2020). *Globalists: The End of Empire and the Birth of Neoliberalism.* Harvard University Press.

Smith, A. (1976a). *An Inquiry into the Nature and Causes of the Wealth of Nations, Vol. I.* Oxford University Press.

Smith, A. (1976b). *An Inquiry into the Nature and Causes of the Wealth of Nations, Vol. II.* Oxford University Press.

Smith, A. (1982). *Lectures On Jurisprudence,* ed. Meek, R.L., Raphael, D.D., and Stein, P.G. Liberty Fund.

Soroos, M. (2015). Garrett Hardin and tragedies of global commons. In P. Dauvergne (Ed.), *Handbook of Global Environmental Politics* (pp. 35–50). Edward Elgar Publishing.

Stiglitz, J. (2002). *Reforming reform: Towards a new agenda for Latin America. Prebisch Lecture.* Cepal.

Stiglitz, J. (2005). More instruments and broader goals: moving toward the post-Washington consensus. In UNU-WIDER (Ed.), *Wider perspectives on global development* (pp. 16–48). Palgrave Macmillan.

Voigt, S. (2019). *Institutional Economics.* Cambridge University Press.

Voigt, S. (2008). The economic effects of judicial accountability: Cross-country evidence. *European Journal of Law and Economics, 25*(2), 95–123.

Weingast, B. (2009). Why developing countries prove so resistant to the rule of law. In J. Heckman, R. L. Nelson, & L. Cabatingan (Eds.), *Global perspectives on the rule of law* (pp. 44–68). Routledge.

Williamson, J. (2005). The Washington Consensus as policy prescription for development. In T. Besley & R. Zagha (Eds.), *Development Challenges in the 1990s: Leading Policymakers Speak from Experience* (pp. 33–61). Oxford University Press.

Witt, U. (2016). *What is specific about evolutionary economics?* Edward Elgar Publishing.

World Bank. (2005). *Economic Growth in the 1990s: Learning from a Decade of Reform.* Washington, DC.: World Bank.

Yusuf, S., Rode, A., & Mohtar, A. (2022). *Budget Transparency in Malaysian States: MyObi 2022.* Institute for Democracy and Economic Affairs. https://www.ideas.org.my/publications-item/brief-ideas-no-35-budget-transparency-in-malaysian-states-key-findings-of-malaysias-open-budget-index-myobi-2022/.

Culture, Development and Liberal Values

5

The reality is that for most of human history, development is constrained. This not only means that people were living on extremely low incomes, but that the opportunities they have for pursuing non-material aspirations or realising their social identities are limited. There were indeed episodes of development in certain times and places (see Goldstone, 2002, 2009; Koyama & Rubin, 2022), but even these were short lived. It is only since 1750 onwards has human history witnessed a clear and sustained improvement in living standards in a process that has now become near global, which is understood as 'the Great Enrichment'. This process is one which began in Western Europe, and since then, non-Western regions have increasingly become integrated into the global capitalist system and have experienced its material enrichment. Yet, for all the progress of history, significant portions of the world are still excluded from enjoying the fruits of growth.

Therefore, this warrants reflection of what held back development for most of history, and why was it that some nations experienced a breakthrough. So far, this handbook has established that economic freedom and market institutions are necessary to break nations of out poverty. However, these are insufficient factors. Markets have existed throughout history, but it was only in a certain geographic region (Western Europe) at a certain time period (late 1700s) where the 'Great Enrichment' occurred. The critical factor that sparked this take-off was the role of culture, that is, there were changes in culture in specific times and places in a pro-liberal direction that brought about a sustained process of market-based development.

What is especially significant to note is that these cultural changes are brought about by cultural entrepreneurs. In Western Europe, there was a rise of liberal rhetoric and values, where wealth creation become socially honoured. Just as entrepreneurs put forward new products on the market, cultural entrepreneurs promote new norms and ways of living. The outcome of such a process is of course uncertain, and by no means will always be positive. What Western Europe enjoyed

© The Author(s), under exclusive license to Springer Nature Singapore Pte Ltd. 2023   117
B. Cheang and T. G. Palmer, *Institutions and Economic Development*,
Classroom Companion: Economics, https://doi.org/10.1007/978-981-99-0844-8_5

was a historically contingent set of circumstances where liberal values emerged victorious in this 'cultural marketplace'.

As such, keeping in mind the points made in the previous two chapters, what societies require to enjoy sustained development are not only economic freedom and institutions of property rights and the rule of law, but rather liberal values centred around individual freedom and the dignity of market exchange. Nations need not only 'get prices right' and 'get institutions right', but need to first 'get the culture right'. Markets and its institutions rely on a supportive cultural environment, without which its benefits cannot be unlocked.

Our argument thus differs from other accounts in several ways. First, our promarket argument is not wedded to the tenets of neoclassical economics. Liberal neoclassical economists are right to point out that markets are necessary conditions for a properly functioning economy. But absent the cultural bedrock, the models that they construct are at best textbook fictions. This is because, as Chap. 3 has explained, neoclassical economics is wedded to a positivist methodological outlook; they tend to seek universal laws and thus see the cultural studies as either contradictory to or irrelevant to their methods. Economists tend to model individuals as maximizing (which they term 'rational') agents, and thus discount how culture and other institutional variables may fundamentally shape behaviour in ways that lie outside of rationality (Hodgson G., 2000). Cultural studies and economics, however, need not be at odds. Culture and economics cannot be torn asunder, for they are fundamentally connected. In fact, culture is the very foundation on the basis of which market and political processes operate (Chamlee-Wright & Lavoie, 2000). Cultural analysis is useful for scholars to explore the diverse and plural world of social meanings (Barker, 2004; Thompson et al., 2006; Vivanco, 2018). Second, the cultural argument that we make here, unlike other approaches, is not a deterministic one. Some theorists in this tradition explain the wealth of nations with reference to certain cultural factors that are either 'present' or 'absent' and thus comprising fixed points that determine national development (we call this 'cultural determinism'). We depart from this approach by emphasising the ideational (beliefs, values and ideas) as opposed to materialist aspect of culture (customs, cultural practices or lifestyles). Seen this way, culture is basically *ideas*, i.e. *what people think and believe*. Political ideas like liberalism, socialism and conservatism also fall under this umbrella of *culture as ideas*. Culture is therefore fluid and adaptive (see Palmer, 2004), and is constituted by the discursive struggles of individuals in the cultural marketplace. The outcome of these struggles forms the prevailing ideological contours of society, which has over history cast a long shadow (Rueschemayer, 2006).

Significantly, our argument is also different from two other schools of thought. For one, some accounts emphasise the prevalence of exploitation in historical development as well as the injustices in the evolution of Western capitalism, such as slavery, imperialism and colonialism. While these practices are indeed unjust and ripe targets for condemnation, they cannot explain the sudden and sustained burst in wealth that began in the late eighteenth century. A raft of economic historians has shown that the slave trade, overseas empires and colonies, while understandably enriching specific coalitions, were not central in accounting for the rise of the West (Davies, 2019; Davies & Huttenback, 1988; Eltis & Engerman, 2000; Goldstone, 2009; Olmstead & Rhode, 2018). The exploitation of man over man has unfortunately been a staple in world history, but it was the gradual ascendancy of liberal values, which recognised the dignity of man, that played a major role in fostering wealth. In fact, leading market liberals have always been fiercest critics of empire, and it was the unfortunate loss of these insights which led to a disjuncture between pro-market and anti-colonial ideas in modern development thinking (Easterly, 2021).

Our account is also different, though not totally unrelated, from purely institutionalist accounts of the rise of liberal institutions (see for instance North & Weingast, 1989; Rosenberg & Birdzell, 1987). In our view, cultural entrepreneurs drive change in the climate of ideas which in turn affect other institutions, making their impact felt over the course of history.

This chapter is structured as follows. The first section will review the contributions of Lawrence Harrison on culture's contributions to development. This approach to culture is ultimately rejected because it is too deterministic and does not recognise the priority of culture's ideational foundations. The second section will focus on the specific ideas that are associated with market exchange. Theory and empirical data suggests social cooperation works best when individual liberty, including the rights to associate and to disassociate and to differentiate oneself and to innovate, is indispensable to the historical 'Great Enrichment'. The presumption of the liberty of the individual to act and the culture—the norms, values and expectations that undergird it—continue to be important today. We then draw implications for understanding development challenges today, showing that those values are under threat from a lingering hostility of market exchange and market-tested betterment, specifically how they are construed as based on exploitation, unequal power relations and historical injustices. Liberal values may have been extensively realised to a greater degree initially in 'the West', but they are decidedly not exclusively Western constructs, as those who habitually move 'between cultures' can attest.

Culture: Deterministic or Fluid?

Arguably the leading theorist of culture in development was Lawrence Harrison, who famously developed a typology distinguishing progress-prone and progress-resistant cultures. His project was based on the observation that there are ethnic and religious minorities situated within wider cultural contexts whose members are more prosperous than the average for the wider societies of which they are part. Even within a given society, country or national group, some groups may prosper more than others, without any legal or political advantages, and sometimes even in spite of systematically imposed disadvantages.

Harrison's cultural project was motivated by a rejection of cultural relativism and multiculturalism. Cultural relativism is closely associated with multiculturalism, with the former claiming that all cultures are equal, and the latter emphasising the need to embrace all cultures, a combination that has led to the decline of the cultural school of thought in development studies (Harrison, 2008, 2012). It smacks of 'political incorrectness' to say that one culture is more conducive to development and prosperity than another and that some core values and norms will be more successful at generating social harmony and rising incomes than others. This is unfortunate, because the cultural school of thought has much to offer. On an individual level that is intuitive. Performance psychologists, business experts and behavioural scientists have shown that certain traits are more conducive to career success and to the development of expertise than are others. For example, grit, emotional resilience and deliberate practice are the bedrock for expert success, rather than mere 'innate abilities or basic capabilities' (Ericsson, 2004). Additionally, the belief that one can grow in knowledge and skills is as important if not more important than the actual skill level itself (Dweck, 2016). What we believe about ourselves will affect whether we do well in life. If this is true, why not consider it in the context of a nation? Why did East Asia grow rapidly in the late twentieth century? More interestingly, why did some parts of Europe gain head starts in the eighteenth and nineteenth centuries? *Culture-as-ideas* explanations have much to offer.

Yet, it is also possible to take the other extreme, where culture becomes too deterministic as an explanation, leaving little room for individual agency. In the case of Lawrence Harrison, this results from too broad a definition of culture, as compared to the ideational version we use. Additionally, the middle ground that we take is consistent with the account of institutional change adopted in this handbook, one that relies on a culturally embedded (but not fully socialised) view of human action (see Chap. 4).

Progress-Prone Values

An early framework developed by Lawrence Harrison and Samuel Huntington (2000) examined ten values that separate 'progressive' from 'static cultures'. To the extent that a society exhibits traits of a progressive culture the more the economic prosperity of that society. As will be made clear, the tables that follow are drawn from and inspired by the work of Harrison and his colleagues, but in presenting them we are not endorsing all their elements. According to Harrison & Huntington (2000), these are the ten factors that distinguish progressive from static cultures:

1. Time orientation: The progressive culture emphasises the future, the static culture the present or past. Future orientation implies a progressive world view: influence over one's destiny, rewards in this life for virtue and positive-sum

economics in which wealth expands—in contrast to the zero-sum psychology commonly found in poor countries.

2. Work and achievement are central to the good life in the progressive culture, but are of lesser importance in the static culture. In the former, work structures daily life, and diligence, creativity and achievement are rewarded not only financially but also with satisfaction, self-respect and prestige.

3. Frugality is the mother of investment—and financial security—in progressive cultures, a threat to the egalitarian status quo in static, zero-sum cultures in which one person's gains are at the expense of others.

4. Education is the key to advancement in progressive cultures but is of marginal importance except for the elites in static cultures.

5. Merit is central to advancement in the progressive culture; connections and family are what count in the static culture.

6. Community: The radius of identification and trust extends beyond the family to the broader society in the progressive culture, whereas the family circumscribes community in the static culture. Societies with a narrow radius of identification and trust are more prone to corruption, nepotism and tax evasion and are less likely to engage in philanthropy.

7. The societal ethical code tends to be more rigorous in the progressive culture. Every advanced democracy except Belgium, Taiwan, Italy and South Korea appears among the 25 least corrupt countries on Transparency International's 'Corruption Perceptions Index". Chile and Botswana are the only Third World countries that appear among the top 25.[1]

8. Justice and fair play are universal, impersonal expectations in the progressive culture. In the static culture, justice, like personal advancement, is often a function of whom you know or how much you can pay.

9. Authority which tends towards dispersion and horizontality in progressive cultures encourages dissent, while authority which tends towards concentration and verticality in static cultures encourages orthodoxy.

10. Secularism: The influence of religious institutions on civic life is small in the progressive culture; their influence in static cultures is often substantial. Heterodoxy and dissent are encouraged in the former, and orthodoxy and conformity are encouraged in the latter.

This set of ten values has also been expanded into a larger set of 25 factors that are then divided into four categories that determine whether a nation has a progress-prone culture. Those four categories are: Worldview, Social Behaviour, Values and Virtues, and Economic Behaviour (Harrison, 2012, pp. 16–17).

The fourth category of Economic Behaviour is especially salient for the development context. For example, progressive economic behaviour would be characterised by openness to innovation, entrepreneurship and competition, a

---

[1] It should be noted that since 2000, the rankings of countries on the Corruptions Perceptions Index have changed.

widespread belief that advancement is achieved through merit rather than connections, and a mindset that work leads to wealth. Thus, successful economic
development would be undergirded by cultural beliefs that endorse productive
wealth creation (Table 5.1).

Lawrence Harrison on Jewish and Chinese Success

Those typologies allowed Lawrence Harrison to analyse the historic success of
some communities embedded within wider social orders, namely Jews, Confucian Chinese and Protestants. The Jewish people have been especially successful
in various fields, with this success regularly attributed to their high intelligence
and cultural values (see Lynn & Kanazawa, 2008 for a review of this topic
and their assessment). Prominent businesspeople with Jewish backgrounds include
Michael Bloomberg, Michael Dell, Sergey Brin, Larry Page, George Soros, Mark
Zuckerberg and many more. Steven Spielberg comes to mind in the entertainment
industry, and Albert Einstein, a pillar of insight and achievement, in science. Jews
are quite disproportionately represented (compared to their percentage of the population, not only globally, but by country) in a number of fields of achievement,
including Nobel Laureates and chess champions (Rubinstein, 2004; Weyl & Possony, 1963). A specific look into the United States provides further information.
Studies of American household income show the Jewish as the richest religious
group, with more than 40% of them earning at least $100,000 (Masci, 2016; Pew
Research, 2021). A sociological study by Lisa Keister (2003) showed that religion had a big influence on wealth accumulation, with the Jewish people being
the wealthiest demographic group.

Of course, comparisons can be misleading unless confounding variables, such
as median age or geographic distribution, are considered. While American Jews
have a higher median age than many other ethnic groups, which would account
for some of the differential incomes and wealth, Jewish cultural norms and values tend to exhibit many aspects of Harrison's "high cultural capital" culture, i.e.
one that is progress-prone. Several factors are especially noteworthy: education is
regarded as 'indispensable', wealth is thought to be expandable through human
creativity; entrepreneurship is highly regarded, as are investment and creativity;
laws are respected and corruption is prosecuted; and work is believed to lead to
wealth (Harrison, 2012, pp. 64–66).

Lawrence Harrison also singled out the Confucian Chinese in East Asia for
their economic success. There is good reason for this, since this is the region
which saw rapid, some would say miraculous, development in the late twentieth
century. Those East Asian 'Tiger Economies' of South Korea, Taiwan, Hong Kong
and Singapore exhibited development in the span of one generation, overshadow-
ing what other industrialised economies only achieved over multiple generations
and many more years. Figure 5.1 shows the rapid catch-up that the 'four tigers'
enjoyed in the late twentieth century. If the economic growth of Japan and China

Table 5.1 Typology of high cultural capital and low cultural capital societies

No	Factor capital	High cultural capital	Low cultural capital
World view			
1	Religion	Religious worldview in such cultures tends to nurture rationality, pragmatism, and achievement; such a worldview promotes material pursuits, and focuses on the present world	Religious worldview in such cultures tends to nurture irrationality; it inhibits material pursuits, focuses on the other world and is characterised by utopianism
2	Destiny	Belief that one can influence his/her destiny for the better	Existence of a fatalistic mindset
3	Time orientation	Future focus promotes planning, punctuality and deferred gratification	Present or past focus discourages planning, punctuality and saving
4	Wealth	Belief that wealth is a product of human creativity and that it is expandable (positive sum view)	Belief that wealth exists in a fixed, zero-sum manner
5	Knowledge	Knowledge in such cultures are practical and verifiable; facts matter	Knowledge in such societies tend to be overly abstract, theoretical and cosmological; not easily verifiable
Values, virtues			
6	Ethical code	Existence of a rigorous ethical code within realistic norms; feeds trust between individuals	Elastic, wide gap between utopian norms and behaviour, breeding social mistrust
7	The lesser virtues	Lesser virtues matter much in these cultures; people value 'a job well done', tidiness, courtesy and punctuality	Lesser virtues seen as unimportant
8	Education	Education is viewed as indispensable, promoting autonomy, heterodoxy, dissent and creativity	Education has less priority in such cultures; education system promotes dependency and orthodoxy
Economic behaviour			
9	Work/achievement	People in such cultures 'live to work' and believe that work leads to wealth	People in such cultures 'work to live', and do not believe that work can lead to wealth
10	Frugality	Belief that frugality is 'the mother of investment and prosperity'	Belief that frugality is 'a threat to equality'
11	Entrepreneurship	Entrepreneurial activities are directed towards investment and creativity	Entrepreneurial activities are directed towards rent-seeking
12	Risk propensity	Moderate risk propensity	Low risk propensity, with 'occasional adventures'
13	Competition	Belief that competition leads to excellence	Belief that competition is a threat to equality and privilege

(continued)

Table 5.1 (continued)

No	Factor capital	High cultural capital	Low cultural capital
14	Innovation	Open to innovation and rapid adaptation	Suspicious of innovation and slow adaptation to change
15	Advancement	Advancement is due to merit and achievement	Achievement is due to family relationships, patronage or personal connections
Social behaviour			
16	Rule of law/corruption	People in such cultures are reasonably law abiding; corruption is prosecuted	Money and connections matter significantly in such cultures; corruption is tolerated
17	Radius of identification and trust	Stronger identification with the broader society	Stronger identification with the narrow community
18	Family	The idea of 'family' extends to the broader society	The family is seen as a 'fortress' against the broader society
19	Association (social capital)	Existence of high social capital and trust between individuals; participation in civic activities	Lack of social capital in such cultures, where mistrust breeds excessive individualism and anomie
20	The individual/the group	Emphasises the individual but not excessively	Emphasises the collectivity over the individual
21	Authority	Authority in such cultures are dispersed, with the existence of checks and balances	Authority in such cultures is significantly centralised, and may often be unfettered and arbitrary
22	Role of elites	Socio-political elites accept a sense of responsibility to society	Socio-political elites in such cultures focus on the accumulation of power and rent-seeking; exploitative behaviour is the norm
23	Church-state relations	High level of secularisation in such cultures, where a 'wall between church and state' exists	Religion plays major role in the civic sphere in such cultures; lack of separation of church and state
24	Gender relationships	Significant degree of gender equality, and which is at least not inconsistent with the prevailing value system; existence of tolerance of gender preferences	Women in such cultures are subordinated to men in most dimensions of life; LGBTQ individuals are discriminated against
25	Fertility	The belief that the number of children should depend on the family's capacity to raise and educate them	The belief that 'children are gifts of God', and that they are 'an economic asset'

Source Adapted from Lawrence Harrison (2012, pp. 16–17)

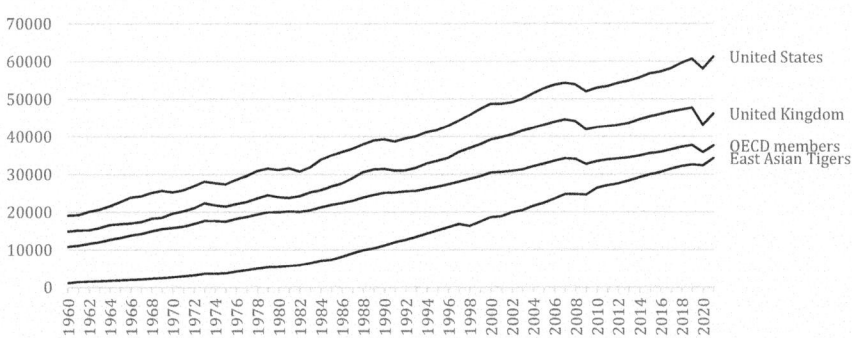

Fig. 5.1 Comparison of GDP per capita of East Asian Tigers with OECD, USA and UK from 1960 to 2020. *Sources* World Development Indicators for all countries and Taiwan's own national statistics (see Republic of China Government, 2022 for Taiwan's data)

are also considered, then this wider conception of East Asia is today an economic powerhouse in its own right.[2]

Notably, these East Asian nations enjoy a common Confucian cultural heritage, to which some scholars have attributed their success. According to Lawrence Harrison (2012, pp. 83–85), Confucian Chinese exhibit many of the traits of 'high cultural capital' societies, including how they prize meritocracy in social advancement and how their frugality spurs investment. Confucian Chinese are also said to have a conception of the family as 'extending to broader society' (Harrison, 2012, p. 85). This last point is interesting, because it explains the familial structure of many Chinese businesses in East Asia's development history (Wong S., 1985, Mackie, 1988; Redding, 1990). Also, Confucian principles of social trust and *guanxi*—or networks of trust, generally based on favours given and owed—explain the close family inter-connexions between and across different business networks (So & Walker, 2013; Wong M., 2007).

Overall, Harrison's work helps illuminate the way specific ethnic groups have enjoyed disportionate success. These groups are by no means limited to the Jewish and East Asians, and as other scholars have shown, they include also the Lebanese, Armenians and Gujeratis. The Indian Gujeratis are especially entrepnreurial, and have been economically successful in most places where they migrate to (Gillion, 1962; Mattausch, 1998). These cultural communities are often economic diasporas who have been enriched by the development process (Pomeranz & Topik, 2014). It has also been shown, for example, that development tends to initially enrich specific minorities, and these groups, with their cultural values, then further succeed and drive development (Chua & Rubenfeld, 2014).

---

[2] There is ongoing debate about whether East Asia's growth has simply been limited to 'catch-up', and lacks the innovation of 'cutting-edge growth'. Heterodox political economists also write about the developmental state approach that East Asia undertook, which supposedly challenges the free market model. We will visit this issue in the next chapter.

Markets and Liberal Values

While Harrison and his colleagues' scholarship provides a useful starting point to understand the role of culture in development, it is not without its flaws. In fact, their approach has been usefully criticised from various quarters. Significantly, it is subject to criticisms made by scholars concerned about Western ethnocentrism in the development discourse. These scholars have pushed back, against the Western-centric variants of modernisation theory which expect developing countries to conform to Western moral standards, moving from one stage of development to ever higher stages (Bordoloi & Das, 2017; Karreth, 2018; Tatsuo, 1999). By putting forward a list of ideal cultural qualities that progress-prone cultures are said to have, and then evaluating national cultures against that benchmark, Harrison's approach opens itself to legitimate concerns of ethnocentrism.

Importantly, 'cultures' are not free-floating entities, but are articulated, activated and transmitted by cultural agents for good or for ill. For example, some of the values mentioned by Harrison, especially Confucianism, have been used in competing ways. While it is said that Confucianism and its personalistic basis facilitated the rise of Chinese business networks, it has at the same time paved the way for widespread corruption and crony capitalism, rather than free market capitalism (Pye, 2000). The political operationalisation of Asian values has not always been conducive to development as well, since some countries, Singapore and China in particular, have weaponised this rhetoric of Asian values to justify authoritarianism, which in both societies has had negative effects on their development prospects (Cheang, 2022; Huang, 2008). As such, it is not clear that 'Confucianism' does most of the work of development; in fact, Pomeranz and Topik (2014) show that the Chinese economic diaspora which has been so successful in development were not merely 'Confucian', but were specifically Fukienese.

Involving the role of cultural entrepreneurs also addresses problems of timing. If it was merely culture alone that was doing the work, then why is it that Confucian values and beliefs, which are often highly praised and have existed for a long time, have led to uneven development at different times in different places? Our answer is that at specific critical junctures in history, cultural entrepreneurs succeed in shifting the intellectual climate of opinion and thereby foster productive wealth creation. There are two quick examples from Asian history that are illustrative. The first is that of Tokugawa Japan, which saw cultural contestation between various groups. While one side of its culture was deeply conservative, and was grounded on the value system of 'bushido' of the samurai class, another was the emergent culture of 'chōnin-dō' which arose largely in Osaka in the early 1700s. Significantly, this new culture was developed by a group of thinkers in the mercantile class who championed the virtues of hard work, craftsmanship and artistic excellence (Davies, 2011). Specifically, it was a *specific variant* of Confucianism that emphasised that moral virtue was compatible with the pursuit of profit. Another example was the immigrant class in colonial Hong Kong and Singapore, two of the most successful development cases in history. These were largely Chinese migrants who arrived in search of economic opportunities and in so doing forged a productive partnership with local British authorities, which was in turn based on the common values of commercialism and meritocracy (Cheang, 2022). Over the years, the *Anglo-Chinese* relationship survived and formed the social glue that facilitated trade-based development, making Singapore and Hong Kong what they are today (Cheang, 2023).

Individualism and Freedom

The root of successful development is a culture that is conducive to individual achievement and that such cultural values need not be historically tied to or rooted in Judaism, Islam, Confucianism, Protestant Christianity or any other historical culture. The individual must be free to work, to exchange, to imagine new possibilities and to introduce new products, technologies and services to the test of market exchange. Wider cultural, intellectual and institutional climates ought to incorporate such beliefs if they are to be conducive to rising incomes, longer and healthier lives, and scientific, technological and economic progress. That means that the market institutions explained in the previous chapter, while necessary for success, are not by themselves, but must also be embedded in a wider cultural context that applauds, rather than condemns, wealth-*creating* achievement and prosperity.

Importantly, it should be noted that these values so described have been found in different forms in different places, even in non-Western contexts. The problem, however, is that they have often been slighted or subordinated by political elites, thus suppressing the growth potential of nations. It is only from the late eighteenth century onwards did the Great Enrichment occur, beginning in Europe. Crucially, the values that we argue to be instrumental for development are at their core, *liberal* values. As this section explains, liberal values are individualist, not in the sense that collectivities do not matter, but revolves around this core precept: that the moral dignity of the individual is held in highest regard and should not be easily abrogated.

The value of individualism has been explored empirically and found to be highly associated with positive development outcomes. This insight is part of ongoing efforts to better measure the importance of cultural values in development (see Guiso et al., 2006; Petrakis & Kostis, 2013). A recent survey of the academic literature revealed that the most studied cultural traits are generalised trust, individualism, family ties, attitudes towards work and people's perception of poverty (Castellani, 2019). Those traits have an impact on institutions, which was the focus of the previous chapter. Specifically, it is shown that the two most important aspects are whether the culture places an importance on the individual and her achievement, and whether the larger society affords equality of opportunity to all individuals—not just to some—and is based on generalised trust. Those traits in turn affect five key domains:

1. the level of economic activity
2. financial markets
3. labour markets
4. innovation activity
5. the quality of institutions.

Most significantly, it has been found that cultures that promote individual effort while ensuring that all enjoy equal opportunities are more likely to generate sustained economic growth (Castellani, 2019). This theory is further supported by Maridal's (2013) analyses, which found that the individual's achievement orientation and cultural values that support such an orientation, coupled with social capital that facilitate exchange, are fundamental in determining economic success. Notably, the influence of individual motivation is even more significant than the combined influence of the quantity of formal education and the quality of formal institutions (Maridal, 2013).

Studies by Yuriy Gorodnichenko and Gerard Roland (2011, 2012, 2017) documented the significant role of individualism in development success. Acknowledging that culture is a significant variable, they observe that the individualism-collectivism dimension is the key cultural variable that affects national development (Gorodnichenko & Roland, 2011). They make an argument in favour of individualism: since it emphasises personal freedom and achievement, it 'awards social status to personal accomplishments such as important discoveries, innovations, great artistic or humanitarian achievements and all actions that make an individual standout' (Gorodnichenko & Roland, 2017, p. 402). Such a culture thus leads to more innovation, and thus higher growth. To clarify, this does not mean that collectivist cultures do not have their own attractions. Being group-oriented, collective action is usually easier in such cultures, with more robust social networks and easier civic mobilisation for collective projects (Gorodnichenko & Roland, 2012). The problem is that it at a cost of conformity, which harms national development prospects.

What is significant from the study of Gorodnichenko and Roland is that cultural characteristics beyond individualism and collectivism do not have significant effects on long-run growth. In analyzing which dimensions of culture matter for long-run growth, only individualism was found to have a significant effect on output per capita (Gorodnichenko & Roland, 2011, p. 492). They drew from three major databases that provide cross-country measures of culture to draw that conclusion (Table 5.2).

In sum, there is strong evidence to conclude that individualism has a robust causal effect on innovation and long-run growth. Not only is culture important in our understanding of long-run growth, with the difference between individualism and collectivism proving to be the most important dimension. Market-based development must be grounded to some extent on individualism, because it requires that the individual be free from coercion to own property, to transact and exchange unmolested. This way, individuals may reap the gains from trade and innovation. It

Table 5.2 The three main international databases providing cross-country measures of culture

	Dutch sociologist Geert Hofstede[a]	Cross-cultural psychologist Shalom H. Schwartz[b]	World values survey[c]
Scope of data collected	Surveys of IBM employees in 30 countries collated to study differences in corporate culture Has been expanded to almost 80 countries	Gathered survey responses from K-12 schoolteachers and college students; for a total of 195 samples drawn from 78 nations and 70 cultural groups between 1998 and 2000 Each sample generally consists of 180–280 respondents for a total of over 75,000 responses	Surveys were conducted in four multi-year waves: 1981–1984, 1989–1993, 1994–1999, and 1999–2004 More than 90 countries have been surveyed, some in multiple waves with a total of nearly 200 surveys Over a quarter million respondents worldwide have provided responses to nearly a thousand questions
Measure-ments of culture utilised	*1. Individualism* – Measures the extent to which it is believed that individuals are supposed to take care of themselves as opposed to being strongly integrated and loyal to a cohesive group – Looks positively on valuing individual freedom, opportunity, achievement, advancement and recognition – Looks negatively on valuing harmony, cooperation and hierarchical relations with supervisors *2. Power Distance* – Measures the extent to which the less powerful members of organisations accept and expect that power to be distributed unequally. A culture that gives great deference to people of higher authority is a 'High Power Distance' culture, and a culture that values the equal treatment of everyone, despite their positions, is a 'Low Power Distance' culture. *3. Masculinity* – Measures the dominance of men over women and to the prevalence of 'masculine' values such as assertiveness and competitiveness versus 'feminine' norms of caring and modesty *4. Uncertainty Avoidance* – Measures the extent to which members of a society feel either uncomfortable or comfortable in situations that are novel and unknown	Consists of approximately 57 questions that ask respondents to indicate the importance of each as 'a guiding principle in my life' Some examples: *1. Autonomy* – Measures the extent to which people view themselves as autonomous, independent entities and the degree to which they feel free to express their own preferences and feelings *2. Embeddedness* – Measures the propensity to maintain the status quo and engage in self-retraining actions to prevent disruption of social solidarity *3. Hierarchy* – Measures the preference for hierarchical social relations in society and in politics, so as to maintain political stability, tradition and conformity *4. Egalitarianism* – Measures a preference for norms of universalism and equality *5. Harmony* – Measures the preference for harmonious social relations and the avoidance of change and conflict	Questions focus on personal attitudes about life, family and society; the environment; attitudes toward work; the importance of traditionalism; gender roles; democracy and government; health; education; religion; spirituality and morality; and honesty

(continued)

Table 5.2 (continued)

	Dutch sociologist Geert Hofstede[a]	Cross-cultural psychologist Shalom H. Schwartz[b]	World values survey[c]
Correlation with national income and economic performance	– No other cultural variable from the Hofstede database other than individualism can be seen to have robust effects in development. – Only the power distance index, which is strongly negatively correlated with individualism, has a negative effect in some specifications. – Masculinity and uncertainty avoidance are not statistically significant.	– None of the Schwartz variables are as robust as the individualism index in Hofstede's approach. – Autonomy and egalitarianism, and to a lesser extent embeddedness, have significant, albeit less robust, effects. These variables are also themselves strongly correlated with the individualism index.	– Trust and tolerance are the most robustly significant in development, though again not as robust as the variable of individualism. These variables are themselves also significantly correlated with individualism. – Hard work and thrift, market orientation, public goods provision and preference for equality of income are not robustly significant in the context of development. – Separate regressions on other WVS questions have been done, and no robust effect has been found on these other variables.
Conclusion	Individualism has a strong and robust effect on log GDP per capita		

Source Gorodnichenko and Roland (2011, pp. 492–493)

[a]First, the database by Geert Hofstede (2001) is a collection of surveys completed by IBM employees in 30 countries. He comes up with four measures for culture: individualism, uncertainty avoidance, masculinity and power distance. This survey allowed for comparison between people with equivalent jobs in the same company, but from different countries, so as to measure cultural discrepancies.

[b]Second, Shalom H. Schwartz (1994) developed a database by collecting survey responses from K-12 schoolteachers and college students. Between 1998 and 2000, 195 samples were drawn from across 70 cultural groups in 78 countries. In this survey, participants were asked to evaluate 56–57 value items with regards to how important they were in being a guiding principle of life. Schwartz then differentiates cultures along the dimensions of autonomy and embeddedness. For the former, people are perceived as autonomous, and are encouraged to express their personal preferences, emotions, and ideas. For the latter, people are identified through their relationship to the group and its shared goals. Additionally, 'embedded cultures' seek to maintain the status quo.

[c]Thirdly, the World Values Survey (WVS) are surveys which were administered in four multi-year waves. Since the first wave of surveys, 90 countries have been surveyed, totalling up to a quarter million respondents worldwide. Nearly a thousand questions have been put forth, focusing primarily on personal attitudes towards life, family and society, and so on (see Inglehart, 2000).

is when an individual's achievement is protected will he have an incentive to inno-vate, and when individual achievement is celebrated, further impetus for innovation is created.

Individualism, however, does not imply atomism, which has often been a com-mon conflation. Individuals are and have always been social creatures, and in fact, it is their mutual interactions that form social constructions and many of the cus-toms, conventions and institutions that have evolved over history (Hayek, 2010; Lewis, 2014). Individuals in our conception are not the *homo economicus* of eco-nomics textbooks, but social beings with the propensity for moral sentiments, and in fact moral improvement. This must be heavily stressed, because individualism has often been seen in a purely 'masculine' lens, as one which is solely centred around the accumulation of wealth, aggressive competition and the preference for strict rules and hierarchy.

Such a conflation is unfortunate. *Liberal* individualism, in our view, is 'femi-nine' as much as it is 'masculine' (see Hofstede, 2001, p. 297 for a dichotomy). A liberal culture is also one where there is high ethical valuation for openness and differences, and 'low conscientiousness', where people prefer general rules of living rather than explicit commands. 'Masculine individualism' may in the end turn out to be hierarchical, illiberal social orders, which are unconducive for human flourishing. In fact, as liberal historian Deirdre McCloskey (2007) pointed out, liberalism is very much grounded on the seven virtues of justice, courage, temperance, prudence, faith, hope and love.

At this point, it is worth reflecting on whether liberal values so described are necessarily Western. Does liberalisation imply Westernisation? The short answer is both 'yes' and 'no'. 'No' because liberal values can be and indeed have been found in many places of the world. A respect for the dignity of the individual and his rights to non-interference need not require an endorsement of Western cultural values, a theme which will be further revisited in the following chapter. However, it is to some extent the case that it was in Western Europe where such liberal values were most pronounced and more fully developed, facilitating a Great Enrichment from the late eighteenth century onwards.

The development success of the West has been a subject of rich study by aca-demic scholars. Various explanations have been given, ranging from the evolution of geography (Diamond, 1998), to the genetic basis for the spread of middle-class values (Clark, 2007), to institutional changes (Acemoglu & Robinson, 2012; North & Weingast, 1989) and to the presence of certain cultural traits (Landes, 1998; Mokyr, 2011a; Weber, 1905). These explanations all contribute something valuable to the discussion, but on their own are limited, because the variables they emphasise have existed in many times and places without a development break-through resulting. The cultural school is most aligned with our account, but should also incorporate the active role of cultural creators and entrepreneurs, which allow one to identify the key critical moments of change and specific change agents.

Consider the famous Protestant Work Ethic argument. It is said that Protes-tant Christianity encouraged a strong work ethic, thrift and capital accumulation. A recent alternative formulation of the 'Protestant Work Ethic' suggests that it was the promotion of biblical reading that gave rise to the literacy and thus to the formation of the human capital necessary to economic prosperity (Becker & Woessman, 2009). What should be noted here is not the Protestant Ethic on its own that made the difference, but the active role played by Calvinist-inspired cultural entrepreneurs in the development context. These change agents, in the UK and elsewhere, facilitated a culture of innovation and enterprise that birthed the industrial revolution and modern economic growth. These entrepreneurs (both in the economic and in the cultural sense) were instrumental in elevating the importance of 'useful knowledge', the belief that improvement is possible through knowledge, as explained by Joel Mokyr (2006, 2011a, b) in his exploration of the Industrial Enlightenment.

Joel Mokyr's (2011b) work is instrumental in highlighting the importance that *culture-as-ideas* played in Britain, and the practical, economic effects they manifested. Rather than portraying the Industrial Revolution as a product of improved incentives or material factors, he locates ideas and values as the key agent of change; particularly he focused on intellectual developments in the eighteenth century associated with the Enlightenment, where there was a spread of a scientific outlook, applying science and reason to foster social progress. In that sense, the Industrial Revolution was a gradual and practical manifestation of earlier periods of the Scientific Revolution and Enlightenment. This line of reasoning was extended by historian Anton Howes (2017), who documented how tit was the spread of an 'improvement mentality' that catalysed the British Industrial Revolution. Importantly, this mentality was one centred on improving the state of the world, i.e. innovation, and transcends a specific skill or body of knowledge. Many of Britain's leading innovators at the time, according to Howes (2017), were also 'committed to spreading the mentality further—they became innovation's evangelists'. They did so by 'creating new institutions and adopting social norms conducive to openness and active sharing', and one example was Henry Brougham, who championed the improvement mentality through his founding of the Society for the Diffusion of Useful Knowledge (Howes, 2017).

This account by Mokyr-Howes is consonant with our emphasis on cultural entrepreneurs. Just as economic entrepreneurs are necessarily leaders who bring forth a new idea for mass consumption, cultural entrepreneurs usually comprise a small elite group who champion new values which then become widely received. Joel Mokyr (2002) acknowledges in his early book *Gifts of Athena* that it was indeed a small group of innovators who drove technology forward and sustained the Industrial Enlightenment. The 'innovation evangelists' in Howe's account is of a similar nature; they are cultural entrepreneurs who promoted market-based development.

In our account, the birth of knowledge and reason, so central in the West's industrialisation, is deeply associated with an emerging climate of liberal freedom that created the space for individual flourishing, for the 'pursuit of happiness', with the emphasis on 'pursuit'—effort, activity—as a constitutive part of happiness. The history of mass prosperity cannot be divorced from the history of liberty. What made the difference was the ascendancy of liberal values in the eighteenth century. Joel Mokyr's own account of the Industrial Enlightenment is situated within this rise of liberal ideas; other European countries too had many scientists and innovators, but what made British scientific culture unique was the way in which its intellectuals opposed rent-seeking and embraced open inquiry and open markets.[3] It was not just the Baconian idea of scientific reason that was ascendant in British public culture at the time, but also the Smithian idea that the economics was positive-sum (Mokyr & Snowdon, 2007).

Significantly, for the first time, ordinary people could become entrepreneurs, innovators and merchants and be accorded liberty and dignity: liberty entails permissionless innovation, risk-taking, exchange and improvement, whether just for its own sake or in the pursuit of wealth; dignity is no longer a rank demanded by the powerful, but a condition of recognised moral worth and standing recognised by the wider society. The world was transformed, connected and enriched by what Deirdre McCloskey calls the 'Bourgeois Deal', a 'mind your own business' ethic which propelled prosperity, and which has proven more conducive to mass prosperity and flourishing than all other modes of social arrangement, whether the aristocratic 'blue-blood deal', the socialist 'Bolshevik deal', or the welfarist 'Bismarckian deal' and statist 'Bureaucratic deal' (see McCloskey & Carden, 2020, Chap. 20). Liberalism is the beating heart of modern prosperity.

'The Great Enrichment', in the words of McCloskey, entailed a dramatic explosion of living standards that made all previous periods of enrichment pale in comparison. Per capita income was not merely doubled, as had happened in other eras, before slipping back to previous levels, but has increased 30-fold and more. Most people who today enjoy modern standards of living, including the ability to speak with distant friends and family at the push of a few buttons, to live into their sixties and beyond with the use of their natural teeth, and to fly through the air, possibilities that were considered fantasies just a few generations ago, rarely stop to think about how much their lives differ from those of their parents, grandparents, great grandparents and great-great grandparents. Human life has changed in such regards more in the past two hundred years than in the previous four thousand years.

Such transformations cannot be adequately explained by other factors, even that of the 'work ethic' and the accumulation of savings and investment, two popular explanations of modern capitalism. Modern prosperity was not born of mere hard work, nor of a spirit of accumulation, for work can be hard and come to little, and more bricks may make buildings higher, but will not of itself install central heating or indoor plumbing. Those innovations required something more than hard work; indeed, much innovation has been precisely a means to the avoidance of 'hard work', as tools have multiplied the results of human labour (think of the impact

---

[3] Joel Mokyr also identified the fact that Europe experienced political fragmentation, which provides an institutional basis that facilitated the rise of these ideas, as compared to other continents where centralisation was the norm.

of such humble machines as the wheelbarrow and the lever) or replaced human labour and freed people to do other things, including acquiring education, reading imaginative literature, undertaking research, and spending more time raising literate and educated children.

How did liberal values arise in the West? An understanding of this mechanism is crucial if we wish to apply lessons for today. The acceptance of the liberal Bourgeois Deal was enabled, as McCloskey documents, by a change in rhetoric, a process that first occurred in northwestern Europe, and which then spread outward and now embraces much of the planet. First occurring in the Dutch Republic in the seventeenth century, and spreading then to Britain and other parts of Europe, people began to *think and talk differently* about commerce. Such developments did not occur in a neatly linear fashion however, for they arose in an unplanned manner and are products of unique historical accidents. In the words of historical sociologists, starting in the seventeenth century, there were 'critical junctures,' shifts in opinion, which led to dramatic improvements in the conditions of life, including material living standards, that no one could have foreseen at the time.[4]

Some clarifications are in order. First, it bears remembering that exchange on markets was not unique to Europe. Markets and trade have always existed through history, but what was novel in northwestern Europe was the greater and more widespread social dignity and liberty that ordinary people enjoyed, as well as the social respect accorded to those who succeeded in creating wealth through work, innovation or exchange. A 'critical threshold' was reached. Bourgeois values were most extensively realised socially, and later institutionally, in the West. There are thus good reasons to learn from the lessons of Western history if we wish to understand how developing nations may similarly achieve a transition to 'trade-tested betterment', or 'innovism', to use McCloskey's preferred terms. In fact, the term 'capitalism' rests on a misleading notion of how prosperity is achieved: the accumulation of more and more capital. Accumulating capital is how you or I may become wealthy compared to others in our societies, but capital accumulation is not the source of rising incomes generally. For one thing, capital investment faces diminishing returns; adding another windmill may be a good thing, but the return on that investment is likely to be less than on the previous windmill. What causes incomes to rise as we have seen them do for the last two centuries is not more windmills, but shifting from windmills to steam power, from steam power to electricity and so on, and that required *innovation*, the human mind.

It was neither the accumulation of capital that gave northwestern Europe and its offshoots a head start, nor their good geography and colonial empire that accounted for modern mass prosperity; it was a change in how people thought about and treated each other (McCloskey, 2015). Ideas matter above all else. Too many modern economists, who are typically wedded to restrictive social science

---

[4] For more on concepts like 'critical junctures' and 'path dependence', refer to James Mahoney (2006).

methodologies rooted in positivist social science, have failed to adequately incorporate ideas, ethics and talk into their accounts of how dramatically human life has changed in the past few centuries (McCloskey, 2010, 2016; Smith & Wilson, 2019).

Cultural Entrepreneurship: Good or Bad?

If *culture as ideas* matters for development, and if cultural entrepreneurs drive change in the climate of opinion, then the outcome of this contestation may very well be uncertain. The liberal values that are critical for development, as presented above, may be supplanted by other values that run in an illiberal direction. Ultimately, as the final chapter of this volume will elucidate further, the outcome of this discursive struggle is unclear, just as the outcome in the economic marketplace is unclear.

Liberal values have been criticised for various reasons and by different scholars. In the philosophical realm, liberalism is criticised by a series of authors, such as Erich Fromm and Karl Marx, who stressed capitalism's alienating effects. Similarly, Herbert Marcuse saw liberal capitalism as repressive, because individuals were held hostage by modern consumer culture and unable to realise their true selves and needs. To some extent, these positions mirror that of liberal capitalism's contemporary communitarian critics, such as Charles Taylor (1985) who argue that liberalism is over-individualistic, neglecting the social nature of human beings. Likewise, the communitarian Alasdair MacIntyre (1981, 220) believes that the institutions of liberal capitalism may be socially corrosive, since it cannot sustain a sense of 'community united in a shared vision of the good of man'.

Liberal capitalism has also been criticised in historical quarters. According to some, capitalism is 'historically tainted', since Western nations grew rich through colonialism, and the unjust practices associated with empire, most notably slavery. The popularity of this argument is evident by the recent surge in writings under the label 'New History of Capitalism' (see Burnard & Riello, 2020). In some way, this literature is also connected to dependency theory which also shares in the view that capitalism has historically been exploitative. Dependency theory posits a polarizing tendency inherent in global markets, whereby some countries in the 'periphery' are stuck in certain structures of production in relation to 'core' nations, which advance through capital investment, and thus are constrained and prevented from developing (see Kvangraven, 2021 for a recent restatement of dependency theory as a research program). Poor countries remain poor because they are exploited by these entities, or in some ways become victims of 'hegemonic structures of domination and control' (Tandon, 2016).

Most recently and especially after the 2008 financial crisis, liberal capitalism is also criticised for its inegalitarian effects. Disparities of wealth and income are also accompanied by a range of other inequalities, whether of race, gender and sexuality. It is not within the scope of this volume to unpack these complicated concerns of the contemporary era. But suffice to say, the climate of opinion has shifted significantly, and liberal capitalism today is seen with much scepticism. Opinion polls—such as those by YouGov, Gallup and Pew—in the United States show that over the past decade, young people have displayed less and less favourable views of 'capitalism'. The Economist Magazine (2019) has labelled this trend the rise of 'millennial socialism'. Apparently, fewer than half of young Americans view capitalism positively, and they are as positive about socialism as they are about capitalism (Newport, 2018). While market capitalism still remains popular in some polls of Americans, it is fast declining and socialism's favourability has been going up (Wronski, 2021; YouGov, 2019). These trends are not exclusive to the United States, but also in the UK, where youths are found to be more favourable of broadly 'socialist' policies than older generations—according to a survey, 67% of them (Niemietz, 2021). Such a negative trend is not universal, of course. Some countries, such as Greece, have seen increases in positive views about liberal principles and principles (Friedrich Naumann Stiftung, 2020), as have countries in the former Communist empire of Eastern Europe (Wike & Fetterolf, 2021). The ten countries with the highest positive evaluations of markets among young people, as measured by the Global Index of Economic Mentality, which examines data derived from the World Values Survey, are (in order) Czechia, Estonia, New Zealand, Poland, Georgia, Belarus, Bulgaria, Armenia, Denmark and Sweden (Czeglédi et al., 2021).

These popular perceptions seem to mirror, not only historical experience, but to some extent trends in academia and the arts, as well. In the United States and the UK, at least, academia, television and film tend to be dominated by those who believe that government direction is generally preferable to spontaneous order (Gross & Fosse, 2012; Langbert et al., 2016). Intellectual monocultures tend to become sterile and even tyrannical and to foster conformity and lack of critical thinking, which has led some to call for a frank revival of the withering ideas of intellectual and academic freedom (Williams, 2016). To the extent that academics influence public policy and popular opinion, the domination of much of the intellectual world by avowed enemies of liberal values and institutions is a worrying trend and bodes ill for continued economic development and widespread prosperity.

Cultural Entrepreneurship as a Key Driver of Change

If values are crucial for development, then how do changes in values or values becoming more influential happen? In our account, cultural entrepreneurship is the key driver of change. It is with such an account can we better trace how ideas evolve, and how they are actually applied on the ground in specific local contexts. This is because cultures are heavily contested (as the example above of Confucianism shows). Additionally, local communities need to identify ways in which cultural values or ideas are to be applied, rejected or modified according to local circumstances, in order to improve their economic welfare. As previous chapters have shown, foreign intervention by development experts have often failed because they did not have local participation or knowledge. This highlights the importance of local individuals, organisations and change agents, whether in terms of promoting reforms, improving governance and in this case promoting ideas.

In this section therefore, we explore some historical and contemporary examples of cultural entrepreneurship. Historically, we briefly explore the role of migration and conquests in shaping the cultural content of certain communities. In the contemporary world, we present two case studies of actual organisations that the present authors have interviewed. Both are local African organisations, in Sudan and Burundi, who have engaged in educational work in order to change social opinion about the role of women. Both countries have faced a problem where women, largely due to the prevailing cultural mindset, have not been able to own property on equal terms. The unequal status of women in property ownership is not unique to these two countries, but in many other developing countries (Gaddis et al., 2021).

Historical Migration and Conquest

Historically, the mass migration of people across space have shaped culture. As host societies receive foreigners, they are both changed by new cultural inputs, and at the same time shape the culture of the new migrants. Migration has occurred for a whole host of reasons throughout history, including the search for employment, for better political conditions or for interpersonal reasons (see Cheng & Yang, 1998 for an analysis of motivations of highly skilled migrants to the USA). Sometimes, migration is connected to wars of conquests, when foreign invaders import their own cultures, practices and populations into the subjugated lands. The cross-border trade of civilisations past also facilitated tremendous cultural exchanges which have shaped the modern world. Thus, the culture of a nation is never static, but shaped at different times and places by factors such as these. In turn, these factors contribute to the theme of cultural entrepreneurship we discuss, because they determine at any one point in time the dominant cultural groups that exist in a given society and their ability to transmit their values more widely.

Due to the migration of peoples, cultural values are transmitted, and these contribute to socio-economic disparities within nations. There is much evidence showing that specific cultural groups within nations have higher socio-economic attainment. These include the examples of Jews and Chinese abovementioned, but have also include Overseas Indians, the Japanese, Italians and Germans, among others, though their ethnic composition vary from society to society (see Sowell, 1995). While there are many reasons for such attainment gaps, one reason is clearly that of culture, which may affect individual motivation and economic skill. One particular group is that Indians, who have emigrated significantly to many Western countries. In the UK for example, from 1955 to 1975, they emigrated in large numbers, and were motivated by push factors such as the 1947 partition of India, status competition between local migrant families as well as the economic attraction of the UK (Ram, 1987). Indian migration to the UK has built on itself ever since. Most recently, it is found that most migrants in the UK hail from India (896,000), just one position higher than Polish migrants to the UK (Rienzo & Vargas-Silva, 2017). Notably, the 57th Prime Minister of the UK, and the current one as of November 2022, is Rishi Sunak, of Indian origin. British Indians, according to available data, perform very well in academic performance, their relatively low poverty rates and their consistently high position in terms of average hourly pay (Palmer & Kenway, 2007; UK Government, 2022a, b). Their achievements on a global level are impressive. As of the late twentieth century, they excelled in many of the same professions as the Jews (like real estate, finance and trading), achieving prominence in key technical fields, and owned more than 100bn in real estate (Kotkin, 1993). While many factors have of course contributed to their success, culturally, they are observed to be frugal, tenacious and persistent in their endeavours, and also strikingly exhibit a high restraint-low indulgence ratio on Hofstedes's cultural indicators (Tinker, 1977).

Migration and the cultures they bring fundamentally shape the societies that receive them. That is because the values that migrants bring have an impact on development prospects. The most obvious and dramatic example of this would be the United States, which has historically been an immigrant society. While there were various waves of migration into the United States, the most historically significant period was from 1492 onwards which saw successive waves of European settlers, which in turn gradually transformed the United States into a neo-Europe (see Gabaccia, 2013 for a historical overview). The peopling of the Americas was also closely tied to European colonisation and conquests, which had an adverse impact on indigenous populations. This period was succeeded by arguably the golden age of migration to the United States, where from 1820 to 1940, about 32 million foreigners arrived. As with most phenomena, migration patterns in the United States are complex, and they also demonstrated racial exclusion of certain groups, e.g. Asians. However, what is important from a development perspective is that the nineteenth century, which was a generally liberal period of economic openness, enriched the American economy, which to a large extent also benefitted from its dynamic immigrant society.

The migration of peoples and the cultural values they bring are historically tied to numerous factors, mostly cross-border trade, and at times conquests and colonisation.[5] Cross-cultural exchange has been common throughout history, but started becoming significant during the era of the ancient silk roads (200BC to 400AD), where trade facilitated contact between civilisations of the East and West. The seventh century onwards then saw the rapid spread of Islam, most extensively through the Umayyad caliphates. Islam's early and rapid spread was due to many factors, including its enjoyment of good transportation technology, the zealousness if its military conquests, as well as state sponsorship of the religion, which provided incentives for conversion to the faith (Hodgson M., 1974; Lapidus, 2014). In the

---

[5] See Thomas Sowell's (1995, 1997, 1999) three-volume work on migration and wars of conquests as drivers of cultural change in history.

next few centuries, other major religions also spread: Buddhism in Asia, Confucian values in Southeast Asia and Christianity in Northern Europe, all aided by long distance exchange that overshadowed the era of the early silk roads. Importantly, all through the mediaeval period, the spread of these values was also hastened by the emergence of larger imperial structures and state power, which acted as inducements to local populations to accept the values of conquering peoples. At times, rulers insisted that subjugated peoples accept their new cultural values, and others, the cultural diffusion was achieved through gradual acceptance of the population who desired the rewards of assimilation. The pre-modern period of history also witnessed another driver of cultural change: the missionary activities of Europeans, who spread Christian values far beyond their origins. China increasingly was for instance a target of European missionaries from the thirteenth century onwards, but their efforts were understandably frustrated in this period due to a failure to effectively communicate their message in Mongol society, which leaned towards Buddhism.

In sum, the historical period of 1000 to 1500 was arguably the one which most accelerated cross-cultural interaction. While the period before witnessed the rise of large civilisations in the East which advanced trade and communications, post 1000, these settled societies were overrun by nomadic Turkish and Mongol peoples, who formed powerful empires that spanned vast regions and further accelerating cross-cultural contact (see Abu-Lughod, 1991). It was in this period that also saw the early voyages of Western explorers into the Eastern hemisphere (such as Marco Polo and his family), setting in motion new processes (and mutual East–West interactions) that would form the basis for subsequent Western hegemony in the modern era (Brotton, 2010).

The cross-cultural contact in various historical junctures led to a range of outcomes: from voluntary acceptance of new ideas, i.e. 'conversion through voluntary association', 'conversion induced by political, economic or social pressure' and 'conversion by assimilation', according to historian Jerry Bentley's (1993) seminal analysis. In the first case, individuals may be motivated by prospects for alliances with foreigners, thus adopting alien beliefs and eventually embracing them for themselves. In other instances, social conversion to foreign beliefs was achieved through some degree of pressure, though not always outright coercion; such pressure could be a result of tactics such as 'differential taxation, diversion of financial resources from established institutions to those associated with a new cultural alternative, preference of adherents to a particular tradition when recruiting officials', etc. (Bentley, 1993, p. 12). Importantly, in this process of cross-cultural exchange, Jerry Bentley notes that cultures are never transplanted or accepted wholesale, as there is often a process of mixing between old and new beliefs—what he called 'syncretism'—which allow foreign cultural values to win support in their new alien contexts. Christianity, for instance, had always had to accommodate pagan values and rituals in order to remain relevant.

Even though cross-cultural exchange has always existed throughout history and were driven by a myriad of civilisations, it cannot be denied that it was in the sixteenth century onwards that European power most deeply shaped world history, and thus the cultural character of its conquered territories. Arguably, the Europeans enjoyed unprecedented technological superiority and also favourable disease conditions which in some cases wiped off indigenous communities entirely. Of course, it should be noted at the outset that not all colonial empires were initiated by the West, for example significant entities included the Islamic Empires of the medieval period, and later the Chinese and Japanese Empires. That said, European imperialism of the past four centuries is most significant in terms of its shaping of modern society and its cultural character. Modern institutions that people live under, whether language, law or politics, are products of the West (Ferguson, 2012). The West continues to dominate global institutions and the global economy, though power has recently started to shift towards the East (Mahbubani, 2022).

The realisation that European imperialism has shaped much of world history is of course seen by many in negative terms. For example, the achievements of the West are seen by some to be morally tainted or achieved on the backs of exploited natives. It should not be denied that imperialism, and the use of force more generally, has always been brutal in history and should be defended. However, some points of consideration are in order. Before Europe became an imperial power, it too was a target of foreign conquest. In fact, modern Europe is the son of the Roman Empire, with its language, cultural beliefs and numerous institutions. Europe was also the beneficiaries of philosophies, scientific knowledge and breakthroughs from the Arabic and Islamic world, imported through wars of conquest (Lindberg, 1976). In a way, wars have fundamentally shaped the world in which we live, and are societies are to some extent a product of past conquests.

What is the impact of colonisation and conquest on developing nations? The answer is mixed. On one hand, many former colonies have suffered, but some have also prospered. Additionally, the fact that many former colonies have languished in poverty does not mean that colonialism is its cause. Some poor nations have never been colonies (e.g. Ethiopia and Liberia), and some countries that have suffered the negative legacy of colonialism have turned the tide (e.g. India and China). The basic premise to remember here is that no two historical experience is the same; it is for instance generally accepted by British colonisation was relatively less brutal than that of other European powers, such as the Belgians and French, who were especially violent in their colonies. In fact, the differences in colonial rule and the degree of force they used determined whether there was a peaceful transfer to power, or violent anti-colonial movements in the aftermath of World War II (see Tarling, 2000 for an analysis of Southeast Asian decolonisation). The realisation that colonial rule was heterogeneous allows for nuanced comparative analysis, and investigation into how institutions and culture were transmitted into colonies.

From a development perspective, there are generally two perspectives on the impact of colonialism onto institutional development. The first emphasises the character of the colonial entity itself, for example, that British colonies have tended to do better because they inherit superior common law, the English language, and because their institutions were more liberal in character (La Porta et al., 2008; Lange et al., 2006). Strikingly, Australia, Canada, United States, Singapore and

Hong Kong, who are economic successes, are all former British colonies. The second emphasises the local conditions faced by colonisers themselves, for example soil, climate, demography and disease conditions may cause colonisers to establish extractive institutions to the detriment of future generations (Acemoglu et al., 2001; Engerman & Sokoloff, 2002). However, the present author believes that both may be fruitfully synthesised to account for how positive culture and institutions create development.

The present author (Bryan Cheang) has separately written about the colonial experiences of Singapore and Hong Kong, who are arguably two of the most successful case studies in global development (see Cheang, 2022; 2023). Both city states benefitted from post-war globalisation, foreign investment, good geographical location as well as generally good governance, but there has been little attempt to systematically investigate the contributions of British colonialism, particularly with regard to culture and institutions. Bryan Cheang (2022, Chap. 5) has separately shown that both city states were fortunate beneficiaries of British values and institutions, in an account that recognises both local conditions and the character of the British. First, unlike other colonies, Hong Kong and Singapore were very sparsely populated when the British arrived, creating an 'institutional tabula rasa' which allowed the British to realise their political designs in an unimpeded fashion. Second, through a set of contingent circumstances that no one could have predicted, it was the British (not other European colonies) who established their rule there, which means that the liberal flavour of British institutions at home could be imported (Cheang, 2023). The confluence of both factors meant that for the next century, trade and immigration exploded, positioning Hong Kong and Singapore as one of the wealthiest places today.

Culture plays an important role in this account. This is because the arrival of the British attracted mass migration of Chinese people, who dominated the local economy. These Chinese migrants started out as 'middlemen entrepreneurs', who are economic intermediaries that facilitate exchange between various social groups (see Min, 2013 for a survey of this concept). In Singapore and Hong Kong, they acted as intermediaries between the British mercantile class and larger Chinese population, thereby linking the domestic and global economy through trade. What is significant is that the Chinese were not mere intermediaries but formed a mutually productive partnership with the British based on common values. Notably, the Chinese demonstrated much of the 'bourgeois virtues' abovementioned, values which were ascendant in liberal Britain at the time (Cheang, 2023). The close Anglo-Chinese relationship not only facilitated economic development, but meant that specific Chinese leaders were also political leaders and representatives of their community. In turn, their prominent position within society and (gradually) in formal governance, perpetuated the meritocratic, bourgeois values of the Chinese community and sustained them through subsequent generations (Cheang, 2023).

In sum, the Hong Kong and Singapore cases are valuable for several reasons. They establish that it is not merely 'culture' that play a role in development, but it is specific cultural entrepreneurs we should look at, and who in specific times and places manage to gain social prominence and sustain their values in wider society.

In Hong Kong and Singapore, the values of the dominant Anglo-Chinese coalition happened to be oriented towards commerce and were largely liberal in character, thus contributing to positive development in the colonial era.[6] However, as has been stressed before, there is no guarantee that any particular cultural group win out in the cultural marketplace.

Liberal Cultural Change in Contemporary Africa

In the contemporary era, there are understandably numerous organisations, individuals and groups who seek to improve the development prospects of their countries. One of the important roles that they play—which will be further elucidated in the final chapter—is to promote cultural change through intellectual and educational outreach activities. This is based on the realisation that what people think and believe matters, and if there are indeed cultural values inimical to development, then the task of development requires one to *change* these mindsets. Two organisations in Africa, interviewed here, are especially noteworthy in their efforts at cultural change in a pro-liberal direction.

In South Sudan, the Students' Organization for Liberty and Entrepreneurship (SOLE) was founded in 2015. One of their key projects have been to promote a cultural change towards women. In addition to their multitude of conferences and lectures which are regularly attended by government officials, SOLE launched a project between February and March 2022 to train government stakeholders on the right of women to own land in South Sudan (Students' Organization for Liberty & Entrepreneurship, 2022). SOLE noted that some of the institutions and stakeholders who have the authority to uphold and enforce the rights of women to own property in South Sudan are inadequately equipped with the knowledge and tools necessary to defend the women, who are often victims of bad cultural practices. The project was hence targeted at equipping these stakeholders with the necessary tools and information, such as to allow them to speak up and transcend the cultural practices that hinder women from owning private property in South Sudan. This was accomplished through a variety of programs: for example, SOLE conducted a one-day stakeholders' training session to 52 and 48 participants in the towns of Yambio and Nzara, respectively, whereby the participants were comprised of women leaders, village chiefs, youth leaders, police and church leaders, all of whom are often directly involved in land ownership disputes. Participants were also given T-shirts printed with the message 'Promoting the Right of Women to Own Land in South Sudan', thereby extending the message beyond participants of the training session. Additionally, SOLE conducted two two-hour radio talk shows on Yambio FM station, which was facilitated by two participants who had

---

[6] The post-war period saw significant changes, where independent Singapore rolled back the liberal flavour of British governance while Hong Kong sustained the same arrangements till 1997.

attended the training session and one SOLE staff. The radio talk shows are estimated to reach 30,000 listeners, with 49 and 61 listeners calling in on the first and second day, respectively, to pose questions. Additionally, SOLE conducted community dialogues in the towns of Yambio and Nzara to 82 and 71 participants, respectively, which was attended by key community leaders and met with strong approval from participants.

A similar educational effort has been underway in Burundi. While statutory law in Burundi upholds the notion of gender equality, customary law, which remains dominant in state and legal apparatus, routinely discriminates against women in relation to land and inheritance rights. Most land holdings in Burundi are acquired by succession: Burundi, however, has failed to successfully pass a succession bill, despite one being prepared since 2004 (Centre for Development & Enterprise Great Lakes, 2021b). A legal void hence exists with regards to matters of succession or specifically the ability of women to inherit land: even formal land policy in Burundi which outlines the main orientations of the government of Burundi in organizing access to land, the appropriation of land and the securing of related rights failed to address women's access to land (Centre for Development & Enterprise Great Lakes, 2021a). Given this legal void, custom hence remains the only reference for succession of properties: under customary law, however, land under intestate succession generally devolves to male members of the paternal line. As noted in the Family Code section, customary laws provide that women cannot inherit land from their fathers or husbands: resultantly, women have few legal rights over the land that they farm despite them playing a key role in agriculture (International Organization for Migration, 2023).

Other factors further complicate land ownership for women. Firstly, the use of the French official language in legal texts governing land, while translated into Kirundi, remains relatively obscure in lieu of the high illiteracy rate in Burundi (Centre for Development and Enterprise Great Lakes, 2022a). This legal ignorance entails that some women who purchase properties continue to certify them at the household level under the name of their husbands. Registration procedures are additionally extremely complicated and time-consuming: per the World Bank's *Doing Business* report, registering a property in Burundi requires six steps that take an average of 120 days, and costs around 9% of the total land value (Centre for Development and Enterprise Great Lakes, 2022b). Land registration hence requires high costs that most Burundian women cannot afford: one specific example here is Law No. 1/05 ratified in 20 February 2020, which sets the tariffs for registration fees for the creation or the transformation of the land certificate into a land title at 40,000 Burundian Francs per page of writing, a price that is excessively high relative to the low purchasing power of Burundian women (Centre for Development and Enterprise Great Lakes, 2022b). Additionally, insufficient legal coverage, the high cost of justice and the slowness of the courts deter women from seeking restitutions, even in instances whereby land ownership is unfairly taken from them.

According to USAID (2017), the largest economic barrier Burundian women face is unequal access to property ownership: while 80.2% of people own land, only 17.7% of them are women. It is important to note the gap between formal and informal law: even though women were the main rights holders to nearly 25% of the land, in actuality only a small fraction of these rights were actually formally registered in their name (International Development Law Organisation, 2017). Given that 90% of the Burundian population live on subsistence agriculture, of which women account for more than 90%, the lack of property rights enjoyed by women entails that females in Burundi are disproportionately disadvantaged: understandably, poverty, unemployment and illiteracy rates in Burundi are disproportionately higher among females (United Nations, n.d.).

Additionally, women are financially excluded from society, since they are unable to obtain credit by pledging their land as collateral: women are hence economically dependent upon their spouses (Inside Burundi, 2022; Centre for Development and Enterprise Great Lakes; 2021c). Per the Bank of the Republic of Burundi, the financial inclusion rate of women was 30.6%, 30.3%, 28.3% in 2013, 2014 and 2015, respectively, which is significantly lower than the financial inclusion rate of men at 69.4%, 69.7% and 71.7% in the same period (Inside Burundi, 2022). Burundi's persistently poor economy is thus attributable to the lack of rights enjoyed by women: since the lack of rights deprive women the means to improve their lives, Burundi loses the value that these women could bring to the economy. Notably, this is evidenced empirically in academic research: in studies conducted in Honduras, Tanzania and Nepal, women who have access to land ownership contribute a greater proportion of family income than men, while malnutrition is reduced by half when women have access to land ownership (Inside Burundi, 2022).

As an aside, women have throughout history played an important role in generating progress, and liberation and dignity for women are only to the benefit of the nation. Despite prejudice against women in the seventeenth and eighteenth centuries, some women played a big role in scientific development at the time (see Fara, 2011). Most notable of course was Emilie du Chatelet, who translated Isaac Newton's seminal book and who contributed much to mathematics, calculus and physics. Women also played an important role in the Age of Revolution where ideals of liberty and equality were fought for: Olympe de Gouges, Mary Wollstonecraft, Elizabeth Stanton and many more. Importantly, pro-liberal cultural change often involves a move away from stereotypical masculine or warrior values. In pre-modern Japan for example—before the Meiji reforms—the merchant class occupied the bottom rung of a social hierarchy which had at the top the samurai class, a striking example of the hegemony of warrior values. This soon reversed in subsequent periods, as Japan underwent modernisation. In an interesting paper, it was pointed out that the merchant class—contrary to other positions that heavily focus on the role of the state—played 'a much more important role as entrepreneurs and capitalists in Japan's industrialisation than has been accepted' (Yamamura, 1969, p. 119). In the field of political theory more generally, liberal progress needs to involve not just formal equality of the sexes, but also a move away from traditional assumptions about women's roles in political society (see Okin, 2013).

It is in this context that the work of another African organisation may be appreciated. Enter Centre for Development and Enterprise Great Lakes, and their Why Women Project, which committed to influencing the implementation of a law that recognises and solidifies the right of women to inherit land, such as to promote the economic inclusion of women and promote economic growth (Centre for Development & Enterprises Great Lakes, 2021). Specifically, the Why Women Project aims to find suitable solutions such as to reconcile the legitimacy of customary land practices presently entrenched within society with legislative and regulatory texts in favour of women, such as to facilitate women's access to justice and land security. Primarily, this is achieved through advocacy efforts along all dimensions of civil society, such as through press briefings, engagement sessions with members of the public such as in the districts of Rugeregere and Ruvumera, regional workshops with leaders of political parties and religious denominations, women's' rights activists, representatives of civil society and media professionals, and roundtables with local elected officials on the need to eliminate barriers to access to land for Burundian women. This educational aspect is crucial, because land reform in Burundi requires a change in mindset towards women owning land. This is because surveys show that even though the Burundian people support women rights in general, a majority still reject land inheritance by women (Ndikumana, 2015).

The work they do is ongoing, and progress remains challenging. But recently, CDE Great Lake's work has recently received recognition amidst members of the Burundian government. Notably, the Burundian Head of State, President Evariste Ndayishimiye, has recently on International Women's Day, reiterated the importance of women in the nation's development and renewed commitments to tackling the problem of women's inheritance rights (UN Women, 2022).

Conclusion

In conclusion, economic progress requires the establishment of pro-growth institutions and policies, but these must also be accompanied by a supportive cultural environment. Past efforts at development, especially plans imposed by foreign organisations, have often failed because they did not cohere with the local culture and did not feature the participation of local communities. Achieving development requires getting the culture right.

Getting the culture right is in turn complicated, because various scholars have different theories about which particular values contribute most to economic development. There is reasonable agreement however, that a culture that respects the individual, and the dignity of and freedom for commerce, is a critical though insufficient ingredient for economic progress. Various nations in history have to various extents embraced such liberal values, though it was the Western World that most fully institutionalised them in the eighteenth century onwards. The spread of such values, liberal or not, are in turn a product of numerous factors, such as migration of peoples and wars of conquests. At specific critical junctures in history, specific cultural groups succeed in perpetuating and spreading their values. The propagation of values by cultural entrepreneurs therefore has a long run, though highly uncertain impact, on the wealth of nations.

Discussion Questions

1. What is 'culture' and what does it include (or exclude)?
2. To what extent is Lawrence Harrison's distinction between Progress-Prone and Progress-Resistant cultures valid and/or relevant?
3. Why did the Western world gain a head start in development and to what extent did its unique cultural values play a role?
4. How important is 'individualism' as a cultural ingredient of development?
5. How do cultures change or evolve, and what does this mean for development policy?
6. How have migration and conquests shaped the cultural character of major nations today?
7. What are some barriers for cultural entrepreneurs to overcome if they are to contribute to positive pro-development cultural change?

References

Abu-Lughod, J. L. (1991). *Before European hegemony : The world system A.D. 1250–1350*. Oxford University Press.

Acemoglu, D., Johnson, S. H., & Robinson, J. A. (2001). The colonial origins of comparative development: An empirical investigation. *American Economic Review, 91*(5), 1369–1401. https://doi.org/10.1257/aer.91.5.1369.

Acemoglu, D., & Robinson, J. A. (2012). *Why nations fail: The origins of power, prosperity, and poverty*. Currency.

Barker, C. (2004). *Cultural studies*. SAGE Publications Ltd.

Becker, S., & Woessman, L. (2009). Was weber wrong? A human capital theory of protestant economic history. *The Quarterly Journal of Economics, 124*(2), 531–596. https://doi.org/10.1162/qjec.2009.124.2.531.

Bentley, J. H. (1993). *Old world encounters: Cross-cultural contacts and exchanges in pre-modern times*. Oxford University Press.

Bordoloi, S., & Das, R. J. (2017). Modernization Theory. In D. Richardson, N. Castree, M. F. Goodchild, A. Kobayashi, R. A. Marston, & W. Liu (Eds.), *International Encyclopedia of Geography: People, the Earth, Environment and Technology*. Wiley. https://doi.org/10.1002/9781118786352.wbieg1174.

Brotton, J. (2010). *The Renaissance bazaar : From the Silk Road to Michelangelo*. Oxford University Press.

Burnard, T., & Riello, G. (2020). Slavery and the new history of capitalism. *Journal of Global History, 15*(2), 225–244. https://doi.org/10.1017/s1740022820000029.

Centre for Development and Enterprise Great Lakes. (2022a). *L'accès de la Burundaise au droit foncier: cinq barrières judiciaires à surmonter (Burundian women's access to land rights: five legal barriers to overcome)*. Centre for Development and Enterprise

Great Lakes. https://centrefordevelopmentgreatlakes.org/2022/06/17/lacces-de-la-burundaise-au-droit-foncier-cinq-barrieres-judiciaires-a-surmonter/.

Centre for Development and Enterprise Great Lakes. (2022b). *Sécurisation des droits fonciers des femmes : trois contraintes à lever (Securing women's land rights: three constraints to overcome).* Centre for Development and Enterprise Great Lakes. https://centrefordevelopmentgreatlakes.org/2022/06/29/securisation-des-droits-fonciers-des-femmes-trois-contraintes-a-lever/.

Castellani, M. (2019). Does culture matter for the economic performance of countries? An overview of the literature. *Journal of Policy Modeling, 41*(4), 700–717. https://doi.org/10.1016/j.jpolmod.2018.06.006.

Centre for Development and Enterprise Great Lakes. (2021a). *Pourquoi la femme burundaise devrait hériter? (Why the Burundian woman should inherit?).* Centre for Development and Enterprise Great Lakes. https://centrefordevelopmentgreatlakes.org/2021/07/30/pourquoi-la-femme-burundaise-devrait-heriter.

Centre for Development and Enterprise Great Lakes. (2021b). *La loi sur la succession : une urgence pour la femme burundaise.* Centre for Development and Enterprise Great Lakes. https://centrefordevelopmentgreatlakes.org/2021/08/02/la-loi-sur-la-succession-une-urgence-pour-la-femme-burundaise/.

Centre for Development and Enterprise Great Lakes. (2021c). *Libérer les droits de la femme pour un développement durable (Liberating women's rights for sustainable development).* Centre for Development and Enterprise Great Lakes. https://centrefordevelopmentgreatlakes.org/2021/09/07/liberer-les-droits-de-la-femme-pour-un-developpement-durable/.

Centre for Development and Enterprises Great Lakes. (2021d). *Why Women Project.* Centre for Development and Enterprises Great Lakes. https://centrefordevelopmentgreatlakes.org/why-women/.

Chamlee-Wright, E., & Lavoie, D. (2000). *Culture and enterprise: The development, representation and morality of busines.* Routledge.

Cheang, B. (2022). *Economic Liberalism and the Developmental State: Hong Kong and Singapore's Post War Development.* Palgrave.

Cheang, B. (2023). Anglo-Chinese Capitalism in Hong Kong and Singapore: Origins, Reproduction & Divergence. *The Journal of Development Studies,* 1-24. https://doi.org/10.1080/00220388.2023.2182685.

Cheng, L., & Yang, P. Q. (1998). Global interaction, global inequality, and migration of the highly trained to the United States. *International Migration Review, 32*(3), 626–653. https://doi.org/10.1177/019791839803200303.

Chua, A., & Rubenfeld, J. (2014). *The triple package: How three unlikely traits explain the rise and fall of cultural groups in America.* Penguin.

Clark, G. (2007). *A farewell to Alms.* Princeton University Press.

Czeglédi, P., Lips, B., & Newland, C. (2021). The Economic mentality of nations. *Cato Journal, 41*(3), 657–689. https://www.cato.org/cato-journal/fall-2021/economic-mentality-nations.

Davies, L. E., & Huttenback, R. A. (1988). *Mammon and the pursuit of empire: The economics of british imperialism.* Cambridge University Press.

Davies, S. (2011, June 22). *The Virtues of Commerce: Lessons from Japan.* Foundation for Economic Education. Retrieved from: https://fee.org/articles/the-virtues-of-commerce-lessons-from-japan.

Davies, S. (2019). *The wealth explosion.* Edward Everett Root.

Diamond, J. M. (1998). *Guns, germs and steel: A short history of everybody for the last 13,000 years.* Random House.

Dweck, C. (2016). What having a "growth mindset" actually means. *Harvard Business Review.* https://hbr.org/2016/01/what-having-a-growth-mindset-actually-means.

Easterly, W. (2021). Progress by consent: Adam Smith as development economist. *Review of Austrian Economics, 34*(2), 179–201. https://doi.org/10.1007/s11138-019-00478-5.

Economist. (2019). Millennial socialism. *The Economist Magazine.* https://www.economist.com/leaders/2019/02/14/millennial-socialism.

Eltis, D., & Engerman, S. L. (2000). The importance of slavery and the slave trade to industrializing Britain. *The Journal of Economic History, 60*(1), 123–144. https://doi.org/10.1017/S00220507 00024670.

Engerman, S. L., & Sokoloff, K. L. (2002). Factor endowments, inequality, and paths of development among new world economies. *Economía, 3*(1), 41–109. https://doi.org/10.1353/eco.2002. 0013.

Ericsson, K. A. (2004). Deliberate practice and the acquisition and maintenance of expert performance in medicine and related domains. *Academic Medicine, 79*(10), S70–S81. https://doi.org/ 10.1097/00001888-200410001-00022.

Fara, P. (2011). *Pandora's breeches: Women, science, and power in the enlightenment.* Random House.

Ferguson, N. (2012). *Civilization: The West and the rest.* Penguin.

Friedrich Naumann Stiftung. (2020). *Liberalism in Greece today. Do we live in a liberal country?.* Kapa Research. Retrieved from: https://kaparesearch.com/wp-content/uploads/2020/11/Libera lism_FNF_2020_EN.pdf.

Gabaccia, D. R. (2013). Migration history in the Americas. In S. J. Gold & S. J. Nawyn (Eds.), *Routledge international handbook of migration studies* (pp. 64–74). Routledge.

Gaddis, I., Lahoti, R., & Swaminathan, H. (2021). *Women's legal rights and gender gaps in property ownership in developing countries.* World Bank Blogs; World Bank. https://blogs. worldbank.org/developmenttalk/womens-legal-rights-and-gender-gaps-property-ownership-developing-countries.

Gillion, K. L. (1962). *Fiji's Indian migrants: A history to the end of indenture in 1920.* Oxford University Press.

Goldstone, J. A. (2002). Efflorescences and economic growth in world history: rethinking the "Rise of the West" and the Industrial Revolution. *Journal of World History, 13*(2), 323–389. https:// doi.org/10.1353/jwh.2002.0034.

Goldstone, J. A. (2009). *Why Europe? The rise of the West in world history 1500–1850.* McGraw-Hill Higher Education.

Gorodnichenko, Y., & Roland, G. (2011). Which dimensions of culture matter for long-run growth? *American Economic Review, 101*(3), 492–498. https://doi.org/10.1257/aer.101.3.492.

Gorodnichenko, Y., & Roland, G. (2012). *Understanding the individualism—collectivism cleavage and its effects: Lessons from cultural psychology.* International Economic Association.

Gorodnichenko, Y., & Roland, G. (2017). Culture, institutions, and the wealth of nations. *Review of Economics and Statistics, 99*(3), 402–416. https://doi.org/10.1162/REST_a_00599.

Gross, N., & Fosse, E. (2012). Why are professors liberal? *Theory and Society, 41*(2), 127–168. https://doi.org/10.1007/s11186-012-9163-y.

Guiso, L., Sapienza, P., & Zingales, L. (2006). Does culture affect economic outcomes? *Journal of Economic Perspectives, 20*(2), 23–48. https://doi.org/10.1257/jep.20.2.23.

Harrison, L. (2008). The end of multiculturalism. *National Interest.* https://nationalinterest.org/art icle/the-end-of-multiculturalism-1933.

Harrison, L. (2012). *Jews, confucians, and protestants: Cultural capital, and the end of multiculturalism.* Rowman and Littlefield.

Harrison, L., & Huntington, S. (2000). *Culture matters: How values shape human progress.* Basic Books.

Hayek, F. (2010). Individualism: True and false. In B. Caldwell (Ed.), *Studies on the abuse and decline of reason.* University of Chicago Press.

Hodgson, G. (2000). What is the essence of institutional economics? *Journal of Economic Issues, 34*(2), 317–329.

Hodgson, M. G. S. (1974). *The venture of Islam—conscience and history in a world civilization : The classical age of Islam* (Vol. 1). The University of Chicago Press.

Hofstede, G. (2001). *Culture's consequences: Comparing values, behaviors, institutions and organizations across nations.* SAGE Publications.

Howes, A. (2017). *The spread of improvement: Why innovation accelerated in Britain 1547–1851.* Unpublished.

Huang, Y. (2008). *Capitalism with Chinese characteristics: Entrepreneurship and the state*. Cambridge University Press.

Inglehart, R. (2000). *World value surveys and European value survey 1981–84, 1990–93, 1995–97*. European Values Survey Group and World Values Survey Group.

Inside Burundi. (2022). *Access to land ownership would enable women to be economically independent, says law academician*. Inside Burundi. https://insideburundi.org/1383-2/.

International Development Law Organisation. (2017). *Strengthening women's customary rights to land*. International Development Law Organization. https://www.idlo.int/news/highlights/strengthening-womens-customary-rights-land.

International Organization for Migration. (2023, March 20). *Not Merely Soil: Access to Land Rights for Women in Burundi Means More*. International Organization for Migration; United Nations. https://storyteller.iom.int/stories/not-merely-soil-access-land-rights-women-burundi-means-more.

Karreth, A. (2018). Development in theory and practice: Culture, ethnocentrism, and the liberal model. *Polity, 50*(4), 664–675. https://doi.org/10.1086/699635.

Keister, L. A. (2003). Religion and wealth: The role of religious affiliation and participation in early adult asset accumulation. *Social Forces, 82*(1), 175–207. https://doi.org/10.1353/sof.2003.0094.

Kotkin, J. (1993). *Tribes: How race, religion, and identity determine success in the new global economy*. Random House Incorporated.

Koyama, M., & Rubin, J. (2022). *How the World Became Rich: The Historical Origins of Economic Growth*. John Wiley & Sons.

Kvangraven, I. H. (2021). Beyond the stereotype: Restating the relevance of the dependency research programme. *Development and Change, 52*(1), 76–112. https://doi.org/10.1111/dech.12593.

La Porta, R., Lopez-de-Silanes, F., & Shleifer, A. (2008). The economic consequences of legal origins. *Journal of Economic Literature, 46*(2), 285–332. https://doi.org/10.1257/jel.46.2.285.

Landes, D. (1998). *Culture counts*. Routledge.

Langbert, M., Quain, A. J., & Klein, D. B. (2016). Faculty voter registration in economics, history, journalism, law, and psychology. *Econ Journal Watch, 13*(3), 422–451.

Lange, M., Mahoney, J., & Vom Hau, M. (2006). Colonialism and development: A comparative analysis of Spanish and British colonies. *American Journal of Sociology, 111*(5), 1412–1462. https://doi.org/10.1086/499510.

Lapidus, I. M. (2014). *A history of Islamic societies*. Cambridge University Press.

Lewis, P. (2014). Hayek: From economics as equilibrium analysis to economics as social theory. In R. Garrison & N. Barry (Eds.), *Elgar companion to Hayekian economics* (pp. 195–223). Edward Elgar Publishing.

Lindberg, D. (1976). *Science in the middle ages*. University of Chicago Press.

Lynn, R., & Kanazawa, S. (2008). How to explain high Jewish achievement: The role of intelligence and values. *Personality and Individual Differences, 44*(4), 801–808. https://doi.org/10.1016/j.paid.2007.10.019.

MacIntyre, A. (1981). *After virtue*. University of Indiana Press.

Mackie, J. (1998). Business success among Southeast Asian Chinese: the role of culture, values, and social structures. In R. Hefner (Ed.), *Market Cultures. Society and Morality in the New Asian Capitalisms* (pp. 129–146). Westview Press.

Mahoney, J. (2006). Analyzing Path Dependence: Lessons from the Social Sciences. In A. Wimmer & R. Kössler (Eds.), *Understanding Change: Models, Methodologies and Metaphors* (pp. 129–139). Palgrave.

Mahbubani, K. (2022). *The Asian 21st Century*. Springer

Maridal, J. H. (2013). Cultural impact on national economic growth. *The Journal of Socio-Economics, 47*, 136–146. https://doi.org/10.1016/j.socec.2012.08.002.

Masci, D. (2016). *How income varies among U.S. religious groups*. Pew Research Center. Retrieved from: https://www.pewresearch.org/fact-tank/2016/10/11/how-income-varies-among-u-s-religious-groups/.

Mattausch, J. (1998). From subjects to citizens: British 'East African Asians.' *Journal of Ethnic and Migration Studies, 24*(1), 121–141. https://doi.org/10.1080/1369183X.1998.9976621.

McCloskey, D. N. (2010). *Bourgeois dignity: Why economics can't explain the modern world.* University of Chicago Press.

McCloskey, D. N. (2015). It was ideas and ideologies, not interests or institutions, which changed in Northwestern Europe, 1600–1848. *Journal of Evolutionary Economics, 25,* 57–68. https://doi.org/10.1007/s00191-015-0392-x.

McCloskey, D. N. (2016). *Bourgeois equality: How ideas, not capital or institutions, enriched the world.* University of Chicago Press.

McCloskey, D. N., & Carden, A. (2020). *Leave me alone and I'll make you rich: How the Bourgeois deal enriched the world.* University of Chicago Press.

McCloskey, D. N. (2007). *The bourgeois virtues: Ethics for an age of commerce.* University of Chicago Press.

Mokyr, J. (2002). *The gifts of Athena.* Princeton University Press.

Mokyr, J. (2011a). *The economics of the industrial revolution.* Routledge.

Mokyr, J. (2011b). *The enlightened economy: Britain and the industrial revolution, 1700–1850.* Penguin.

Mokyr, J., & Snowdon, B. (2007). The power of ideas. *World Economics, 8*(3), 53–110.

Mokyr, J. (2006). Useful Knowledge as an Evolving System: the view from Economic history. In L. Blume & S. Durlauf (Eds.), *The Economy as an evolving, complex system III: current perspectives and future directions* (pp. 309–336). Oxford University Press. https://doi.org/10.1093/acprof:oso/9780195162592.003.0013.

Ndikumana, A. (2015). *Gender equality in Burundi: Why does support not extend to women's right to inherit land?* Afrobarometer. https://www.afrobarometer.org/wp-content/uploads/migrated/files/publications/Policy%20papers/ab_r6_policypaperno22.pdf.

Newport, F. (2018). *Democrats more positive about socialism than capitalism.* Gallup. https://news.gallup.com/poll/240725/democrats-positive-socialism-capitalism.aspx.

Niemietz, K. (2021). *Left turn ahead: Surveying attitudes of young people towards capitalism and socialism.* Institute for Economic Affairs. https://iea.org.uk/publications/left-turn-aheads urveying-attitudes-of-young-people-towards-capitalism-and-socialism/.

North, D. C., & Weingast, B. R. (1989). Constitutions and commitment: The evolution of institutions governing public choice in seventeenth-century England. *The Journal of Economic History, 49*(4), 803–832. https://doi.org/10.1017/S0022050700009451.

Okin, S. M. (2013). *Women in Western political thought.* Princeton University Press.

Olmstead, A. L., & Rhode, P. W. (2018). Cotton, slavery, and the new history of capitalism. *Explorations in Economic History, 67,* 1–17. https://doi.org/10.1016/j.eeh.2017.12.002.

Palmer, T. G. (2004). *Globalization and culture: Homogeneity, diversity, identity, liberty.* Liberales Institut.

Palmer, G., & Kenway, P. (2007). *Poverty rates among ethnic groups in Great Britain.* Joseph Rowntree Foundation. https://www.jrf.org.uk/report/poverty-rates-among-ethnic-groups-great-britain.

Petrakis, P., & Kostis, P. (2013). Economic growth and cultural change. *The Journal of Socio-Economics, 47,* 147–157. https://doi.org/10.1016/j.socec.2013.02.011.

Pew Research Center. (2021, May 11). *Economics and well-being among U.S. Jews.* Pew Research Center. https://www.pewresearch.org/religion/2021/05/11/economics-and-well-being-among-u-s-jews.

Pomeranz, K., & Topik, S. (2017). *The world that trade created: society, culture, and the world economy, 1400 to the Present.* Routledge.

Pye, L. W. (2000). *Asian values: From dynamos to dominoes?* Harrison, Culture Matters. Basic Books.

Ram, S. (1987). Indians in England: Why did they emigrate? *Population Geography: A Journal of the Association of Population Geographers of India, 9*(1–2), 37–44.

Redding, G. (1990). *The spirit of Chinese capitalism.* Walter de Gruyter.

Republic of China Government. (2022). 中華民國統計資訊網 (專業人士) - 主計總處統計專區 - 國民所得及經濟成長 - 新聞稿. National Statistics of Republic of China (Taiwan); Government of the Republic of China. https://www.stat.gov.tw/ct.asp?xItem=48520&ctNode=497&mp=4.

Rienzo, C., & Vargas-Silva, C. (2017). *Migrants in the UK: An overview*. Compas, University of Oxford.

Rosenberg, N., & Birdzell, L. (1987). *How the West grew rich*. Basic Books.

Rubinstein, W. D. (2004). Jews in grandmaster chess. *Jewish Journal of Sociology, 36*, 35–44.

Rueschemayer, D. (2006). Why and How ideas matter. In R. Goodin & C. Tilly (Eds.), *Oxford Handbook of contextual political analysis* (pp. 227–251). Oxford University Press.

Schwartz, S. H. (1994). Beyond individualism/collectivism: New cultural dimensions of values. In H.C.-C.U. Kim (Ed.), *Individualism and collectivism: Theory, method, and applications* (pp. 85–119). Sage Publications.

Smith, V., & Wilson, B. (2019). *Humanomics: Moral sentiments and the wealth of nations for the twenty-first century*. Cambridge University Press.

So, Y. L., & Walker, A. (2013). *Explaining guanxi: The Chinese business network*. Routledge.

Sowell, T. (1995). *Race and culture: A world view*. Basic Books.

Sowell, T. (1997). *Migrations and cultures*. Basic Books.

Sowell, T. (1999). *Conquests and cultures*. Basic Books.

Students' Organization for Liberty and Entrepreneurship. (2022). *Stakeholders training on the right of women to own land In South Sudan*. Students' Organization for Liberty and Entrepreneurship. https://soless.org/stakeholders-training-on-the-right-of-women-to-own-land-in-south-sudan/.

Tandon, Y. (2016). Development as the struggle for liberation from hegemonic structures of domination and control. In E. Reinert, J. Ghosh, & R. Kattel (Eds.), *Handbook of alternative theories of development* (pp. 256–269). Edward Elgar Publishing.

Tatsuo, I. (1999). Liberal democracy and asian orientalism. In D. Bell (Ed.), *East Asian challenge for human rights*. Cambridge University Press.

Taylor, C. (1985). *Philosophy and the human sciences*. Cambridge University Press.

Thompson, M., Verweij, M., & Ellis, R. (2006). Why and how culture matters. In R. Goodin & C. Tilly (Eds.), *Oxford handbook of contextual political analysis* (pp. 319–340). Oxford University Press.

Tinker, H. (1977). *The banyan tree: Overseas emigrants from India, Pakistan, and Bangladesh*. Oxford University Press.

UK Government. (2022a). *Average hourly pay*. Government of the United Kingdom.https://www.ethnicity-facts-figures.service.gov.uk/work-pay-and-benefits/pay-and-income/average-hourly-pay/latest#by-ethnicity-over-time

UK Government. (2022b). *GCSE English and maths results*. Government of the United Kingdom. https://www.ethnicity-facts-figures.service.gov.uk/education-skills-and-training/11-to-16-years-old/a-to-c-in-english-and-maths-gcse-attainment-for-children-aged-14-to-16-key-stage-4/latest#by-ethnicity-and-gender.

United Nations. *Burundi*. United Nations. https://africa.unwomen.org/en/where-we-are/eastern-and-southern-africa/burundi.

USAID. (2017). *Burundi Gender Analysis Final Report*. US Agency for International Development. https://banyanglobal.com/wp-content/uploads/2017/07/USAID-Burundi-Gender-Analysis-Final-Report-2017.pdf.

UN Women. (2022). *International Women's Day in Burundi: Women in Agricultural Development and Environmental Protection*. UN Women; United Nations. https://africa.unwomen.org/en/stories/news/2022/03/international-womens-day-in-burundi-women-in-agricultural-development-and-environmental-protection.

Vivanco, L. (2018). Culture. In L. Vivanco (Ed.), *A dictionary of cultural anthropology*. Oxford University Press.

Weber, M. (1905). *The protestant ethic and the spirit of capitalism*.

Weyl, N., & Possony, S. (1963). *The geography of intellect*. Henry Regnery.

Wike, R., & Fetterolf, J. (2021). *Global Public Opinion in an Era of Democratic Anxiety*. Pew Research Center's Global Attitudes Project; Pew Research Center. https://www.pewresearch.org/global/2021/12/07/global-public-opinion-in-an-era-of-democratic-anxiety/.

Williams, J. (2016). *Academic freedom in an age of conformity: Confronting the fear of knowledge*. Palgrave Macmillan.

Wong, S. (1985). The Chinese Family Firm: A Model. *The British Journal of Sociology, 36*(1), 58-72. https://doi.org/10.2307/590402.

Wong, M. (2007). Guanxi and its role in business. *Chinese Management Studies, 1*(4), 257–276.

Wronski, L. (2021). *Axios|Momentive Poll: Capitalism and Socialism*. Survey Monkey. https://www.surveymonkey.com/curiosity/axios-capitalism-update/.

Yamamura, K. (1969). The role of the merchant class as entrepreneurs and capitalists in Meiji Japan. *Vierteljahrschrift für Sozial-und Wirtschaftsgeschichte, 56*(H. 1), 105–120.

YouGov. (2019). *2019 Poll*. Victims of Communism Memorial Foundation. https://victimsofcommunism.org/annual-poll/2019-annual-poll/.

State Capacity and the Political Infrastructure of Development

6

Why State Capacity?

Consistent with the framework of institutional economics, it is necessary to consider the political infrastructure of successful economic development. Economic exchange does not take place in a vacuum, and the wider environment of human action influences economic outcomes. Politics matters, and the manner in which the political system is structured will have an effect on the wealth of nations.

Accordingly, this chapter will examine 'state capacity' and 'regime type', two key concepts in the development literature. Specifically, it evaluates the nature and extent to which state capacity is necessary for successful development and the corresponding regime type most conducive to facilitating it. Reflection on the necessity of liberal democracy is also warranted. Liberal democratic institutions are typically advocated as morally superior to other alternatives, and best placed to bring about positive economic outcomes. This liberal perspective will also be evaluated against a prominent challenge arising from the 'East Asian Challenge', which consciously eschewed neoliberal prescriptions of the international establishment and made use of authoritarian or quasi-authoritarian political structures.

This chapter will develop several interrelated contentions. First, the reality of cultural diversity and social complexity means that there is no single institutional arrangement that can be easily and universally transplanted. That said however, successful development requires a state that is both high capacity and constrained at the same time, enjoying the ability to enforce its will but nonetheless subject to limits on the exercise of power. Accordingly, such a social order is best found in the contributions of institutional economist Elinor Ostrom, and the larger Bloomington School of Political Economy of which she was a part. The polycentric social order described by these institutionalists emphasises the importance of inter-jurisdictional competition as a means of preserving liberty and delivering

© The Author(s), under exclusive license to Springer Nature Singapore Pte Ltd. 2023 153
B. Cheang and T. G. Palmer, *Institutions and Economic Development*,
Classroom Companion: Economics, https://doi.org/10.1007/978-981-99-0844-8_6

effective public services, without denying the necessity of a strong central political authority.

On the regime type, it is our contention that some form of commitment to liberal democracy is necessary to development. Such an application of liberal democratic principles may take many forms, depending on local cultural commitments and the direction of local institutional entrepreneurship. However, the basic *sine qua non* of successful development requires at the minimum a commitment to limit arbitrary political coercion. This is because development does not include just material wealth, but also involves the ability to achieve one's conception of the good life.

This chapter is structured as follows. The first section will review the literature on state capacity, looking at what it entails and its various determinants. Drawing on the Ostromian concept of 'co-production', state capacity is closely connected civil society, specifically: state capacity may be enhanced through close and productive interactions with the non-state sector. The second section focuses on the question of regime type, and reviews arguments in favour of liberal democracy as well as the 'East Asian Challenge', which is arguably the most persuasive criticism of the liberal position in the twentieth century. The third section explores the importance of state constraints, which is a necessary countervailing force that prevents state capacity from degenerating into mere predation.

Understanding State Capacity

The academic literature on development has seen a strong emphasis on the concept of 'state capacity' (Acemoglu & Robinson, 2020; Besley & Persson, 2011; Dincecco, 2017; Kugler, 2018). While there are understandably different definitions of this, state capacity is generally understood as the ability of a state to implement and enforce its decisions in society. This is initially used to just mean a state's fiscal capacity to raise taxes from its population, but has come to include a wide range of capabilities involved with public administration. In other words, development assumes the presence of an 'effective state', one that has the ability to 'raise taxes, enforce contracts and organise public spending for a wide range of activities' (Besley & Persson, 2011, p. 1).

The state has some important functions to play in development. Perhaps most pivotal is the role of the state in the provision of the necessary institutions for development, namely rule of law, secure private property rights and military defence against external threats. Such institutions, as discussed in the prior chapter, are crucial in incentivising private investments by individuals, since they reduce the likelihood of expropriation by other individuals, predatory states or hostile foreign governments. It cannot be assumed that such institutions are naturally found in the world, they in fact require an effective state. Additionally, states play a crucial role in fostering competitive and free domestic markets for the exchange of goods and services: apart from the aforementioned institutions which are themselves critical for the functioning of free market systems, states aim for the elimination (or minimally harmonisation) of internal tariffs and trade barriers, thereby improving development prospects through the enforcement of a competitive and free domestic market better able to attain economies of scale. In the United States, for example, this role is codified in the Constitution: Clause 1 of section 6.8 states that 'all duties, imports and excises shall be uniform throughout the United States', while Clause 5 of section 6.10 states that 'No state shall, without the consent of the Congress, lay any imposts or duties on imports or exports'.

Additionally, states are primarily responsible for the provision of public goods, such as the development of physical and human capital critical in economic production. Public goods, which are characteristically non-rivalrous (i.e. use by an individual does not diminish its availability to others) and non-excludable (i.e. nonpayers cannot be feasibly denied access to the good), are generally unprovided in free market systems (Olson, 1965; Samuelson, 1954). Resultantly, the provision of such goods falls upon the state. Direct provision of physical capital such as transportation infrastructure by the state, for example, is necessary: improvements in transportation infrastructure can reduce costs of moving inputs in economic production processes, reduce commuting costs and increasing labour supply, and facilitate domestic trade. Similarly, the onus of providing mass public education falls upon the state: higher human capital arising from the widespread access to quality education increases productivity, allowing for greater technological innovations and improving overall growth prospects. Despite their apparent utility, the nature of such inputs as public goods, however, entails that they have to be provided by the state: resultantly, economic development can only be attained should states be able to fulfil this role.

Modern states that are capable of facilitating economic development have the following capacities (see Savoia & Sen, 2015):

1. Fiscal capacity—the state has in place the means to raise revenue from broad tax bases such as income and consumption;
2. Legal capacity—the state is capable of enforcing contracts and defining and protecting property rights;
3. Bureaucratic and administrative capacity—the state is capable of designing and implementing policies that channel tax revenue efficiently to the production of public goods;
4. Infrastructural capacity—the state is capable of extending its reach over the territory over which it claims sovereignty;
5. Military capacity—the state is capable of deterring or repelling challenges to its authority, whether from within or without its borders, with force.

Determinants of State Capacity

Why, however, do states differ in capacity? Primarily, determinants of state capacity are divisible into three broad categories: historical, geographical and political economy.

Firstly, state history is empirically shown to impact the strength of state capacity: longer histories of statehood, for example, tend to lead to higher state capacity or greater quality of administration due to 'learning by doing' effects (Bockstette et al., 2002). Similarly, engagement in external conflict is shown to booster state formation: specifically, incidence of external conflict supports the demand for defence, a common-interest public good. This demand increases the incentive faced by states to invest in fiscal and legal capacity, thereby fostering conditions that lead to the growth of state capacity. Many studies in the academic literature have accordingly focused on the formation of centralised nation states in European history, and the manner in which this facilitated development (Johnson & Koyama, 2017). In Charles Tilly's (2017) famous conception, states were borne out of war-making. Pre-modern Europe was characterised by a multitude of competing and often warring political entities, and it was in this context that the demand for state functions emerged: the ability to raise taxes to fund standing armies, bureaucracies to mobilise national defence and administer control over citizens, and so on (Besley & Persson, 2010; Dincecco & Wang, 2018). The specific linkage between war and fiscal development has received much attention; it is said that the circumstances of war in the fifteenth and sixteenth centuries spurred the development of new fiscal technologies to consolidate power (Bonney, 1995).

Another aspect of history to consider would be the legacy of empire and the type of political institutions that colonies inherited. It has been said that legal origins of states matter: in particular, Anglo-Saxon common law legal systems supposedly deliver better protection of property rights and a more limited, efficient state than French civil law systems, since the landed aristocracy and merchants in Anglo-Saxon systems were predominantly focused upon the provision of strong protection of property rights by the crown (La Porta et al., 2008). The geographical conditions and starting points of different empires had an impact on subsequent development: colonies where extractive institutions were established characteristically spent little focus on property rights protection or the efficient delivery of public goods, instead focused on collecting as much revenue as they could (Acemoglu et al., 2001). A most obvious contemporary example is the twin city states of Hong Kong and Singapore, arguably the most prosperous former colonies, both of whom inherited pro-growth institutions from the British and which subsequently fostered trade and immigration (Cheang, 2022a). Contemporary examples of the latter are Peru and Mexico, former colonies of an extractive empire that invested little in protection of property rights or the efficient delivery of public goods to the population (Acemoglu & Robinson, 2012).

Alternatively, differences in state capacity can arise from differences in geographical characteristics and political economy mechanisms. Explanations accounting for differences in state capacity through these factors focus upon their impact upon the role of the elites, specifically the type of incentives they face in allowing or facilitating investment in and accumulation of state capacity. Inequality, for example, is suggested to be detrimental to the building of state capacity: societies with extreme inequality are often the result of sociopolitical and economic systems that favour a wealthy minority by ensuring them a disproportionate share of political power (such as through oligarchic rather than democratic politics) (Savoia and Sen, 2015). This political power is then used to implement and propagate rules, laws and policies that give the wealthy minority greater access to economic opportunities than the rest of the population. Such conditions hence create states whereby the prevailing social arragements perpetuate and reinforce the disproportionate influence of the minority elites over the majority, thereby debilitating the development of state capacity and inclusive institutions in the long run. Similarly, social fractionalisation along ethnic, linguistic and religious lines are associated with less efficient states, as groups in power tend to engage more in patronage spending and less in the development of overall state capacity (Savoia and Sen, 2005).

Deconstructing State Capacity

State capacity as a concept may be fruitfully deconstructed. There are three subsections. First, the functions of the state can, and have sometimes, been provided through stateless private arrangements. This is an interesting perspective to consider, though it may not ultimately represent a viable option for most developing societies. The second sub-section will proceed to show that state capacity can be understood in reference to the concept of co-production, where state-society relationships can improve governance. Third, state capacity must also be balanced with state constraints, without which it may degenerate into predation. Consequently, the virtuous balance between state capacity and constraints produces beneficial outcomes.

Private Governance

'State capacity' and 'governance' are not synonymous, for the latter may arise independently of the state sector. acknowledging that social order requires rules that govern behaviour need not always mean that they must be enforced through a central political authority. Private governance has at various times in history been an alternative mode of social organisation apart from the nation state.

In the absence of government, many voluntary and non-state institutional arrangements have emerged throughout history to prevent conflict and to facilitate cooperation (Benson, 2011; Stringham, 2015). Such arrangements, including the use of multilateral punishment among small groups via ostracism or boycott, the promulgation of conflict-inhibiting social norms and the use of arbitration organisations for international trade operate primarily through mechanisms of reputation.

Reputation mechanisms constrain opportunistic behaviour and individual choice, thereby resolving prisoners' dilemma situations and facilitating secure exchange without state enforcement (see Powell & Stringham, 2009 for a useful survey).

Many such mechanisms are more successful among small, close-knit communities, and may be hard to scale to realise the gains from trade as agents deal with increasingly unfamiliar individuals (Leeson, 2007a). The introduction of governments, by reducing the state of uncertainty that surrounds interacting with agents outside of one's social network, hence allows for the improvement of social wealth by enabling additional exchange. On the other hand, non-state voluntary arrangements can also be quite successful in reducing conflict and predatory behaviour, thereby facilitating mutually beneficial cooperation among large numbers of people who are not known to each other.

Central examples include financial reporting, which provides reliable information on investments and other economic activities, trade associations and—perhaps one of the most important for those who travel more than a few kilometres from home, credit card companies and credit bureaus, which maintain and monitor information on the reliability of merchants and customers to deliver goods and pay bills. The global network of credit card companies makes it possible for one to travel to a foreign country for the first time, to interact with someone whom the traveller will probably never see again and who may not even share a common language with the traveller, and after showing a piece of plastic with a magnetic strip embedded in it walk out with the keys to an automobile worth tens of thousands of pounds. State enforcement of contracts and property claims plays a role in the *background* to the global system of credit and debit cards, but the system is operated by private parties who are linked in an extraordinarily complicated network of information sharing and payment facilitation.

In cases where a central government has a track record of predation, reliance on non-state institutions is often the best option available to people who want to reduce predation and facilitate cooperation. Predatory states appropriate economic resources at the expense of the social good and utilise the claim of a monopoly to the legitimate use of violence, not to enable social cooperation, but to award benefits to the few at the expense of the many and to cement the hold of the political authorities on of power.

Many developing countries have poor government structures that are simultaneously weak and incapable when it comes to enabling or facilitating economic development and very predatory. They lack the capacity to do the things that are taken for granted in developed nations. Take for example the enforcement of private property rights, which is a typical function of capable states. In Afghanistan, one of the poorest countries in the world, the formal enforcement of property is weak, and many formal efforts of legal titling have been difficult. Other systems provide what the Afghan government has not. Jennifer and Ilia Murtazashvili (2015) show that the failure to define and enforce property rights in Afghanistan has to some extent been remedied by a 'robust system of self-governance and community-based land reform'. Yet, there is also wisdom to heed the words of former IMF Chief Economist Raghuram Rajan (2004) to 'assume anarchy' when analysing the conditions of developing countries, rather than assuming the presence of properly functioning governance.

Anarchist political economists have pointed to some cases where stateless societies have been economically successful (Friedman, 1979; Friedman et al., 2019; Leeson, 2007b). However, it must be acknowledged that these cases are historically rare, and difficult to replicate. It is safe to assume that the existence of a high-capacity central political authority is a necessary precondition for development. That said, state capacity can still be further deconstructed by looking at its relationship to civil society as well as its internal constraints, both to which we now turn.

Co-production and State-Society Collaboration

State capacity may be studied in relation to the sphere of civil society, a linkage that has been stressed by the branch of institutional economics inspired by Elinor Ostrom and the Bloomington School of which she was a part. The Ostromian view believes that civil society is often able to solve collective action problems, though under specific conditions. Through real-world case studies, Ostrom demonstrated that communities have a high capacity to collaborate, coordinate and conserve their resources, without the need for state oversight or market intervention. Ostrom's work provides a counter-narrative to the presumption that unregulated communities can only ravage their resources—a phenomenon (in)famously known as the 'tragedy of the commons'.

Her work, however, has also been applied to the study of 'public governance' (Aligica et al., 2019). Specifically, the Ostromian framework suggests that civil society has an important role to play in delivering public services as well, which is typically thought to be the exclusive domain of the state. The concept that best explains this is 'co-production', whereby the nature and effective of some public services require the participation of citizens themselves. In such cases, productive ventures may be forged between the state and civil society groups, who can engage in mutual learning (Ostrom, 1998; Ostrom & Ostrom, 1978).

This allows us to make an additional point on the determinants of state capacity: at times, states acquire or maintain capacity through a progress of 'organisational learning'. They do not always acquire capacity by themselves or necessarily due to external pressures such as by war. In contemporary times, through a process of organisational learning, states learn from civil society organisations, especially those that provide knowledge, skills and training to state officials in an effort to improve public administration.

In this context, the following section provides two specific case studies of local organisations in present-day UK who have engaged in work that enhance and support state capacity. These are local institutional entrepreneurs who, as this handbook has suggested, play an important role in social change.

The first noteworthy mention is New Local. As an independent think tank, New Local envisages a community-led approach to public service provision. With a sprawling network of over 70 local councils, it engages local authorities to improve public service delivery. Deeply etched in New Local's modus operandi is the notion of 'community power'. Community power is closely associated to the new 'community paradigm' which 'place[s] the design and delivery of public services in the hands of the communities they serve. In this way, a new, egalitarian relationship can be built between public services and citizens… one that requires communities to take more responsibility for their own well-being' (Lent & Studdert, 2019).

Put differently, the community paradigm reduces government oversight and empowers people to improve their neighbourhoods and the services they receive. Such a contextualised approach is a unique proposition in policy discourse which has long remained mired in the classic state and market paradigms.

The state paradigm, which arose in the wake of World War II, saw the state as the sole purveyor of important public goods. Within this centrally managed, top-down model, people are treated as passive recipients of public goods. This means people have to accept the universal solutions doled out by unsympathetic politicians and experts. The market paradigm, on the other hand, gained traction in the 1980s and had an unshifting focus on efficiency. Economies of scale turned interactions into transactions and individuals into customers. Policymakers often oscillate between these two paradigms when thinking about common-pool resources and public service provision. These approaches, however, fatally neglect contextual complexities and fail to provide the necessary autonomy and agility for adaptation.

The emergence of the community paradigm breaks this long-standing duopoly which has dominated policy discourse. The community paradigm precipitates a power shift away from the centre and distributed among local municipalities. By facilitating community enablement and democratic participation, New Local believes that public service delivery can be improved. Their initiative aimed to operationalise Ostrom's community-centric approach to governance.

In New Local's compelling 2020 report 'Think Big, Act Small', Simon Kaye identifies three instructive insights for an Ostromian approach (New Local, 2020).

First, locality. Ostrom emphasised the need for systems and structures to be tailored to specific settings. This includes the rules of resource access and management, and decision-making processes. These local institutions are more enduring when they emerge organically from the community. Ostrom's work is edifying and shows that overall outcomes can be improved this way. For example, the community group known as 'Friends of Bramley Baths' have been managing Bramley Baths in Leeds since 2012. The city council's approval of this community asset transfer is a show of confidence in the local community's ability and shared interest in managing a common resource.

Secondly, autonomy. Short of granting the autonomy to create and run local systems, small communities may feel dispossessed and disincentivised to manage their resources sustainably. This paves the way for more bureaucratic, 'expert' solutions which may be costly, clumsy and counterproductive. Social trust and legitimacy, therefore, are the indispensable building blocks for local systems to operate and thrive. The funding scheme called 'Big Local' illustrates the

Ostromian point that communities can oversee their own neighbourhood renewal projects. One example is Barrow Island in Cumbria. Here, the community collectively decided to invest in a new community centre and sports facility within an under-utilised plot. Today, the newly built facility is the centrepiece of the neighbourhood where members gather for recreational sports. This resident-led initiative shows that communities can manage financial resources if given the authority to manage a budget.

Thirdly, diversity. Ostrom emphasised the need for a dynamic system that allows for experimentation. When systems are made more diverse, they tend to be more resilient and adaptive, especially in times of crisis. Conversely, a centralised, monolithic system lacks the flexibility and layers to make institutions more robust. Diversity is the key takeaway of Ostrom's eighth design principle which states that complex systems are organised into layers of nested governance.

Taken altogether, New Local's Ostrom-inspired, community-powered approach is a bold re-imagining of devolution and power dispersion in the UK. The multiple, intersectional crises of 2020 have exposed the failures of public service and the need for more experimentation and fine-tuning at the local level. Instead of inflating the powers of central government, local actors, though small, can make outsized contributions to their communities.

Another example to hail from the UK is the educational charity known as 'Reform'. It publishes policy reports across various public service domains, including education, health care, work and pension and digital services. Reform uses an evidence-based approach to make policy recommendations for both Westminster and Whitehall, the UK's intellectual hub for policymaking. Like New Local, Reform seeks to discuss how civil society can be re-centred in order to improve public services. Notably, other policy think tanks tend to be narrowly focussed on expenditure and how public services are either over or under funded.

Dr. Simon Kaye, who serves as the Director of Policy at Reform, has articulated the challenges that beset the British civil service. In particular, he expounds on its inability to adapt and resistance to change. This rigid structure, as Dr. Kaye suggests, made the civil service a 'stable platform' for policy intervention, between different administrations. Therefore, even though government may be a 'revolving door', institutional memory is preserved through the civil service. Such an emphasis on continuity, however, means that adaptation and agility is not a strong suit of the highly bureaucratic British government. In times of crisis, this built-in inertia takes its toll and renders the government highly ineffective.

In its review of the government's COVID-19 crisis management, Reform made a slew of recommendations that required unique structural changes. Below are two recommendations from Reform's, 2021 report 'A State of Preparedness: How Government Can Build Resilience to Civil Emergencies':

> The Government should move a motion in Parliament to *establish a Civil Contingencies Select Committee* to strengthen parliamentary oversight of emergency planning and preparedness. This would improve coordination of parliamentary scrutiny and ensure that it is both proactive and cross-government in focus.

The Government *should reinstate the National Security Council Threats, Hazards, Resilience and Contingencies Subcommittee,* to be chaired by the newly created Minister. This would convene monthly to hold departmental Ministers to account for progress acting on lessons.

These recommendations show that bureaucratic governments are not always adaptive in crisis response. Policy think tanks like Reform push the envelope with structural suggestions to make the government nimbler and more attuned to changing circumstances, illustrating the mutual learning that can take place between state and society.

State Constraints

In this sub-section, we explore the link between state capacity and state constraints. But first, it is important to more closely evaluate the causal link between state capacity and economic development. State capacity may not necessarily have a direct causal effect on development because it may simply be a 'correlative filter'. As argued by Vincent Geloso and Alex Salter (2020), the reason why high development nations are usually those with high state capacity is because in its absence, these nations will be vulnerable to plunder by strong states. As such, state capacity is not a 'causal condition for widespread economic prosperity, but a survivability condition for enjoying this prosperity' (Geloso & Salter, 2020). In other words, state capacity was simply something that wealthy nations had to develop to survive.

The connection between state capacity and state predation invites a deeper consideration of the notion of 'state constraints', which are rules, norms or mechanisms that constraint the arbitrary exercise of political power. While this may not necessarily necessitate Western style liberal institutions, the key principle is about the limitation of arbitrary power. State capacity cannot be unchecked, and in the absence of constraints, it may degenerate from a means of delivering economic development to a means of predation (Boettke & Candela, 2020).

Of course, the precise balance is difficult to strike, since we want a government that is both capacious and constrained at the same time, what has been called a 'shackled leviathan' (Acemoglu & Robinson, 2020). The fundamental political dilemma inherent in economic systems is hence that a government strong enough to protect property rights and enforce rule of law will inevitably be strong enough to confiscate the wealth and engage in coercive activity of its citizens. Functioning markets arising from property rights and rule of law and limited government are therefore complementary aspects of economic development: failure in either domain will impede development in the long run.

The Indian economic writer Gurcharan Das (2012) summed it up neatly the need for an 'enabling state', in the context of India:

> Generally, leftists desire a large state and rightists a small one, but what India needs is an effective state with a more robust rule of law and greater accountability. ... Such a state is efficient in the sense that it enforces fairly and forcefully the rule of law, and contracts and rights guaranteed by the Constitution; it is strong because it has independent regulators who are tough on corruption and ensure that no one is above the law; it is enabling because it delivers services honestly to all citizens; it is not intrusive as the 'licence raj' was, but is rules-based, with a light, invisible touch over citizens' lives.

State constraints must be institutionalised within the constitutional structure of a society in a way that facilitates market-based development. As explained in Chap. 4, institutions necessary for market-development include secure property rights and a legal regime of general, stable and predictable rules. These principles have to be reflected in political institutions. In English history, an important lesson was not only the formation of state capacity, but constitutional constraints on the monarchy following the events of 1688 (North & Weingast, 1989; Weingast, 1995). Crucially, this was not antithetical to, but consonant with state capacity: Mark Dincecco (2011, 2015) explains that the formation of a state's fiscal capacity worked in tandem with the gradual establishment of constraints on state power and thus provided a credible commitment that property rights would indeed be protected.

Informal institutions, including norms, expectations and ethical standards, are also crucial in maintaining state constraints. Social actors outside of the state sector have the capacity to organise, engage in politics and, if necessary, rebel against the state and its elites (Novak, 2021). Social movements throughout history have acted as an important bulwark against the excesses of the state, from the anti-war movement in 1960s' United States, to anti-establishment protests in present-day Hong Kong. These organisations are possible only because of the mobilisation efforts of individuals or coalitions of individuals gathered for common cause. Once again, this suggests the importance of looking at political and institutional entrepreneurs in driving change. Movements around the globe against slavery, to take a quite prominent example, involved ordinary citizens who were mobilised by conscience. The twelve people, nine Quakers and three Anglicans, who formed the Society for the Abolition of the Slave Trade in 1787, managed in twenty years to abolish the slave trade across the British Empire and by 1833 to have passed the Slavery Abolition Act. The movements for women's emancipation and suffrage also called on ordinary citizens to act on their consciences. Millions of acts of 'coming out' to family members, friends and colleagues have led to the elimination of laws persecuting LGBTQ people and, in more and more countries, to liberty and legal equality, a process still underway in much of the world.

Ordoliberalism, State Capacity and German Economic Recovery

State capacity and state constraints are not mutually exclusive. For the state to both possess high capacity and yet be constrained in its power requires deliberate constitutional design, and the political will to sustain such a balance. One case study that best exemplifies this judicious balance is that application of the principles of ordoliberalism to the post-war economic recovery of Germany. Ordoliberalism is a school of thought found within the broader family of classical liberalism, but one that advocates for high state capacity and also the necessity of strong political leadership in designing effective political mechanisms.

After World War II, the German economy lay in shambles. The war, along with Hitler's scorched-earth policy, had destroyed 20 percent of all housing. Food production per capita in 1947 was only 51 percent of its level in 1938, a legacy of the price controls implemented by Hitler in 1936 and the rationing system imposed by Goering in 1939 (Henderson, 2008). Additionally, the continued printing of money by the German government to finance the war had resulted in severe inflation.

In November 1945, the Allied Control Authority, formed by the governments of the United States, Britain, France and the Soviet Union, agreed to retain Hitler and Goering's system of price controls and rationing. They also continued the Nazi conscription of resources, including labour. Industrial output in 1947, however, remained only one-third its 1938 level, partly because a large percentage of Germany's working-age men were dead (Henderson, 2008).

Each of the Allied governments controlled a 'zone' of German territory. In the U.S. zone, a cost-of-living index in May 1948, computed at the controlled prices, was only 31 percent above its level in 1938. Yet in 1947, the amount of money in the German economy—currency plus demand deposits—was five times its 1936 level. With money a multiple of its previous level but prices only a fraction higher, shortages were abundant: resultantly, many turned to informal means of obtaining food, such as growing their own or engaging in barter trade in the countryside. Barter was also widespread in business transactions, insofar that firms hired 'compensators', a specialist who bartered his firm's output for needed inputs and often had to engage in multiple transactions to do so. In September 1947 U.S. military experts estimated that one-third to one-half of all business transactions in the bizonal area (the U.S. and British zones) were in the form of 'compensation trade' (i.e. barter) (Wallich, 1955). Barter, however, was inefficient compared with direct purchase of goods and services for money: Eucken noted that barter and self-sufficiency were incompatible with an extensive division of labour, and that the German economic system had been reduced to a primitive condition. Reflectively, bizonal production in March 1948 was only 51 percent of its level in 1936.

In 1945, Ludwig Erhard was appointed the Bavarian minister of finance in the American zone. Erhard used his position as a platform to advocate market reforms, exhorting the German people through radio broadcasts to accept that they had brought their current tragic circumstances on themselves and that only hard work, savings and self-responsibility could restore their prosperity and gain them a new place among the civilised nations of the world (Ebeling, 2008). In lieu of his anti-Nazi views, which had been made clear by his refusal to join the Nazi Association of University Teachers, Erhard was appointed the director of the bizonal Office of Economic Opportunity in 1947 following the combination of the British and American zones. Erhard worked in close cooperation with U.S. General Lucius D. Clay, the military governor of the U.S. zone.

Ludwig Erhard pursued what is now known as a 'social market economy', which was often framed in terms of being a middle way between a free market and socialist planning. There were various scholars associated with the term 'social market economy', and their ideas included the necessarily of some government regulation of the size and composition of large enterprises, urban and rural planning, a system of 'co-determination', under which all large enterprises and corporations were legally required to have trade-union representatives included in the decision-making bodies of businesses (Müller-Armack, 1982). However, this model should not be conflated with welfare-state social democracy, which was ascendant in Europe at the time—a common misconception. While a certain level of state support for social purposes was deemed necessary, this was always intended to be 'as self-limiting as possible', where assistance was provided in a remedial rather than continuous manner, and where individuals remain primarily responsible for their own welfare (Müller-Armack, 1982; Nicholls, 2000).

What was significant, however, was an emphasis on competition, and the necessity of legal rules, policies and institutions to maintain this. Social market economy, while not synonymous with ordoliberalism, was very much influenced by it (see Glossner, 2013). Ordoliberalism was an economic school of thought associated with scholars of the University of Freiburg at the time, and which included individuals such as Walter Eucken, Wilhelm Röpke, Alexander Rüstow and others. Ordoliberals were concerned about private economic power in capitalism, and the anti-competitive practices of monopolists, cartels and dominant economic entities. They thus saw a role for government legislation to protect competition and prevent market manipulation and abuse (Eucken, 1990; Nicholls, 2000). Ordoliberalism, however, cannot just be reduced to advocacy to antitrust legislation but was a sophisticated body of thought which integrated economic analysis with concerns about social order, law, ethics and institutions. In this way, ordoliberalism stands in the tradition of classical political economy of Adam Smith and David Hume, and shares similar concerns about achieving liberty under the rule of law (Sally, 1996).

German ordoliberalism is not unlike the rules-based liberalism that outlined in this Classroom Companion thus far. In many ways, their ideas anticipated the concept of state capacity which we have discussed. Ordoliberalism envisions a 'policy of order' (*Ordnungspolitik*) defined and enforced by the state: the role of the state, however, is limited to acting as an umpire and enforcer of general rules, rather than being a market player of its own (see Sally, 2016).

Therefore, the political leadership of Ludwig Erhard in West Germany should be seen in its wider intellectual climate, specifically how he translated ordoliberal ideas into a viable political program. The impact of ordoliberalism on postwar political developments in Germany again reinforces our argument about the importance of intellectual ideas and idea entrepreneurs in promoting.

Consistent with his ordoliberal beliefs, Erhard believed in the necessity of currency reform and abolition of price controls. This view was one largely shared by members of the Freiburg school such as Wilhelm Röpke: as articulated by Röpke, both currency reform and abolition of price controls were crucial for the post-war restoration of the economy. While currency reform would end inflation, price decontrol would end repression, thereby allowing the functioning of the free market. Reflectively, Erhard advised General Clay to undertake a currency reform on June 20 1948, after the Soviets withdrew from the Allied Control Authority. The reform involved the substitution of one deutsche mark (DM), the new legal currency, for ten reichsmarks, thereby contracting the money supply substantially. This allowed for the reduction of shortages even at the controlled prices, thereby ending the inflationary after-effects from the Nazi period and restoring monetary stability in the process. The currency reform was highly complex, with many people taking a substantial reduction in their net wealth. The net result was about a 93 percent contraction in the money supply.

The German Bizonal Economic Council further adopted a price decontrol ordinance at the urging of Erhard, which allowed him to eliminate price controls against the opposition of Social Democratic members who were supportive of continued state control and intervention. Throughout the latter half of 1948, Erhard removed price, allocation and rationing regulations from almost all manufactured goods, vegetables, fruit and eggs, and raised ceiling prices on many other goods. Decontrol of prices and the abolishment of the rationing system allowed the reformation of the price mechanisms, allowing buyers to effectively express their demands to sellers, and incentivising sellers to increase their supply.

In addition to the currency reform and decontrol of prices, the German Bizonal Economic Council also reduced tax rates. To remove the repressive effect of extremely high rates, the council implemented new tax laws, drastically reducing the corporate income tax rate from a range to 35 to 65 percent to a flat 50 percent. Similarly, the top rate of individual income, while remaining at 95 percent, was applied only to income above the level of DM250,000 annually, in comparison with the previous threshold of DM6,000. Median income Germans with annual incomes of less than DM2,400, while in the 85 percent tax bracket in 1948, were taxed 18 percent in 1950 (Heller, 1949).

The effect on the West German economy was instantaneous: today West Germany's economic recovery is referred to as *WirtschaftsWunder*, or post-war economic miracle (Vonyo, 2018). On June 21 1948, a day after the currency reforms, shops were filled with goods as sellers realised that the money they sold them for would be worth more than the old money. The reforms quickly re-established money as the preferred medium of exchange and monetary incentives as the prime mover of economic activity. Additionally, absenteeism reduced drastically: while workers had stayed away from their jobs for an average of 9.5 h per week in May 1948 partly because the money they earned was not worth much and partly because they were out foraging or bartering for food, average absenteeism in October was reduced to 4.2 h per week (Henderson, 2008). Reflectively, industrial production increased by more than 50 percent between June and December 1948: in June 1948 the bizonal index of industrial production was at only 51 percent of its 1936 level; by December the index had risen to 78 percent. By 1958, industrial production was more than four times its annual rate for the six months in 1948 preceding currency reform. Industrial production per capita was similarly more than three times as high. While prices initially spiked when the controls were abolished, the greater industrial and agricultural output offered on a more open market by the end of the 1950 significantly reduced the cost of living, thereby setting Germany on an economic recovery path that eventually allowed its rate of growth in output and productivity to far exceed other countries in Western Europe.

West Germany's *WirtschaftsWunder* was especially remarkable given the extent of reconstruction, both economical, infrastructural and social, that was necessitated. As a result of its role as a primary instigator of the war, Germany faced significant backlash from the international community, such as numerous restrictions on imports, much of which lasted beyond the currency and price control reforms in 1948. The division of Germany further disrupted input–output links between the western and eastern industrial districts, birthing severe structural imbalances in manufacturing capacity for both Western and Eastern Germany: West German suppliers of intermediary inputs for highly specialised industrial production, for example, were now geographically separated from the highly specialised industrial production districts in East Germany (Ritschl & Vonyo, 2014). Additionally, the destruction of urban housing by the air war left millions trapped in the rural hinterlands, leaving the urban industry with a significant labour shortage (Vonyo, 2012).

The success of West Germany's economic growth is impressive when compared to the numerous problems faced by its neighbouring countries which significantly impeded their economic growth: countries in Eastern Europe such as Hungary, Romania and Yugoslavia, for example, experienced significant barriers to economic growth such as stagnating or declining populations and the resultant shortage of labour. Similarly, economic growth for countries in Western Europe faced difficulties arising from institutional and geopolitical factors, such as the prevailing command economy, rigid prices and wages, and insufficient foreign currency to import the capital goods necessary to rebuild their infrastructure and restock their factories (Milward 2003; Eichengreen, 2007).

The effect of Erhard's economic reforms was clear and positive, according to historian Henry Wallich (1955, p. 71), 'the spirit of the country changed overnight. The gray, hungry, dead-looking figures wandering about the streets in their everlasting search for food came to life'.

Political Structures, Regime Type and Democracy

In the development literature, not only is state capacity important, but there are also questions about the appropriate regime type most conducive to economic success. While related, these are two separate matters. Questions about regime type, as opposed to that of state capacity, involve greater normative considerations about the ideal political order.

Discussions about state capacity may to some extent—though not fully—avoid normative aspects if the analysis is limited to the degree to which such capacity has historically been necessary to development success. However, considerations about regime type will necessarily involve philosophical reflection about the nature of freedom, rights and justice and the political order necessary to secure these values. In the development literature, the debate has mostly centred around the merits of democracy, which is considered to not only be necessary for development, but a sort of development that is consistent with liberal values. This section accordingly reviews the arguments for and against democratic institutions in the development context.

'Democracies' differ from one context to another. Democracies may simply be electoral in nature, which are those featuring free, fair and regular elections accessible to citizens. Citizens of a 'liberal democracy' also enjoy something more than electoral freedom: legal protections and respect for civil liberties and political constraints on the executive branch (see Lührmann et al., 2019 for definitional clarifications). Over the post-war period of 1945 till present day, there has been a 13.8% increase in the share of liberal democracies in the world, and if electoral democracies are included, there has been a 42.17% increase, with 50.28% of the world under democratic systems as of 2021. The trends since at least 2010 have been in the other direction (Fig. 6.1).

Substantial evidence is available that liberal democracies are more likely to facilitate economic growth. The fundamental reason is that democracies disperse political power and vest it in a large percentage of the people, thus acting as a check against the arbitrary exercise of coercion by political elites. Political leaders in liberal democracies can be held accountable to a larger share of the population and are subject to criticism and contestation, meaning that democracies are more likely to act in the general interest (Olson, 1993). Democratic regimes act as 'meta-institutions' that 'elicit and aggregate local knowledge and thereby help build better institutions' (Rodrik, 2000). Put that way, participatory politics is a foundation for good governance, as citizens contribute their local knowledge to the process of improving social cooperation.

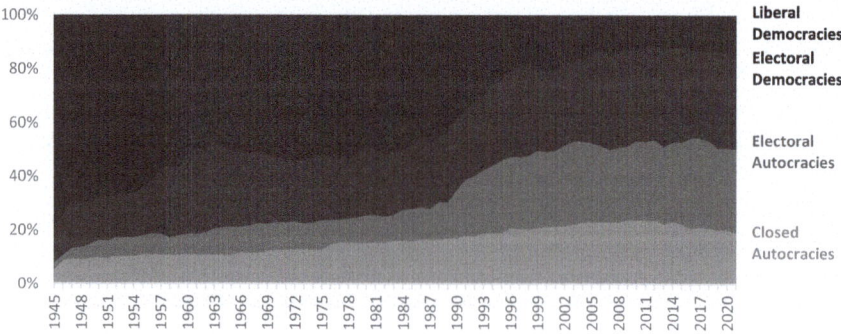

Fig. 6.1 Share of Democracies in the World (1945–2020) *Source* Our World in Data (Roser et al., 2013)

Moreover, a population that is actively engaged in political participation is more likely to carry a similar participative mentality over to economic activities (Sirowy & Inkeles, 1990). Political pluralism and economic plurality both tend to generate improved outcomes and processes through competition for the favour of voters or of customers.

The political pluralism at the foundation of democratic practices is likely to go hand-in-hand with economic pluralism, as well, and the latter fosters conditions conducive to trade, market-based improvements, and entrepreneurial innovation, all of which are crucial preconditions for economic pluralism and economic development.

Examining just liberal democracy alone, which is typically found in Europe and North America, there is a clear association between national income and liberal democratic institutions. The wealthiest countries in the world tend to be democratic, though not always liberally so (Fig. 6.2). The diagram shows a generally positive relationship between national income and liberal democracy, notwithstanding outliers from the trend—countries like Singapore and China come to mind. Most of the world is also clustered in the middle, suggesting great potential for further improvements in both national income and democratic freedoms (see Roser et al., 2013 for further details).

Governments in democracies are more responsive to the expressed desires of their citizens, and accordingly in such systems, there is greater investment in human capital. Education and health care tend to be better under democracies than under other regimes, partly because economic pluralism tends to generate more wealth and partly because political pluralism tends to generate more accountability to the vast majority of the population. While it is arguable that non-predatory dictatorships, for example, allow ruling elites to make long-term investments independent of the desires of its more short-sighted electorate, democracies are shown

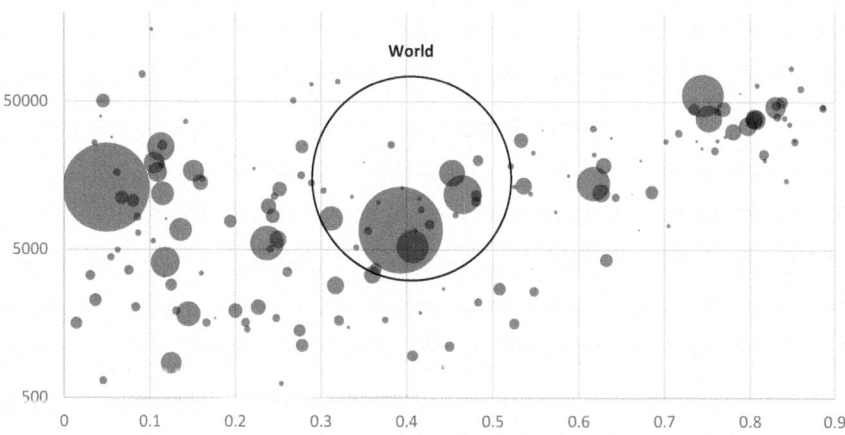

Fig. 6.2 GDP per capita versus liberal democracy in 2018 *Source* Our World In Data (Roser et al., 2013)

empirically to increase the accumulation of human capital (see Baum & Lake, 2003; Tavares & Wacziarg, 2001). The expansion of political participation rights in Western Europe, for example, increased education spending and widened education coverage, while democracy in Africa was similarly shown to have a positive effect on primary education spending in Africa.

Comparatively, democratic regimes are better suited to facilitating technological change and development. Technological change is widely acknowledged by developmental economists to be the most important factor underlying long-term growth: in turn, democratic regimes are shown to have a higher probability of accepting novel projects under uncertainty than are hierarchical regimes (Knutsen, 2012; Sah & Stiglitz, 1986). Additionally, democracies are better able to adapt to technological change and progress and widespread rights of speech and expression tend to be favourable to such innovation. Free and open debate, for example, is instrumental in the growth of knowledge (Halperin et al., 2005). In dictatorship or authoritarian regimes where civil liberties or information diffusion is restricted to reduce threats to their own political survival, absorption and spread of economically productive ideas and technologies is likely to be stifled, as well, thereby rendering democratic regimes the most capable of facilitating the technological change and progress crucial for economic growth.

So far, these benefits outlined are instrumental, in that democracy is said to be welfare-enhancing. Consider also if democracy is desirable on its own terms. Certainly, the economist Amartya Sen (1999) popularised this argument, that the political freedom of democracy is an end of development. He also invoked the notion of justice, showing that the need for public justification of rules requires democratic governance. Freedom is both a means and an end of development (Sen, 2008).

On Authoritarian Development: The Cases of Singapore and China

The case for democracy has received its fair share of criticisms. Some have argued on the basis of empirical evidence that the association between democracy and economic prosperity is not robust, and that democracy may in fact be a by-product rather than an ingredient of development (Barro, 1996). Scholars have used different empirical approaches to measure the effect of democracy on development, and it is safe to say that the consensus is mixed and remains contested (Acemoglu et al., 2019; Ghardallou & Sridi, 2020; Helliwell, 1994; Przeworski et al., 2000).

One important criticism worth addressing is the 'East Asian challenge' to liberal democracy and market capitalism. It is said that East Asian nations adopted a path to development that consciously eschewed the Western liberal democratic capitalist model. Politically, the East Asian Tiger Economies of Singapore, South Korea, Hong Kong, Taiwan and Japan were all authoritarian, or at least non-democratic, to some degree in the late twentieth century. The Confucian basis of East Asian political thought is said to challenge the universality of Western liberalism (see Bell, 2006). In terms of political economy, these East Asian nations adopted a 'developmental state' model of capitalism, rather than the minimal state model championed by the West (see Haggard, 2018 for an overview). At times, these nations consciously rejected 'neoliberal prescriptions', implementing infant-industry protections, industrial policy and maintained state-owned enterprises.

Developmental states are said to enjoy 'state autonomy', which is a concept closely related to state capacity and refers to the ability to pursue developmentalist projects in a way that is free from political pressure (Evans & Heller, 2019; Wade, 1990). Specifically, while democracies are prone to capture from special interest groups such as specific business sectors or pivotal voting blocs, thereby leading to the formulation of policies that are incongruent with the interests of the broader populace, authoritarianism insulates political elites from such pressures, thereby enabling them to enact better policies.

An important clarification must be made. Developmental state theorists stress the concept of state capacity (through what they term 'embedded autonomy'), but state capacity as a wider concept is compatible with various regime types. State capacity and developmental statism are not synonymous, even though the latter do believe that their preferred institutional arrangement is favourable due to its possessing high state capacity.

The fact that East Asia succeeded with developmental state arrangements suggests that liberal capitalism is either unnecessary, or even inimical to development (Amsden, 1994). The two countries that particularly stand out in this regard are Singapore and China. Singapore is particularly interesting, because today it is the last East Asian nation holding onto the authoritarian developmental state model, seeing that Korea, Taiwan and Japan have embraced rapid democratisation in recent times. Its use of industrial policy is arguably the most extensive of them all, and today government-linked corporations continue to shape Singapore's economic structure (Chang, 2011; Lim & Pang, 2016). An understanding of the Singapore case is thus instructive.

One of the fastest-growing countries from 1970 to 2000, Singapore, under the domination of the People's Action Party (PAP), developed rapidly from an economy based on the transhipment of goods produced and resources extracted elsewhere under British colonial rule to an industrialised economy, and then further to a centre for finance and high-tech innovation. Central to Singapore's rapid development was the idea, as propounded by its long-time Prime Minister Lee Kuan Yew, that an authoritarian regime was needed in developing countries to boost economic development (Barr, 2000). Ideologically, Lee argued that Asian cultures were fundamentally incompatible with liberal democracy: in what was referred to as the 'Asian Values Debate', Lee claimed that Singapore's success rested on Confucian values; those values emphasised moral leadership, not political competition. The means to attain good governance, as envisioned by Singaporean leaders, was to install 'Confucian gentlemen (who were) … upright, morally beyond reproach, someone people can trust,… and committed to the public good' into political office

(Goh, 1988). Political pluralism and competition, per Singapore's Prime Minister Goh Chok Tong, would only result in politics becoming 'contentious with groups vying for power, and in trying to do so, appealing to gut feelings of race, language, religion, culture', thereby deepening divisions in Singapore's multi-ethnic society (Roy, 1994).

Additionally, Singaporean leaders argued that Asian values, which placed special emphasis on family and social harmony, were fundamentally incompatible with the individualism promoted by democracy (Bell & Li, 2013). Those arguments were used as elements of an ideology according to which the interest of society took precedence over the interests of the individual. That ideology was, in turn, called on to justify authoritarian actions, such as the suspension of civil liberties in the name of economic growth. Recognising extensive individual rights would come, it was argued, at the expense of the community as a whole and would only result in chaos, unequal distribution of wealth, serious unemployment and economic crises: according to the ruling party's perspective, a high degree of personal freedom was incompatible with order and prosperity (Roy, 1994).

Singapore's model of authoritarianism demonstrated the compatibility of sound economic management with one-party rule, while raising questions about the universality of liberal democracy and liberal capitalism. Furthermore, the lack of corruption and effective governance exemplified by Singapore suggested that such attributes were not the sole product of liberal democracies but could be achieved through pragmatic decision-making by a determined ruling elite under authoritarian rule.

To some extent, the development story of China is similar. Though it moved towards market capitalism with Deng Xiaoping's reforms, it has always remained a mixed economy, with significant state-owned enterprises and active government intervention. Much has been written about China's development and its future prospects, and we will not revisit old ground. However, what is especially noteworthy here is the Singapore-China connection, especially the way in which the latter was influenced by the former in a process of 'authoritarian learning' (see Ortmann & Thompson, 2020 for an excellent exploration of the topic). To put it bluntly, Singapore's practice of authoritarianism has provided lessons for Chinese political elites wishing to enhance their political power.

How so? It was partly a matter of timing, because Singapore's successful development came at a time when China was facing increasing pressures, both externally and internally (as exemplified by the student protests of 1989 in Tiananmen Square), to modernise and open up its economy. Importantly, Singapore embodied the ideal future that the Chinese Communist Party leadership at the time had hoped for: an orderly society with corruption-free government and effective long-term planning to achieve high economic growth, while maintaining sufficient social welfare and guaranteeing authoritarian political stability (Ortmann & Thompson, 2014). Additionally, the Confucian emphasis in Singaporean state rhetoric made Singapore an ideal and crucially culturally appropriate target for emulation. Consequently, China initiated a systematic 'study' of the Singapore model that was directed at transplanting Singaporean policies and practices in the hope of replicating their success in China. Singapore became the model guiding China's development under authoritarian one-party rule. The Chinese Communist Party elites hoped to distil principles of governance from Singaporean experience in the hope that imbibing them would strengthen the grip of China's authoritarian regime (Ortmann & Thompson, 2014).

Evaluating the 'East Asian Challenge'

The 'East Asian Challenge' to democratic capitalism has some problems. First, to fundamentally attribute East Asia's success to an authoritarian model is to ignore other favourable ingredients it enjoyed. East Asia's growth occurred at a time of burgeoning world trade and the growth of global capital (Panagariya, 2019). Though at different time periods, and even though it is true that they adopted a variety of laissez faire and interventionist policies, as did the countries of Europe and North America at various times, the leadership of East Asian countries did make conscious decisions to be plugged into the global economy at a time when globalisation was fast occurring. Further, authoritarianism is not without its costs. Political authoritarianism in East Asia stifled civil society and delayed the development of democratic institutions, though this has very much changed in recent years. While China saw moves towards openness, if not democracy, those were crushed in several waves in the name of maintaining the continuous dictatorship of the Communist Party (Dikötter, 2018). In the Singapore case abovementioned, where authoritarianism and developmental statism have persisted, there have been serious concerns about its poor productivity, innovation and entrepreneurship. This is arguably due to the way home-grown entrepreneurship has been crowded out by government enterprises and the chilling of a 'creative culture' necessary for cutting-edge growth (see Cheang, 2022a, b).

Developmental state theory also has a tenuous relationship with democracy. Recent theorists argue that developmental state arrangements may be compatible with democracy (Evans & Heller, 2015; Huber et al. 2017). However, one must remember that most of the East Asian nations in its early years were authoritarian to some degree. While Japan was admittedly not authoritarian, it nonetheless experienced one-party dominant rule for most its post-war history. In fact, one might argue that the state capacity necessary for developmental states to enforce its will possess a tendency towards authoritarian governance. Stephen Haggard himself admits that 'each policy transition was accompanied by a reconsolidation of authoritarian domination in all the East Asian cases' (Chu, 2016a, p. 10). Even if this extreme is rejected, it is nonetheless true that democratic states are more exposed to popular pressures, divergent concerns and rent-seeking (see Cheang, 2022a). These problems frustrate the state's capacity to impose development plans, which is what occurred in the mid-1980s democratic transitions in South Korea and Taiwan; its democratisation has led to a diminishment of its past developmental state characteristics (Wong, 2004; Chu, 2016b).

The use of developmental state arrangements thus has economic and normative implications. In terms of economic policy, we acknowledge that state-led development, as in the case of China and Singapore, can result in rapid economic growth measured in terms of national income. However, authoritarian governance limits the potential of this very development, and causes it to lack higher-order qualities such as productivity, innovation and entrepreneurship (see Huang, 2008 for an analysis of structural problems in China's development model). Authoritarian developers may easily achieve catch-up growth, but struggle with cutting-edge growth. Innovative economies tend to be those that are open to talk, discussion and criticism, precisely the things that authoritarian states tend to discourage (see Ridley, 2020). The economist and philosopher James Buchanan (1954) embraced majority rule in free societies, not in order to maximise a social welfare function, but:

> precisely because it allows a sort of jockeying back and forth among alternatives, upon none of which relative unanimity can be obtained. Majority rule encourages such shifting, and it provides the opportunity for any social decision to be altered or reversed at any time by a new and temporary majority grouping. In this way, majority decision-making itself becomes a mean through which the whole group ultimately attains consensus, that is, makes a genuine social choice. It serves to insure that competing alternatives may be experimentally and provisionally adopted, tested, and replaced by new compromise alternatives approved by a majority group of ever-changing composition. This is democratic choice process, whatever may be the consequences for welfare economics and social welfare functions.

The values of democracy not only constrain violence, but they create the space for sharing, debating and testing ideas, which means the possibility of entertaining new ones. If innovation is the key to sustained economic growth, then restraints on the freedom to entertain new ideas makes such innovation far less likely.

However, the 'East Asian Challenge' to market liberalism should not be dismissed altogether, as it has important lessons worth remembering. Notably, these East Asians were in no way beacons of economic freedom like market liberals often portrayed them to be. This mischaracterisation stemmed from the way in which Western observers were wedded to their use of aggregate statistics that measure economic freedom on a single dimension, which obscures the micro-level nuances in political economy (Cheang, 2022a). Therefore, the economic freedom statistics, introduced in Chap. 3, should be used with caution. It may be able to generate causal relationships across a large-N basis, such as establishing the links between economic freedom and a variety of welfare indicators like environmental quality, and so forth. However, making policy prescriptions in a specific institutional context with the use of such aggregate data is highly problematic. Top-down blueprints by global development organisations often failed due to such hubris. Once again, the importance of local participation in development policymaking becomes clear.

Polycentric Governance and Freedom

Historically, central political authority has often been essential for development success, notwithstanding the limited cases in which anarchic societies have thrived and where private rules are used in certain legal contexts. State capacity may thus be accepted as a given in an economic development context. However, as explained above, state capacity may, and often has, degenerated into predation, which raises the importance of having constraints on the exercise of power. Western liberal democratic institutions are typically viewed as the best way in which to not only achieve such a limitation of power, but also achieve a form of economic development that is innovative, as opposed to merely accumulative.

However, does an acceptance of a liberal and constrained state necessitate an embrace of Western values? As the 'East Asian Challenge' argument suggested, local communities may have cultural commitments that are opposed to Western values. As has also been stressed throughout this volume, the precise mix of state-market elements in a society also cannot be described in advance. Due to social complexity and differences in local contexts, it is often difficult for outsiders and global development organisations to divine the ideal policy and implement it costlessly.

There is thus a fundamental dilemma that arises: what precise institutional arrangements are best placed to secure some basic commitment to individualism and freedom, but without resorting to a top-down imposition that is often ignorant of local knowledge and context? This dilemma of governance is best addressed by the Bloomington school's articulation of a polycentric social order, which accepts the need for central political authority, but nonetheless advocates a wide degree of choice, flexibility, adaptation and competition *within* government (Aligica & Boettke, 2009).

What does such a system look like in terms of the size and scope of the state? In terms of its role in development policymaking? While difficult to state precisely, some general principles apply. For one, polycentric governance is one where local authorities and devolved jurisdictions are given significant recognition. This could come in the form of federal, power-sharing arrangements as in the United States, as Vincent Ostrom (wife of Elinor Ostrom) articulated in his writings on American federalism (Ostrom, 1997; Ostrom & Allen, 2008). Where state action is unavoidable—and there are indeed many cases where this is true—public policy proceeds on the basis of small, incremental steps rather than 'grand plans', in order to minimise systemic failure. Additionally, regulatory agencies in such a system engage in regular consultations and co-production initiatives with civil society actors in order to engage in learning. Alas, a more radical Ostromian answer to this question suggests that one cannot know the answers to these institutional questions in advance. It is rather when we allow a bottom-up process that the ideal institutional form arises and becomes clear (see Pennington, 2013). The central point is that under polycentric arrangements, there are multiple polities given room for experimentation (albeit under an overall regulatory framework), and inter-jurisdictional competition of said polities allow for evolutionary improvement in governance and policymaking.

The recognition that institutional arrangements are a product of evolutionary competition means that there could exist a wide diversity of state-market arrangements in the world. Rather than nations converging on a single set of arrangements, they may diverge. This means that there may not be a single set of free market institutions that end up being the most ideal, but 'varieties of capitalism' may ensue (Feldmann, 2019; Hodgson, 1996). In fact, one of the major contributions of the East Asian Challenge is to debunk some market liberal beliefs on the universal convergence to a single set of liberal capitalist institutions.

Importantly, the benefit of polycentric governance is that it may be justified without necessarily resorting to the use of Western values or any monistic moral value rooted in a Western context. The political theorist Daniel Bell (2008), as part of the 'East Asian Challenge', has rightly pointed out that democratic institutions, to the extent that they are worthwhile, should be justified according to cultural norms that local people can accept. The benefit of the polycentric vision advocated here is that it provides an epistemic, and thus *culturally agnostic*, justification for these liberal democratic institutions. Freedom is secured through a polycentric framework that allows for ongoing experimentation in public policy. Not only does this provide diversity to fit with the heterogeneous needs of the population, such a system also accords a degree of freedom for people to live according to their own conceptions of the good life.

Polycentricity is justified not with regard to substantive values of individualism, autonomy or justice, but as an institutional *mechanism for discovery*. It strives for what Michael Oakeshott called a 'nomocratic' rather than 'teleocratic' social order. This Ostromian paradigm, with its stress on value pluralism, has been articulated recently by some Hayekian theorists (see Kukathas, 2003; Tebble, 2016; Gaus, 2016).[1] The common theme in these works is the idea that there is no single overriding value to maximise, no allegiance to any particular theory of justice, with which social institutions are to be evaluated. In a compelling essay, Gerald Gaus (2017, 49) explains:

> First and foremost, it (Hayekian liberalism) is not a "moral theory," which formulates normative standards that are then used to evaluate and propose reforms of social orders. The Hayekian approach does not justify the Open Society in terms of efficiency, productivity, utility, utility-based rules, "evolutionary utilitarianism," social welfare, desert, merit, natural rights, autonomy, economic liberty, respect for persons, or progress. This is not to say that it is skeptical whether the Open Society has been a tremendous boon to humanity; having experienced it, the resulting human betterment is manifest to all who truly look. But it was not designed to produce that betterment, nor can it be controlled to secure it in ways that may seem most desirable to us. We know the general features of the Open Society, such as its endless inquiry and innovation, but it has no "maximand"—a value to be maximized, by which our version is to be rated.

---

[1] The close connections and mutual learning between ostromian and hayekian scholars have been explained by Boettke et al. (2015).

In turn, Hayekian liberalism and the polycentric governance structures that flow from it are part of a longer tradition in political philosophy that emphasises value pluralism.[2] According to this tradition, the task of political philosophy is to identify principles that best accommodate the inevitable disagreements in political life, rather than justify a single overarching principle of justice or moral truth. Philosophers writing in this tradition include Stuart Hampshire (2018), John Gray (2000), John Kekes (1993), William Galston (2002) and David McCabe (2010). This value pluralist stance takes the deep heterogeneity of values in society seriously and strives for peaceful co-existence rather than the resolution of such diversity. It is sceptical of the possibility of finding agreement, and the potential for severe and perpetual conflict if such resolution is demanded. In the end, the value pluralism perspective simply calls for radical toleration, or in other words, a 'modus vivendi' as the key operating principle.

Two leading theorists in this regard, David McCabe (2010) and William Galston (2002), defend a liberal social order on such a basis, where the 'value-pluralist liberal state…will not insist on promoting Socratic or Millian ideas as valid for all citizens. It will limit the agreement on principle and practices required of all citizens to constitutional essentials, parsimoniously understood' (Galston, 2002, p. 62). It is our contention that such a defense of liberalism based on value pluralism and Hayekian-Ostromian polycentricity best meets the East Asian cultural challenge and addresses the real issue of cultural diversity in the world today.

In conclusion, development requires both a state with the sufficient capacity to enforce its rules, provide governance and public goods, but at the same time constrained enough to afford a wide scope for private action. The question of regime type is inescapably normative, and on that note, liberal democracy is widely seen as the most attractive in that regard, in addition to its mechanisms to check the excesses of power. Justifying the institutions of liberal democracy, however, runs into the challenge of non-Western cultural commitments, a problem raised by the 'East Asian Challenge'. This challenge may be addressed by the theory of polycentric social orders, which simultaneously achieves state capacity but preserves liberty through a culturally diverse *open society*.

Discussion Questions

1. What is 'state capacity'?
2. Why do some states have high capacity but others do not?
3. Can anarchy ever be desirable from a developmental perspective?
4. What is the role played by civil society organisations in constraining state power?
5. How may state capacity be gained or improved through interactions or joint projects with civil society?

---

[2] I wish to acknowledge paul dragos aligica for, in his work, demonstrating the close interrelationship between the modus vivendi literature and that of polycentric governance.

6. What are 'state constraints' and how do (or should) they interact with 'state capacity'?
7. When does 'state capacity' become political authoritarianism? Is this a concern?
8. Can authoritarianism ever be beneficial to economic development and if so, how?
9. Would technocracy be potentially superior to democracy from a development perspective?
10. What insights from the 'East Asian Challenge' remain relevant today?
11. How may liberal governance be secured in the light of cultural diversity?
12. To what extent may state capacity be achieved through polycentric institutional arrangements?

References

Acemoglu, D., & Robinson, J. A. (2012). *Why nations fail: The origins of power, prosperity, and poverty.* Crown Business.

Acemoglu, D., & Robinson, J. A. (2020). *The narrow corridor: States, societies, and the fate of liberty.* Penguin Random House.

Acemoglu, D., Johnson, S., & Robinson, J. A. (2001). The colonial origins of comparative development: An empirical investigation. *American Economic Review, 91*(5), 1369–1401. https://doi.org/10.1257/aer.91.5.1369.

Acemoglu, D., Naidu, S., Restrepo, P., & Robinson, J. A. (2019). Democracy does cause growth. *The Journal of Political Economy, 127*(1), 47–100. https://doi.org/10.1086/700936.

Aligica, P. D., Boettke, P. J., & Tarko, V. (2019). *Public governance and the classical-liberal perspective: Political economy foundations.* Oxford University Press.

Aligica, P. D., & Boettke, P. J. (2009). *Challenging institutional analysis and development: The Bloomington school.* Routledge.

Amsden, A. (1994). Why isn't the whole world experimenting with the East Asian model to develop?: Review of the East Asian miracle. *World Development, 22*(4), 627–633. https://doi.org/10.1016/0305-750X(94)90117-1.

Barr, M. (2000). Lee Kuan Yew and the "Asian values" debate. *Asian Studies Review, 24*(3), 309–334. https://doi.org/10.1080/10357820008713278.

Barro, R. (1996). Democracy and growth. *Journal of Economic Growth, 1*(1), 1–27. https://doi.org/10.1007/BF00163340.

Baum, A., & Lake, D. (2003). The political economy of growth: Democracy and human capital. *American Journal of Political Science, 47*(2), 333–347. https://doi.org/10.2307/3186142.

Bell, D. (2006). *Beyond liberal democracy.* Princeton University Press.

Bell, D. (2008). East Asia and the West: The impact of confucianism on Anglo-American political theory. In J. Dryzek, B. Honig, & A. Phillips (Eds.), *Oxford Handbook of political theory* (pp. 262–280). Oxford University Press.

Bell, D., & Li, C. (2013). *The East Asian challenge for democracy: Political meritocracy in comparative perspective.* Cambridge University Press.

Benson, B. (2011). *The enterprise of law: Justice without the state* (2nd ed.). Independent Institute.

Besley, T., & Persson, T. (2010). State capacity, conflict, and development. *Econometrica, 78*(1), 1–34. https://doi.org/10.3982/ECTA8073.

Besley, T., & Persson, T. (2011). *Pillars of prosperity: The political economics of development clusters.* Princeton University Press.

Bockstette, V., Chanda, A., & Putterman, L. (2002). States and markets: The advantage of an early start. *Journal of Economic Growth, 7*(4), 347–369. https://doi.org/10.1023/A:1020827801137.

Boettke, P. J., & Candela, R. (2020). Productive specialization, peaceful cooperation and the problem of the predatory state: Lessons from comparative historical political economy. *Public Choice, 182*(3–4), 331–352. https://doi.org/10.1007/s11127-019-00657-9.

Boettke, P. J., Lemke, J. S., & Palagashvili, L. (2015). Polycentricity, self-governance, and the art & Science of association. *Review of Austrian Economics, 28*(3), 311–335. https://doi.org/10.1007/s11138-014-0273-9.

Bonney, R. (1995). *Economic systems and state finance: The origins of the modern state in Europe 13th to 18th centuries.* Oxford University Press.

Buchanan, J. M. (1954). Social choice, democracy, and free markets. *Journal of Political Economy, 62*(2), 114–123.

Chang, H. J. (2011). Reply to the comments on 'Institutions and economic development: Theory, policy and history.' *Journal of Institutional Economics, 7*(4), 595–613. https://doi.org/10.1017/S174413741100035X.

Cheang, B. (2022a). *Economic Liberalism and the Developmental State: Hong Kong and Singapore's Post-War Development.* Palgrave Macmillan.

Cheang, B. (2022b). What can industrial policy do? Evidence from Singapore. *Review of Austrian Economics.* https://doi.org/10.1007/s11138-022-00589-6.

Chu, Y. W. (2016a). *The Asian developmental state.* Palgrave Macmillan.

Chu, Y. W. (2016b). Democratisation, emergence of the knowledge-based economy and the changing developmental alliances in South Korea and Taiwan. In Y.-W. Chu (Ed.), *The Asian developmental state* (pp. 117–138). Palgrave Macmillan.

Das, G. (2012). *India grows at night: A liberal case for a strong state.* New Delhi.

Dikötter, F. (2018). *Mao's great famine: The history of China's most devastating catastrophe, 1958–62.* Bloomsbury Paperbacks.

Dincecco, M. (2011). *Political transformations and public finances: Europe, 1650–1913.* Cambridge University Press.

Dincecco, M. (2015). The rise of effective states in Europe. *The Journal of Economic History, 75*(3), 901–918. https://doi.org/10.1017/S002205071500114X.

Dincecco, M. (2017). *State capacity and economic development: Present and past.* Cambridge University Press.

Dincecco, M., & Wang, Y. (2018). Violent conflict and political development over the long run: China versus Europe. *Annual Review of Political Science, 21*, 341–358.

Ebeling, R. M. (2008, April 1). *The German Economic Miracle and the "Social Market Economy."* Foundation for Economic Education. https://fee.org/articles/the-german-economic-miracle-and-the-social-marketeconomy/.

Eichengreen, B. (2007). *The European economy since 1945: Coordinated capitalism and beyond.* Princeton University Press.

Eucken, W. (1990). *Grundsätze der Wirtschaftspolitik.* Mohr.

Evans, P., & Heller, P. (2019). The State and Development. In D. Nayyar (Ed.), *Asian transformations: An inquiry into the development of nations* (pp. 109–135). Oxford University Press.

Evans, P., & Heller, P. (2015). Human development, state transformation, and the politics of the developmental state. In S. Leibfried, E. Huber, M. Lange, J. Levy, & J. Stephens (Eds.), *The Oxford handbook of transformations of the state.* Oxford University Press.

Feldmann, M. (2019). Global varieties of capitalism. *World Politics, 71*(1), 162–196. https://doi.org/10.1017/S0043887118000230.

Friedman, D. (1979). Private creation and enforcement of law: A historical case. *The Journal of Legal Studies, 8*(2), 399–415. https://doi.org/10.1086/467615.

Friedman, D., Leeson, P., & Skarbek, D. (2019). *Legal systems very different from ours.* Independent Publisher.

Galston, W. A. (2002). *Liberal pluralism: The implications of value pluralism for political theory and practice.* Cambridge University Press.

Gaus, G. (2016). *The tyranny of the ideal*. Princeton University Press.

Gaus, G. (2017). Hayekian "classical" liberalism. In J. Brennan, B. van der Vossen, & D. Schmidtz (Eds.), *The Routledge handbook of libertarianism* (pp. 34–52). Routledge.

Geloso, V. J., & Salter, A. W. (2020). State capacity and economic development: Causal mechanism or correlative filter? *Journal of Economic Behavior & Organization, 170*, 372–385. https://doi.org/10.1016/j.jebo.2019.12.015.

Ghardallou, W., & Sridi, D. (2020). Democracy and economic growth: A literature review. *Journal of the Knowledge Economy, 11*(3), 982–1002. https://doi.org/10.1007/s13132-019-00594-4.

Glossner, C. L. (2013). *The making of the German post-war economy: political communication and public reception of the social market economy after World War II*. I.B. Tauris; New York.

Gray, J. (2000). *Two faces of liberalism*. Polity Press.

Goh, C. T. (1988). *Why we had no choice but to react*. Straits Times, Singapore.

Government of India. (1964). *Report of the Committee on the Prevention of Corruption*. Central Vigilance Commission. https://cvc.gov.in/sites/default/files/vm21ch9/vm17ch9/1,2.%20S anthanam%20Committee%20Report-.pdf.

Haggard, S. (2018). *Developmental states*. Cambridge University Press.

Halperin, M., Siegle, J., & Weinstein, M. (2005). *The democracy advantage: How democracies promote prosperity and peace*. Routledge.

Hampshire, S. (2018). *Justice is conflict*. Princeton University Press.

Heller, W. W. (1949). Tax and monetary reform in occupied Germany. *National Tax Journal, 2*(3), 215–231. https://doi.org/10.1086/NTJ41789824.

Helliwell, J. (1994). Empirical linkages between democracy and economic Growth. *British Journal of Political Science, 24*(2), 225–248. https://doi.org/10.1017/S0007123400009790.

Henderson, D. R. (2008). German economic miracle. *The Concise Encyclopedia of Economics*. https://www.econlib.org/library/Enc/GermanEconomicMiracle.html.

Hodgson, G. M. (1996). Varieties of capitalism and varieties of economic theory. *Review of International Political Economy, 3*(3), 380–433. https://doi.org/10.1080/09692299608434363.

Huang, Y. (2008). *Capitalism with Chinese characteristics: Entrepreneurship and the state*. Cambridge University Press.

Huber, E., Evans, P., & Stephens, J. (2017). The political foundations of state effectiveness. In M. Centeno, A. Kohli, D. Yashar, & D. Mistree (Eds.), *States in the developing world* (pp. 380–408). Cambridge University Press.

Johnson, N., & Koyama, M. (2017). States and economic growth: Capacity and constraints. *Explorations in Economic History, 64*, 1–20. https://doi.org/10.1016/j.eeh.2016.11.002.

Knutsen, C. H. (2012). Democracy and economic growth: A survey of arguments and results. *International Area Studies Review, 15*(4), 393–415. https://doi.org/10.1177/2233865912455268.

Kekes, J. (1993). *The morality of pluralism*. Princeton University Press.

Kugler, J. (2018). *Political capacity and economic behavior*. Routledge.

Kukathas, C. (2003). *The liberal archipelago: A theory of diversity and freedom*. Oxford University Press.

La Porta, R., Lopez-de-Silanes, F., & Shleifer, A. (2008). The economic consequences of legal origins. *Journal of Economic Literature, 46*(2), 285–332. https://doi.org/10.1257/jel.46.2.285.

Lim, L., & Pang, E. F. (2016). Labor, productivity and Singapore's development model. In L. Lim (Ed.), *Singapore's economic development: Retrospection and reflections* (pp. 135–168). World Scientific.

Leeson, P. (2007a). Efficient anarchy. *Public Choice, 130*(1), 41–53. https://doi.org/10.1007/s11127-006-9071-7

Leeson, P. (2007b). Better off stateless: Somalia before and after government collapse. *Journal of Comparative Economics, 35*(4), 689–710. https://doi.org/10.1016/j.jce.2007.10.001.

Lent, A., & Studdert, J. (2019). *The community paradigm - Why public services need radical change and how it can be achieved*. New Local. https://www.newlocal.org.uk/wp-content/uploads/2019/03/The-Community-Paradigm_New-Local-2.pdf.

Lührmann, A., Grahn, S., Morgan, R., Pillai, S., & Lindberg, S. I. (2019). State of the world 2018: Democracy facing global challenges. *Democratization, 26*(6), 895–915. https://doi.org/10.1080/13510347.2019.1613980.

McCabe, D. (2010). *Modus vivendi liberalism.* Cambridge University Press.

Milward, A. (2003). *The reconstruction of Western Europe, 1945–1951.* Routledge.

Müller-Armack, A. (1982). The second phase of the social market economy: An additional concept of a humane economy. In *Standard texts on the social market economy: Two centuries of discussion* (pp. 49–61). Stuttgart–New York: Fischer.

Murtazashvili, I., & Murtazashvili, J. (2015). Anarchy, self-governance, and legal titling. *Public Choice, 162*(3), 287–305. https://doi.org/10.1007/s11127-014-0222-y.

New Local. (2020). *Think big, act small: Elinor Ostrom's radical vision for community power.* New Local. https://www.newlocal.org.uk/wp-content/uploads/2020/10/Think-Big-Act-Small_.pdf.

Nicholls, A. (2000). Erhard and the realization of the social market economy. In A. Nicholls (Ed.), *Freedom with Responsibility: The Social Market Economy in Germany 1918–1963* (pp. 322-366). Oxford University Press. https://doi.org/10.1093/acprof:oso/9780198208525.003.0017.

Norberg, J. (2020) *Open: The story of human progress.* Atlantic Books.

North, D., & Weingast, B. (1989). Constitutions and commitment: The evolution of institutions governing public choice in seventeenth-century england. *The Journal of Economic History, 49*(4), 803–832. https://doi.org/10.1017/S0022050700009451.

Novak, M. (2021). *Freedom in contention: Social movements and liberal political economy .* Rowman and Littlefield.

Olson, M. (1965). *The logic of collective action.* Harvard University Press.

Olson, M. (1993). Dictatorship, democracy, and development. *American Political Science Review, 87*(3), 567–576. https://doi.org/10.2307/2938736.

Ortmann, S., & Thompson, M. (2020). *China's Singapore model and authoritarian learning.* Routledge.

Ortmann, S., & Thompson, M. (2014). China's obsession with Singapore: Learning authoritarian modernity. *Pacific Review, 27*(3), 433–455. https://doi.org/10.1080/09512748.2014.909522.

Ostrom, V., & Ostrom, E. (1978). Public goods and public choices. In E. S. Savas (Ed.), *Alternatives for delivering public services: Toward improved performance* (pp. 7–49). Westview Press.

Ostrom, E. (1998). The comparative study of public economies. *The American Economist, 42*(1), 3–17. https://doi.org/10.1177/056943459804200101.

Ostrom, V. (1997). *The meaning of democracy and the vulnerability of democracies: A response to Tocqueville's challenge.* University of Michigan Press.

Ostrom, V., & Allen, B. (2008). *The political theory of a compound republic: Designing the American experiment.* Lexington Books.

Panagariya, A. (2019). *Free trade and prosperity: How openness helps the developing countries grow richer and combat poverty.* Oxford University Press.

Pennington, M. (2013). Elinor Ostrom and the robust political economy of common-pool resources. *Journal of Institutional Economics, 9*(4), 449–468. https://doi.org/10.1017/S1744137413000258.

Powell, B., & Stringham, E. (2009). Public choice and the economic analysis of anarchy: A survey. *Public Choice, 140*(3), 503–538. https://doi.org/10.1007/s11127-009-9407-1.

Przeworski, A., Alvarez, R. M., Alvarez, M. E., Cheibub, J. A., Limongi, F., & Neto, F. P. (2000). *Democracy and development: Political institutions and well-being in the world, 1950–1990.* Cambridge University Press.

Rajan, R. (2004). Assume anarchy? Why an orthodox economic model may not be the best guide for policy. *Finance and Development, 41*(3), 56–57.

Reform. (2021). *A state of preparedness: How government can build resilience to civil emergencies.* Reform UK. https://reform.uk/index.php/research/state-preparedness-how-government-can-build-resilience-civil-emergencies.

Ridley, M. (2020). *How innovation works - and why it flourishes in freedom.* Harper.

Ritschl, A., & Vonyo, T. (2014). The roots of economic failure: What explains East Germany's falling behind between 1945 and 1950? *European Review of Economic History, 18*(2), 166–184. https://doi.org/10.1093/ereh/heu004.

Rodrik, D. (2000). Institutions for high-quality growth: What they are and how to acquire them. *Studies in Comparative International Development, 35*(3), 3–31. https://doi.org/10.1007/BF0 2699764.

Roser, M., Herre, B., & Ortiz-Ospina, E. (2013). *Democracy.* Our World in Data. https://ourworldi ndata.org/democracy.

Roy, D. (1994). Singapore, China, and the soft authoritarian challenge. *Asian Survey, 34*(3), 231–242. https://doi.org/10.2307/2644982.

Sah, R. K., & Stiglitz, J. E. (1986). The architecture of economic systems: Hierarchies and polyarchies. *The American Economic Review, 76*(4), 716–727. https://doi.org/10.3386/w1334.

Sally, R. (1996). Ordoliberalism and the social market: Classical political economy from Germany. *New Political Economy, 1*(2), 233–257. https://doi.org/10.1080/13563469608406254.

Sally, R. (2016). *Ludwig Erhard's social market economy—a liberal, not a social democratic concept.* Institute of Economic Affairs. https://iea.org.uk/blog/ludwig-erhards-social-market-economy-a-liberal-not-a-social-democratic-concept.

Samuelson, P. (1954). The pure theory of public expenditure. *Review of Economics and Statistics, 36*(4), 387–389. https://doi.org/10.2307/1925895.

Savoia, A., & Sen, K. (2015). Measurement, evolution, determinants, and consequences of state capacity: A review of recent research. *Journal of Economic Surveys, 29*(3), 441–458. https://doi.org/10.1111/joes.12065.

Sen, A. (1999). *Development as freedom.* Anchor.

Sen, A. (2008). The idea of justice. *Journal of Human Development, 9*(3), 331–342. https://doi.org/10.1080/14649880802236540.

Sirowy, L., & Inkeles, A. (1990). The effects of democracy on economic growth and inequality: A review. *Studies in Comparative International Development, 25*(1), 126–157. https://doi.org/10.1007/BF02716908.

Stringham, E. (2015). *Private governance: Creating order in economic and social life.* Oxford University Press.

Tavares, J., & Wacziarg, R. (2001). How democracy affects growth. *European Economic Review, 45*(8), 1341–1378. https://doi.org/10.1016/S0014-2921(00)00093-3.

Tebble, A. J. (2016). *Epistemic liberalism: A defence.* Routledge.

Tilly, C. (2017). War making and state making as organized crime. In E. Castañeda, & C. L. Schneider (Eds.), *Collective violence, contentious politics, and social change.* Routledge.

Vonyo, T. (2012). The bombing of Germany: The economic geography of war-induced dislocation in West German industry. *European Review of Economic History, 16*(1), 97–118. https://doi.org/10.1093/ereh/her006.

Vonyo, T. (2018). *The economic consequences of the war: West Germany's growth miracle after 1945.* Cambridge University Press.

Wade, R. (1990). *Governing the market: Economic theory and the role of government in East Asian industrialization.* Princeton University Press.

Wallich, H. C. (1955). *Mainsprings of the German revival.* Yale University Press.

Weingast, B. (1995). The economic role of political institutions: Market-preserving federalism and economic development. *Journal of Law, Economics & Organization, 11*(1), 1–31. https://doi.org/10.1093/oxfordjournals.jleo.a036861.

Wong, J. (2004). The adaptive developmental state in East Asia. *Journal of East Asian Studies, 4*(3), 345–362. https://doi.org/10.1017/S1598240800006007.

Conclusion—Humane Liberalism, Bottom-Up Change and Institutional Entrepreneurship

7

The institutional economist Douglass North (1981, p. 20) captured the dilemma of development: "the existence of the state is essential for economic growth; the state, however, is the source of man-made economic failure". State capacity, while a necessary condition, must at the same time be balanced with meaningful constraints on the exercise of power and be grounded in liberal values of dignity, rule of law and respect for the individual. The polycentric social order explained previously provides the institutional flesh to this liberal vision.

Knowing the ingredients of development is one thing, but achieving positive change is another. Knowing that various factors inputs like land labour and capital feed into a 'black box' production process tells us nothing about how they are combined by entrepreneurs. Similarly, the process of development, in our view, should also include a consideration for institutional entrepreneurs, who spot opportunities to advocate for positive change.

Accordingly, this chapter outlines the role of civil society groups as *change agents* in the development process. As important as markets and market institutions are, they cannot be successfully imposed onto a community from afar, by development experts or well-meaning Western powers. Development is best achieved through homegrown, organic efforts. Theorising the role of such bottom-up change driven by local actors once again brings to the fore the insights of Elinor Ostrom, who brought to bear a focus on the third sphere of civil society that lies beyond state and markets. Crucially, this third sphere contributes to development by fostering the necessary liberal values in society, challenging state power and providing the necessary knowledge, skills and community involvement for sustainable development.

© The Author(s), under exclusive license to Springer Nature Singapore Pte Ltd. 2023
B. Cheang and T. G. Palmer, *Institutions and Economic Development*,
Classroom Companion: Economics, https://doi.org/10.1007/978-981-99-0844-8_7

Humane Liberalism

A central question in development is which mechanism should be relied upon to allocate scarce resources and to coordinate human affairs. In the past few centuries, the debate has been largely between coordination through a centrally planned, command economy or voluntary exchange. Today, the market model has largely won out, although there is much variation among the mixes of state and market (Feldmann, 2019).

This handbook has made the case that markets are indispensable for development. If the aim is to achieve increases in standards of living, real wages, life expectancy and the like, development driven by exchange, trade and innovation is a must. But what are 'markets'? Do markets simply refer to trade activity, which requires institutions? Or are markets themselves institutions? To answer these questions, a full understanding of 'markets' will require a holistic reading of Chaps. 3, 4 and 5, which analysed markets through a tri-fold prism of 'getting the prices right', 'getting the institutions right' and 'getting the culture right'.

Basically, markets simply refer to the networks of exchange that link producers and consumers. But markets are embedded within larger rules and values that make them work. Collectively, the *market-based social order*, in our conception entail:

1. Economic freedom to exchange, trade and associate (getting the prices right);
2. Institutions of private property rights, rule of law and contract enforcement (getting the institutions right);
3. Cultural values that dignify and support wealth creation (getting the culture right).

Market-based development is that which is driven by the presence of these factors. These three layers have a nested structure: where the economic policies of the first layer are nested within formal legal-political institutions, and which is itself embedded within a larger ideational envelope. There has of course been debate over which of these three aspects take primacy. Institutionalists tend to emphasise the second layer while culturally sensitive scholars emphasise the third. For example, Deirdre McCloskey (2022b) has wholly rejected neo-institutionalism and posits that values (layer 3) are often *sufficient* and prime agents of change.

It is not this book's aim to settle the debate, but rather to provide an overview of all three layers and emphasise their inter-connections. Neoclassical economists often operate on the first layer without considering institutions and values, an omission that makes for sterile analysis. Some sociologists and cultural studies experts have on the other hand not engaged in economic analysis or are largely hostile to market organisation; the interdisciplinary field of economic sociology is thus a worthy addition to our knowledge (see Chamlee-Wright, 2002). In actual development practice, as Chap. 4 has shown, global efforts to promote economic reforms have backfired whenever governance problems in developing nations were neglected.

Contrary to McCloskey's rejection of institutional economics, this handbook believes it is possible to approach development from an institutional perspective, one that takes a broad view of how institutions are defined and which rejects a *homo economicus* conception of behaviour. Thus, as explained in Chap. 4, old institutional economics' conception of human action as *habit-following* is important and allows us to recognise the way a range of institutions, including 'soft' institutions like culture and values, influence outcomes. The central institutional question of development is 'what are the rules and norms in society which facilitate economic progress?', and the answer presented herein is the contributions from liberal political economy.

At this point, the many criticisms of markets must be acknowledged, some of which explained in Chap. 3. Such criticisms include market failure arguments to moral charges of exploitation, commodification and injustice (Anderson, 2017; Sandel, 2012). It is important to remember though that many of these flaws identified in markets tend to be those found in every form of human interaction and are not unique to market systems. That does not mean that they are unimportant, but they are not generally flaws of free exchange.

There is reason to believe that market exchanges strengthen desirable moral values. People in market-based societies are more generous and charitable, engage in greater levels of environmental action and are more accepting of social differences (see, for example Berggren & Nilsson, 2013; Cai et al., 2021). Markets are not merely amoral instrumental tools for economic enrichment—though they are also that—but social spaces within which moral virtues are cultivated (Storr, 2012). Scholars have also shown that the concerns that motivate those seeking social justice, the lifting up of the least well-off among us, may be best served through market principles (Cowen, 2021; Tomasi, 2012).

Liberalism, as we understand it, is a humane approach to human cooperation. It is humane because it recognises that ordinary have an extraordinary capacity to flourish if given the chance to 'have a go', as Deirdre McCloskey puts it. People can achieve happiness and prosperity when they are not coerced, ordered about or threatened with violence, but treated as dignified and free moral agents to be persuaded rather than to be compelled (McCloskey, 2019). The Great Enrichment sustainably lifted humanity out of poverty.

Global Applications

In the context of global development, the principles of humane liberalism so described are highly relevant. While a context-sensitive approach to domestic market reforms is necessary, as described in this handbook, there are two high-impact reforms that have the potential to do much good for the global poor. These are in the area of trade and migration policy, both of which are in much need of liberalisation. While these are not the only aspects in need of change, a greater embrace of such humane liberal principles promises to improve global justice and empower the least-advantaged (see Lomasky & Teson, 2015; Van der Vossen & Brennan, 2018).

Poor countries need foreign trade; they benefit disproportionately from trading with wealthier nations; exporting agricultural goods and importing vaccines and life-saving medications mean wealthy people get fresh fruit and clothing and that poor people get to live longer and much healthier lives. Moreover, foreign investment increases wages and spurs the development of numerous domestic industries. The poor desperately need global markets. The increases of incomes in India and China in recent years are largely connected to their integration with the world economy. National case studies of specific countries have also shown how export-led growth and foreign investment go together with poverty reduction (Hanson, 2007; Bhagwati, 2020).

Therefore, rising protectionism in the Western world in recent years limits the export earnings of developing countries and harms poor nations. Tariffs foster negative macroeconomic consequences for the country imposing them in the first place (Furceri et al., 2018). Because a tax on imports has, in the aggregate, the same impact as a tax on exports, attempts to restrict imports and simultaneously expand exports are doomed (Irwin, 1997). A study showed that since the 2008 financial crisis, the world's top 60 economies adopted more than 7000 trade barriers, with tariffs specifically worth more than $400 billion (Jones, 2017). Since 2018, these protectionist policies have more than tripled (Gowling WLG, 2020).

Available data also shows that trade integration has slowed over the last decade. Since World War II, there was an explosion in global trade, measured in terms of trade as a percentage of world GDP, but this has since slowed as seen in the following measure (Fig. 7.1).

Closely related to the free movement of goods and services is the free movement of people across borders. Even though the world has seen a growth in world trade in the late twentieth century—despite some slowing in recent times—the global movement of people has lagged behind, due to immigration controls maintained by governments. Data shows that even though the absolute number of migrants internationally have increased, as a proportion of the world's population, the change has been minimal (Fig. 7.2).

Immigration controls today remain a major barrier to the free movement of people. Interestingly, a famous article by migration economist Michael Clemens

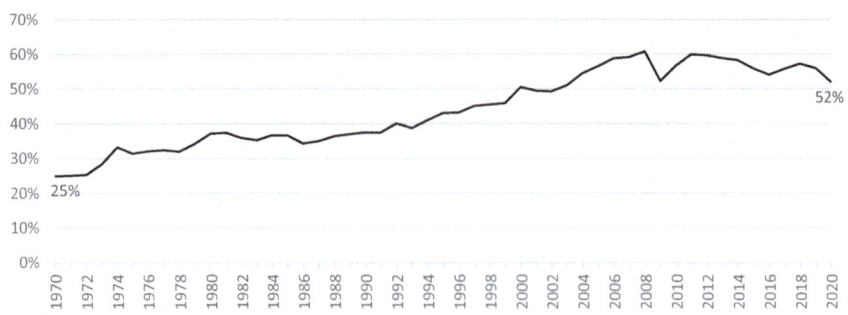

Fig. 7.1   Trade as a percentage of World GDP (1970–2020) *Source* World Bank (2021)

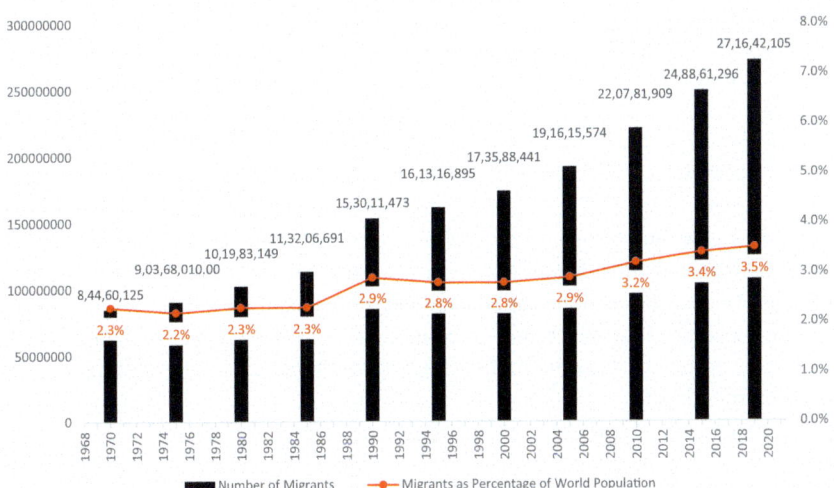

Fig. 7.2 Absolute number of migrants compared with migrants as percentage of world population (1970–2020) *Source* International Organisation for Migration (2020)

(2011) argues that there are 'trillion-dollar bills' on the sidewalk to be gained through immigration freedom, since the gains to eliminating migration barriers are 'one or two orders of magnitude larger than' trade liberalisation itself, amounting to approximately 78 trillion dollars. He has since declared that relaxing these restrictions is perhaps the 'biggest idea in development no one has ever tried' (Clemens, 2009). The magnitude of this impact should not be underestimated. Much empirical research estimates that eliminating migration barriers would lead to growth in up to 150% of world national income (Hamilton & Whalley, 1984; Iregui, 2005; Moses & Letnes, 2004).

Free movement is not only economically beneficial, but also a moral imperative (Kukathas, 2021). Billions of people in the world today continue to live in poor nations, without the sound institutions and values that the rich world enjoys. The poverty is not because of the people, but because of their institutional surroundings. It's not that the people are inherently poor, because when they move to other countries, they cease being poor. It's the countries that are poor, that inhibit economic growth and thereby keep people poor. As we have outlined, changing governance is easier said than done, and may even take a generation or more. It is far easier to allow people in poor countries to move to countries where good institutions already exist than to implement those institutions, or suitable versions of them, in poor countries. The productivity of the human capital of the poor will immediately increase just by allowing them to enjoy the type of governance that so many take for granted.

Of course, the debate over migration has many aspects, including socio-cultural concerns. Many fear that unfettered migration could potentially dilute the national culture of the recipient nation, which might undermine the basis of the liberal democratic institutions that created the wealth that attracted the migrants in the first place. If migrants come from cultures that do not respect liberal values, then liberal societies that accept them may end up being worse off. We are unable to settle this debate in the limited scope of this chapter, but we make two responses. First, as important as cultural concerns are, if the focus is on economic well-being, for both sending and receiving countries, the data on migration freedom is clear. The more people are free to move to where their talents are best used, the greater the world's economic productivity and prosperity (see Leeson & Gochenour, 2015, for an overview of the economic literature). Second, the potential for cultural erosion may be real, but should not be overstated, and can be in many ways resolved through 'keyhole' solutions (which are targeted interventions) or regulations, without giving up on the benefits of free migration altogether (Nowrasteh & Powell, 2020; Somin, 2020).

Ultimately, the degree to which immigrants are accepted into a community, and how public policy can be changed to embrace migrants, is a matter for local communities to decide. That is why, once again, the deliberation that takes place across civil society plays such an important role. Without such deliberative processes in the community at large, any top-down policy to liberalise immigration is likely to trigger public backlash. Immigration-centric CBOs can provide specialist knowledge on immigration policy reform to governments, taking into account local conditions and challenges. Once again, it is this bottom-up process of policy reform, which takes into account the voices of local actors, that is most likely to realise the benefits of migration.

Necessary but Imperfect

There are certain well-known criticisms of markets that are worth revisiting at this stage. The first is the concern of market failure (discussed in Chap. 3), which posits that markets fall short of the standards of Pareto efficiency. At this point, it must be clarified that we do not view markets as perfect systems that operate according to textbook depictions in mainstream economics, where there is perfect information, competition and zero externalities. We are well aware that markets are highly imperfect and perhaps especially so in developing countries. Our case for markets is a realistic one: that as compared to centrally planned societies they are less likely to be subject to abuses of power and systemic errors of judgement. A market-based society decentralises power and the use of knowledge, thereby facilitating experimentation and the growth of new ideas (Pennington, 2011). Such a 'market process' conception (explained in Chap. 3), as opposed to equilibrium theory, allows us to appreciate the evolutionary nature of economic and also social change. With such a view, we appreciate how markets not only facilitate economic progress, but also social progress. A decentralised polycentric order based on private property allows 'cultural innovators' to break away from the status quo, just like economic innovators do, promoting new ways of living, new norms and new mental models. It is for this reason that those concerned with social oppression or domination should find reasons to support polycentric governance (see Horwitz, 2015).

Another objection to our position is that markets are embedded in politics and thus do not exist independently. This criticism is best exemplified by the heterodox economist Ha-Joon Chang (2011, 2012), who has argued that there is 'no such thing as a free market', since market exchange and even market reforms are all rooted (and embedded) in political decisions and political structures (see Chap. 2). There is some truth in this criticism, in that we must pay attention to politics, especially when analysing development. Understanding development and what it takes to achieve it requires us to consider politics, not just economics. The one-dimensional methodology of neoclassical economics may be rejected, but that need not imply a rejection of markets.

It is true that markets do not just exist in a vacuum, and certainly, in developing countries, to construct markets successfully, people need a functioning political system that is responsive to them, that invests in public goods and can effectively enforce law. The absence of effective central authorities has often been a source of civil instability and 'traps' a nation in a cycle of under-development. A proper and delicate balance must be struck between states and markets. For us, this ideal balance is when states have the capacity to enforce general rules that are clear, predictable and stable, but at the same time leaves a large degree of freedom to the private sector to operate.

The 'sweet spot' between how much state control and market freedoms to have in a society, however, cannot be predicted in advance. It is not for us or any development organisation to prescribe to a developing nation. This is why we are sceptical of efforts, even well-intentioned ones, by external agencies to pursue development programs—whether massive injections of foreign aid, Washington Consensus-type reforms or nation-building programs to establish democracy—in poor countries. These have often been subject to failure due to a lack of local knowledge and cultural fit, leading to a range of unintended consequences (Boettke et al., 2015a, b; Coyne, 2008).

So where does this leave us? Today, there is a broad consensus among development economists that institutions are foundational to economic development, and that among them those that make possible and facilitate market exchanges are central. But there is an added element that is often overlooked by those who propose just adding the right institutions to the recipe. Not only do we need to 'get the institutions right', one must also 'get the cultures right'. Some countries have achieved mixes of institutional and cultural ingredients and have achieved great success. But that doesn't tell us a great deal about how to achieve good mixes in particular contexts.

The economic historian Deirdre McCloskey (2022a), who most emphatically argued for humane liberalism in the development context, herself admitted that the rhetorical and intellectual shifts in Western Europe that preceded the Great Enrichment was itself a product of historical accidents. The contingency, time and specific nature of these changes mean that it may be very difficult to replicate the confluence of factors that brought about such rapid development.

Situating this concern within institutional economics, the development economist Dani Rodrik (2006, p. 11) expressed this dilemma best:

> Taken to its logical conclusion, the focus on institutions has potentially debilitating side effects for policy reformers. Institutions are by their very nature deeply embedded in society. If growth indeed requires major institutional transformation—in the areas of rule of law, property rights protection, governance, and so on—how can we not be pessimistic about the prospects for growth in poor countries?

Possibly, one may look back in retrospect and trace how certain countries or regions experienced development, and the kind of institutions and policies they adopted. But if the Great Enrichment was a product of historical accidents, then that makes it difficult for one to replicate the accident(s) and to achieve the desired outcome. Knowing the ingredients of development is one thing, putting them together to create a 'finished product' is another. Does that mean that we can only *describe* successful development *after the fact?*

Institutional Entrepreneurship and Social Change

An understanding of how institutions change is therefore needed. So far, there is much knowledge about the institutions and other ingredients needed for long-run development, but less is known about how they change and why such change is often slow to come. Such a lack of knowledge means that ultimately, it is difficult to predict or engineer institutional or even policy change.

First, it is worth reviewing the reasons why nations often do not have good institutions, and why such sub-optimal states are often prolonged. There are generally four leading explanations in this regard, best outlined by institutional economist Mary Shirley (2005):

1. Colonial heritage—countries inherited poor institutions from their colonial masters;
2. Colonial heritage plus—countries had valuable resources, people that could be enslaved, or land suitable to plantation agriculture, enticing colonisers to design institutions to exploit these endowments;
3. Political conflict—countries had too little political competition over their borders or between their elites so their rulers were less motivated to appeal to the wider population for support in their battles and faced little effective opposition when they built institutions to serve their selfish interests; and
4. Beliefs and norms—countries had beliefs and norms that were inhospitable to markets or engendered mistrust, preventing them from building institutions that encourage trade and investment.

The 'colonial heritage' school emphasises geographical and historical factors that affect nations' institutional development. Often, poor countries have inherited extractive institutions from colonial masters. The reason for this is also subject to debate: some argue that it is the character of colonisers themselves that affect the type of institutions they transmit (La Porta et al., 2008; Lange et al., 2006), and some refer to the geographic conditions that affect whether they import inclusive institutions (Acemoglu et al., 2001; Engerman & Sokoloff, 2002). The 'political conflict' school emphasises the vested interests that stand to lose if pro-growth institutional reforms are pursued. As Acemoglu and Robinson (2000) put it well, there are 'political losers' in transition, and they block change. The last perspective emphasises the beliefs and norms that persist, preventing people from embracing change (see Chap. 5 for our discussion of why cultural values matter).

Whichever position one takes, there is a wide consensus that institutional change—the rules and norms in society—while possible, is rare. Once such change happens, it can be easily observed and identified, but it is much harder to foresee when they will happen again. In the academic literature, such a view is understood with reference to the concept of 'critical junctures' and 'path dependence' (Fioretos et al., 2016). It is said there are certain 'critical junctures', where conditions for change are more permissive than usual. After change occurs in such critical junctures, society tends to settle into an equilibrium, which persists in a path-dependent manner until future critical junctures open the window for change.

Such a 'punctuated equilibrium' view of institutional change is one that has much to favour. However, in this section, we argue that it can be supplemented with an analysis of the role of institutional entrepreneurs. This contributes to ongoing work to consider endogenous factors that drive change even in the face of institutional constraints (Thelen & Conran, 2016). First, such institutional entrepreneurs increase the likelihood of critical junctures occurring, as they shift conditions on the ground to make change more amenable. Second, once critical junctures actually occur, the direction of change (what kind of institutions and policies are being embraced by those in power) is determined by institutional entrepreneurs. As this handbook has documented, there are numerous individuals and organisations in local contexts who engage in this sort of work: discovery, promulgating and implementing institutional improvements.

Institutional entrepreneurs are actors 'who have an interest in particular institutional arrangements and who leverage resources to create new institutions or to transform existing ones' (Maguire et al., 2004). They are analogous to entrepreneurs in markets for goods and services. Just as economic entrepreneurs try out novel solutions under conditions of uncertainty, institutional entrepreneurs develop and market new proposals for institutional and policy changes in society. The process of development is not a linear one with a predetermined outcome. At critical moments of change, and in the light of the changing external environment, certain proposals break through and take hold in the public's imagination. The last century and a half, for instance, saw the pendulum swing from liberalism to central planning and back.

Much institutional entrepreneurship involves what is called 'discursive struggles', in other words, ideas, rhetoric and social meanings (see Hardy & Maguire,

2008). In the context of development, people debate and reflect on what development means for them, the proper balance of material vs non-material goals, the role of the state in development, the relationship their nation takes vis-à-vis the outside world and so on. In post-war Southeast Asia, for example, this 'discursive struggle' saw nations take different paths. Ho Chi Minh implemented communism in Vietnam, with deleterious economic consequences. Less radical but still harmful was Sukarno's preference for economic nationalism, which was rooted in his nationalistic ideology of 'Pancasila' (Hainsworth, 1983; Marktanner & Wilson, 2015). Indonesia soon closed itself to foreign capital. These political leaders made use of traditional ideas of communalism such as 'gotong royong' and 'bayanihan' in their pursuit of power, hence the appeal of these leftist ideas and communism (Owen, 1993). In other Singapore, the rhetoric of 'modern growth' held sway under the leadership of Lee Kuan Yew, though he was almost initially outcompeted by communist leaders who would have taken the nation onto the path that others in Southeast Asia took. In a society where trade had accounted for such a huge portion of economic activity for more than a century, the discursive appeal of communism and of village-based communalism was limited in Singapore. Ideologies are potent, and the outcome of these struggles has grave consequences for the wealth of nations.

As such, even though a nation's institutional development may be thwarted by vested interests (who wish to block change) or delayed by historical path dependence, there is good reason to be optimistic in the ability of institutional entrepreneurs to disrupt the status quo. A new mentality breaks forth into the public imagination. The past decade especially has witnessed the emergence of new social movements advancing their agenda, from environmental movements that point to the climate emergency, to those dedicated to social causes, such as protecting the rights of minorities and limiting the power of police to target and harass them.

Elinor Ostrom and Bottom-Up Change

Institutional entrepreneurship so described may also be analysed with reference to once again the work of Elinor Ostrom. This is because the Ostromian and Bloomington mode of analysis provides one with an endogenous view of institutional change and focuses on the actions of civil society actors.

Civil society plays a central role in formulating policy recommendations, enhancing state capacity, mobilising civic action and changing the climate of opinion and the moral framework of a nation, all of which have an impact on a nation's development prospects. Consequently, this is very much a central feature of Ostrom's work, which has focused on how democratic citizens can devise rules of self-governance and thereby overcome collective action problems. Through extensive fieldwork, she was able to show that local communities are not necessarily consigned to 'tragedy of the commons' type scenarios and are able to construct social rules to manage common-pool resources (see Ostrom, 1990). Those rules are locally created and contextually sensitive and are distinct from the two traditional policy approaches of either privatising common-pool resources or putting them under state management. Her pioneering work has contributed much to our understanding of bottom-up processes (and why they are often preferred to top-down processes) in climate change management, natural resource management and environmental governance as a whole (Cai et al., 2022; Ostrom, 2010; Dorsch & Flachsland, 2017).

Her work of course has implications for how we understand a myriad of policy issues. Among the implications of her work is understanding how a self-governing citizenry is essential for sustaining democratic life (Boettke et al., 2015a, b; Wagner, 2005). Ostrom (2014) noted that 'a frequently overlooked precondition of democracy' is 'citizens knowledgeable about and engaged in collective action'. Seen that way, the associational life of democratic citizens becomes a ripe focus of study: the way people identify issues of concern, mobilise fellow citizens, protest government policies and generate norms of behaviour. Ostrom's framework is rich in insights into the nature of bottom-up development.

The most obvious application of this framework is the realisation that non-governmental organisations (NGOs) play a big part in development. This is nothing new, and much has been written about it (Bebbington et al., 2008). Much attention is devoted to such international 'Development Oriented NGO' organisations, such as Mercy Corps, the Gates Foundation, Doctors Without Borders and the Red Cross.

Development NGOs have been characterised as 'implementers', 'catalysts' and 'partners' in the development community (Lewis et al., 2021, pp. 14–15). As implementers, NGOs deliver goods and services of their own, for example, by providing humanitarian relief, monetary aid or even 'intangibles' such as policy advice, training and research. As catalysts, they seek to inspire change through a range of activities, such as grassroots activism, acting as pressure groups to office-holders and disseminating ideas to mobilise social action. They are also partners, engaging in joint projects with national governments, individual donors and global organisations like the World Bank. The roles of NGOs in development have been understandably subject to much debate.

We're not convinced that 'more NGOs are better' in the world of development. In fact, the actions of some NGOs have been rightly criticised. Poor countries suffer from poor governance, and they require institutional, policy and even cultural reforms which facilitate inclusive growth. The actions of some NGOs thwart such progress, especially those who are part of the broken aid industry that has made local governments more accountable to global organisations than to their own citizens, thereby propping up predatory government leaders and delaying much-needed governance reforms (Palmer & Warner, 2022). That said, there are certainly many NGOs that do good work, notably in the area of humanitarian relief.

The incentives of NGOs and their leaders may not always be aligned to that of beneficiaries. There are cases where NGOs end up serving the interests of their donors, rather than their intended stakeholders. Cases of corruption and malfeasance involving NGOs are not hard to find. Oxfam, a leading NGO, has been accused of sexual exploitation failing to take appropriate corrective measures to stop such exploitation by their aid workers (Khan, 2018). The Red Cross' relief projects in Haiti saw hundreds of millions of dollars unaccounted for (Sullivan, 2015). The United Nations, for all the good it has done, has been subject to recent criticism over sexual abuse, corruption and misogyny, as documented in a recent BBC documentary (see Seale, 2022). They may also act paternalistically, imposing onto local communities the NGO's preferences without actually giving local communities real stakes in the policy agenda. NGOs may end up serving the agendas of foreign elites rather than those of local communities. Their interventions may also upset political and social arrangements and favour particular groups at the expense of others. The World Bank is a particularly tragic example. Even though its research arm has rightly pointed out the need for poor countries to adopt market-oriented reforms, many of the actual projects of its implementation divisions have either been ineffectively implemented or did not get root of the problem: poor governance (Aiad-Toss, 2020; Johnson, 1996).

For Elinor Ostrom, the preferred term is that of CBOs: Community-Based Organisations, which differ from development-oriented NGOs (Dongier et al., 2003). CBOs are narrower associations formed around common interests and aimed at advancing said interests, such as farmers associations, youth clubs and industry groups. Despite uncertainties of measurement, some estimates suggest that there are hundreds of thousands, even millions of such CBOs worldwide, and they manage increasing amounts of funds—from both government donations and private funding—that amount to billions of dollars. There are two ways in which CBOs differ from NGOs. First, CBOs may not have an explicit humanitarian or development-oriented mission, unlike NGOs, which are typically formed to promote the social good (think Oxfam or Gates Foundation). CBOs are more like civil society groups which may have a wide range of common goals, including 'mundane' ones like chess clubs or dance clubs. Second, CBOs are typically smaller in scale than NGOs; being 'community based', they rely on the participation of members and are bound by strong communal ties. In contrast, some NGOs are global in scale; the largest one being Building Resources Across Communities (BRAC) in Bangladesh which employs tens of thousands of employees. In the end, the line between CBOs and NGOs is not entirely clear, as some organisations may be both.

As John Maynard Keynes rightly pointed out, the course of society is influenced by the prevailing political-economic ideas in the intellectual environment: 'the ideas of economists and political philosophers, both when they are right and when they are wrong are more powerful than is commonly understood. Indeed, the world is ruled by little else. Practical men, who believe themselves to be quite exempt from any intellectual influences, are usually slaves of some defunct economist'. However, what is important to note for our purposes is that these ideas typically take shape in *organisational settings*. The 'economists and political philosophers' that Keynes speaks of, and the audiences that they communicate to, are usually found in universities, think tanks, pressure groups and many others, who promote specific ideological agendas. In other words, CBOs that concern themselves with political change matter. This is not difficult to visualise, for in recent years we have seen the rise of specific CBOs centred around the liberation of black, queer and various minorities. Public attention to such issues has understandably been greater than ever before.

The reason why CBOs are worth analysing is twofold. First, the number of CBOs itself is an important reflection of the associational life of any nation. As Elinor Ostrom and various authors have written, a healthy democratic society comprises more than procedural rules and electoral processes but are rooted in the norms and ties between people. The constraints on state power described previously are also rooted in the desire of people for self-governance. Additionally, such CBOs provide individuals with the opportunity to transcend material goals, and pursue meaning with fellow citizens. The expansion of civil society and CBOs is thus a means and an end of development. Second, the inter-organisational competition between CBOs, especially those that deal with intellectual and political ideas, has a significant influence on the course of institutional development. Specifically, think tanks, research organisations, ideology-centric groups and political activist groups are CBOs that have a direct impact on development, for they promulgate concrete policy ideas, mobilise citizen action and also more abstract principles for social improvement.

CBOs and Institutional Change

In the context of development, CBOs, being community-centric, fill an important gap between theory and practice. Often, knowledge about the ingredients for development remains at an abstract level, but local citizen participation translates these abstract principles into workable projects. The necessity for such knowledge was articulated by development economist Dani Rodrik (2005, p. 32) who wrote:

> Economics is full of big ideas on the importance of incentives, markets, budget constraints, and property rights. It offers powerful ways of analysing the allocative and distributional consequences of proposed policy changes. The key is to realize that these principles do not translate directly into specific policy recommendations. That translation requires the analyst to supply many additional ingredients that are contingent on the economic and political context and cannot be done a priori. Local conditions matter not because economic principles change from place to place, but because those principles come institution free and filling them out requires local knowledge.

The contributions of CBOs to institutional change may be understood with regard to two dimensions of human action: knowledge and incentives. For institutional change to occur (or be made more permissive), there must be incentives for the relevant stakeholders to break away from the status quo and also the necessary knowledge of how and what to change. Just as prices provide the necessary knowledge and incentives in the market process, CBOs provide the knowledge and incentive in the laboratory of institutional change. Of course, it is worth remembering that not all CBOs have an equal influence in development, since they are not all focused on political, development or ideological work. The local chess club for instance will not be as impactful to development outcomes as a think-tank. The relevant CBOs (we may call them 'Development-Relevant CBOs'), however, play an incentive and knowledge function. First, they make institutional change more likely by improving political incentives for change. They also provide the necessary knowledge to key stakeholders, and the content of this knowledge will affect the type of change that happens (Table 7.1).

Development-relevant CBOs provide four important functions. First, they enhance state capacity by providing policy advice and knowledge. Government officials may not always have the necessary information about the best course of action to take. State bureaucracy may not always be staffed with the best talent and officials may not possess the expertise to implement sound policies, problems which are especially acute in developing nations. Development-relevant CBOs supplement low state capacities by engaging in policy research, providing advice to policymakers and at times even offering policy-related skills to such officials.

Table 7.1 Contributions of development-relevant CBOs

Dimension of human action	Relationship to other actors	Function	Strategies
Knowledge	State	Providing policy advice & knowledge	Policy research and advice, provision of training to civil servants, joint projects with government bodies
	Society at large	Highlighting necessity of change and improving knowledge on change methods	Development of new ideas, intellectual thought leadership by academics and opinion-makers, dissemination of ideas by educators, journalists and the media, organisation of events and outreach activities
Incentives	State	Lower the political costs of policy reforms, making change more likely to occur	Engaging in advocacy work, providing donations or intangible support to decision-makers, public criticism of officials
	Society at large	Mobilising the public to act, participate and join change efforts	Organising protests, forming social movements and mobilising other forms of collective action

Think tanks are especially relevant here, since they occupy a knowledge niche, and they produce research publications aimed at influencing the policy environment.

At the same time, state officials may not always have the incentive to do what's right, even if they know what must be done. What is good for the society generally may not always be the best for the policy holders, who often enrich themselves at the expense of the general public. Political incentives may lead state officials to engage in profoundly destructive policies. Development-relevant CBOs can play the important role of making sound policies align with the political self-interest of decision-makers, for example by helping them to get credit for successful reforms that generate greater general prosperity.

CBOs do not just engage state officials, but in fact have a wide variety of stakeholders. The public at large is also important, since their interests and values will be reflected in government through the democratic process. Increasing the level of economic literacy can generate widespread benefits for all, as can educating marginalised populations about their rights. Development-relevant CBOs disseminate ideas to the public, educating people about social problems and improving methods of social change. This contribution is related to the writings of intellectuals by the famous economists John Maynard Keynes and F. A. Hayek. Keynes had spoken about original academic ideas from universities—he referred to them as 'academic scribblers'. For Hayek, the wider knowledge dissemination infrastructure was more important: the 'second dealers of ideas', such as bloggers, vloggers, columnists, teachers, preachers and radio commentators. Regardless, both recognised the power that ideas have. These ideas are in turn often connected to the work of development-relevant CBOs, especially ideas-centric ones like research institutes, think tanks and university departments.

Of course, people must also be motivated to act. An especially difficult hurdle to overcome is the collective action problem, since individuals can free ride on the efforts of others without themselves putting in the effort at social organisation (Olson, 2009). Social movements can be quite difficult to organise, and those that are organised sometimes fizzle out quickly. Development-relevant CBOs, especially those that involve citizen mobilisation and activism, encourage individuals to organise and generate valuable common identities. They overcome the collective action problem by providing its members with a sense of shared identity in their struggle for change. Importantly, they shift society's 'Overton Window' on what is considered acceptable and unacceptable in the realm of institutional and policy change. For example, the work of environmental organisations and activist groups has now brought the climate agenda front and centre of policymaking, on both national and global levels.

Is Institutional Change (Always) Liberal?

This handbook has argued that the principles of humane liberalism are valuable in development. There is an obvious irony however: the direction of institutional change (if and when it does occur) is not always liberal.

On the one hand, the future of liberal society both relies on the existence of a robust civil society. A liberal society, with its freedom of association, is bound to witness robust CBO action. Conversely, authoritarian societies typically limit civil society, and thus, policy-oriented CBOs are stunted. For example, the East Asian nations mentioned in Chap. 6 may have experienced rapid growth under authoritarian governance, but some of them have had their civil society stunted, for example, in Singapore, which has perpetuated soft authoritarianism till present day. A healthy liberal democratic society therefore requires robust civil society and ideological inbucation by various CBOs.

However, there are two ways in which liberal change is not guaranteed. The first is the uncertainty associated with CBO contestation, and the second is that liberal societies may at times generate problematic internal tendencies that threaten to undermine its future.

The first problem is that of uncertainty. Just as the outcome of the market process is uncertain—since it is an evolutionary discovery process—the outcome of CBO competition is similarly uncertain. The organisations that prevail at any given time in history—and their success in mobilising support around their ideas and policies—are different. It is widely understood, for example, that reception towards market-liberal ideas reached a high point in the late twentieth century due to the influence of specific CBOs in the form of market-oriented think tanks. However, the reception of liberal ideas may wax and wane depending on the outcome of organisational competition. To champion liberal change requires not only CBO participation, but specific CBOs that are grounded in liberal principles. Whether or not this happens, and whether they succeed, depends on the ideological struggles that take place in society, and how larger macro-forces make these ideas palatable to the wider public (López & Leighton, 2012).

Certainly, in the current context, there is much reason to worry. Even though there is much more CBO competition than ever before (witness the rise of powerful social movements and activist groups in recent years), many of these groups and their practices are deeply illiberal, as seen by the rise of far-left and far-right groups. Often, the content of their message and the methods they use threaten to undermine the liberal norms of civility, free debate and reasonable discourse. Populist forces make use of the freedom that liberal society offers, but if successful may end up undermining it.

This brings us to the second problem about the internal tensions of liberalism. The market-based economy that this handbook has championed, ironically, may not be internally self-sustaining. The theorist of creative destruction Joseph Schumpeter himself acknowledged (in a prologue to his *Capitalism, Socialism & Democracy*) that capitalism cannot survive on its own. The success of capitalism leads to the formation of an intellectual class that 'cannot help nibbling...at the foundations of capitalist society', because this class 'lives on criticism and its whole position depends on criticism that stings' (Schumpeter, 1942, p. 150). Additionally, the success of capitalism brings about large corporations and bureaucratic structures, who strangle the spirit of individualism and entrepreneurialism. Such corporate structures start engaging in rent-seeking, and in the end, market liberalism ends up descending down a 'road to crony capitalism' and becomes institutionally sclerotic (Olson, 2008; Munger & Villareal-Diaz, 2019). In the political sphere, as just mentioned, the freedom to associate may mean that some groups use it for illiberal ends. The question that liberal theorists have asked is the extent to which toleration should be given to even groups with extreme messages and with the potential to undermine liberal norms. This is a complex dilemma to which we have no answer, except to say that it is up to citizens, we who live in liberal democratic societies who have the responsibility to counter-organise against illiberal CBOs.

The future of development, liberalism and human welfare is in the end, uncertain, but nonetheless in all our hands.

Discussion Questions

1. What are Non-Profit Organisations and Community-Based Organisations? How important are they in the world of development?
2. If culture and institutions are slow to change and engineering the right mix is difficult, what practicable insights may policymakers apply?
3. Is positive social change something that can be engineered top-down or is it a product of unplanned evolution?
4. How important is trade and immigration liberalisation in promoting development today, and how may this be achieved?
5. How concerned about we be about the rise of populism today?
6. Is capitalism self-sustaining?
7. What can citizens do to preserve the future of liberal society?

References

Acemoglu, D., & Robinson, J. A. (2000). Political losers as a barrier to economic development. *American Economic Review, 90*(2), 126–130. https://doi.org/10.1257/aer.90.2.126.

Acemoglu, D., Johnson, S. H., & Robinson, J. A. (2001). The colonial origins of comparative development: an empirical investigation. *American Economic Review, 91*, 1369–1401. https://doi.org/10.1257/aer.91.5.1369.

Aiad-Toss, K. (2020). *World Bank Group Failing at Remedies for Project Abuses*. Human Rights Watch. https://www.hrw.org/news/2020/08/24/world-bank-group-failing-remedies-project-abuses.

Anderson, E. (2017). *Private government*. Princeton University Press.

Bebbington, A. J., Hickey, S., & Mitlin, D. C. (2008). *Can NGOs make a difference?: The challenge of development alternatives*. Bloomsbury Publishing.

Berggren, N., & Nilsson, T. (2013). Does economic freedom foster tolerance? *Kyklos, 66*(2), 177–207. https://doi.org/10.1111/kykl.12017.

Bhagwati, J., & Krishna, P. (2020). Protectionist Myths. In C. Erbil, & F. Rivera-Batiz (Eds.), *Encyclopedia of international trade and globalisation*. World Scientific.

Boettke, P. J., Coyne, C. J., & Leeson, P. T. (2015a). Institutional stickiness and the new development economics. In L Grube & V. Storr (Eds.), *Culture and Economic Action* (pp. 123-146). Edward Elgar Publishing.

Boettke, P. J., Lemke, J. S., & Palagashvili, L. (2015b). Polycentricity, self-governance, and the art & science of association. *The Review of Austrian Economics, 28*(3), 311–335. https://doi.org/10.1007/s11138-014-0273-9.

Cai, M., Caskey, G. W., Cowen, N., Murtazashvili, I., Murtazashvili, J. B., & Salahodjaev, R. (2021). Individualism, economic freedom, and charitable giving. *Journal of Economic Behavior and Organization.*

Cai, M., Murtazashvili, I., Murtazashvili, J., & Salahodjaev, R. (2022). *Toward a Political Economy of the Commons: Simple Rules for Sustainability.* Edward Elgar Publishing.

Chamlee-Wright, E. (2002). *Culture and enterprise: The development, representation and morality of business.* Routledge.

Chang, H. J. (2011). Institutions and economic development: Theory, policy and history. *Journal of Institutional Economics, 7*(4), 473–498. https://doi.org/10.1017/S1744137410000378.

Chang, H. J. (2012). *23 things they don't tell you about capitalism.* Bloomsbury Publishing USA.

Clemens, M. (2009). *The Biggest Idea in Development that No One Really Tried.* YouTube. https://www.youtube.com/watch?v=bB1hRNMGdbQ.

Clemens, M. (2011). Economics and emigration: trillion-dollar bills on the sidewalk? *Journal of Economic Perspectives, 25*(3), 83–106. https://doi.org/10.1257/jep.25.3.83.

Cowen, N. (2021). *Neoliberal social justice: Rawls unveiled.* Edward Elgar Publishing.

Coyne, C. (2008). *After war: The political economy of exporting democracy.* Stanford University Press.

Demsetz, H. (1982). *Economic, legal, and political dimensions of competition.* North-Holland Publishing Company.

Dongier, P., Van Domelen, J., Ostrom, E., Ryan, A., Wakeman, W., Bebbington, A., & Polski, M. (2003). *Community driven development.* World Bank Poverty Reduction Strategy Paper.

Dorsch, M. J., & Flachsland, C. (2017). A polycentric approach to global climate governance. *Global Environmental Politics, 17*(2), 45–64. https://doi.org/10.1162/GLEP_a_00400.

Engerman, S. L., & Sokoloff, K. L. (2002). Factor endowments, inequality, and paths of development among new world economies. *Economía, 3*(1), 41–109. https://doi.org/10.1353/eco.2002.0013.

Feldmann, M. (2019). Global varieties of capitalism. *World Politics, 71*(1), 162–196. https://doi.org/10.1017/S0043887118000230.

Fioretos, O., Falleti, T. G., & Sheingate, A. (2016). Historical institutionalism in political science. In O. Fioretos, T. G. Falleti, & A. Sheingate (Eds.), *The Oxford handbook of historical institutionalism.* Oxford University Press.

Fowler, A. (2011). Development NGOs. In M. Edwards (Ed.), *The Oxford handbook of civil society.* Oxford University Press.

Furceri, D., Hannan, S. A., Ostry, J. D., & Rose, A. K. (2018). Macroeconomic consequences of tariffs. *National Bureau of Economic Research.* https://doi.org/10.3386/w25402.

Gowling WLG. (2020). *Protectionist policies adopted by countries more than triples—gowling wlg research finds.* Gowling WLG. https://gowlingwlg.com/en/news/firm-news/2020/protectionism-a-new-era/.

Hainsworth, G. B. (1983). The Political Economy of Pancasila in Indonesia. *Current History, 82*(483), 167–171, 178–179.

Hamilton, B., & Whalley, J. (1984). Efficiency and distributional implications of global restrictions on labour mobility. *Journal of Development Economics, 14*, 61–75. https://doi.org/10.1016/0304-3878(84)90043-9.

Hanson, G. (2007). *Globalization and poverty.* University of Chicago Press.

Hardy, C., & Maguire, S. (2008). Institutional entrepreneurship. In R. O. Greenwood, R. Suddaby, & K. Sahlin (Eds.), *The SAGE Handbook of organizational institutionalism* (pp. 198–217). SAGE Publications.

Horwitz, S. (2015). *Hayek's modern family: Classical liberalism and the evolution of social institutions*. Palgrave Macmillan.

International Organization for Migration. (2020). *World Migration Report 2020*. United Nations International Organization for Migration. https://publications.iom.int/books/world-migration-report-2020.

Iregui, A. M. (2005). Efficiency gains from the elimination of global restrictions on global mobility. In G. Borjas & J. Crisp (Eds.), *Poverty, international migration and Asylum* (pp. 211–238). Palgrave Macmillan.

Irwin, D. (1997) *Three simple principles of trade policy*. American Enterprise Institute.

Johnson, B. (1996). *The World Bank and Economic Growth: 50 Years of Failure*. Heritage Foundation. https://www.heritage.org/trade/report/the-world-bank-and-economic-growth-50-years-failure.

Jones, M. (2017). *World has racked up 7,000 protectionist measures since crisis: Study*. Reuters. https://www.reuters.com/article/us-global-economy-protectionism-idUSKBN1DF005.

Khan, M. (2018). Oxfam: Sex scandal or governance failure? *Lancet, 391*(10125), 1019–1020. https://www.thelancet.com/journals/lancet/article/PIIS0140-6736(18)30476-8/fulltext.

Kukathas, C. (2021). *Immigration and freedom*. Princeton University Press.

La Porta, R., Lopez-de-Silanes, F., & Shleifer, A. (2008). The economic consequences of legal origins. *Journal of Economic Literature, 46*(2), 285–332. https://doi.org/10.1257/jel.46.2.285.

Lange, M., Mahoney, J., & Vom Hau, M. (2006). Colonialism and development: A comparative analysis of Spanish and British colonies. *American Journal of Sociology, 111*(5), 1412–1462. https://doi.org/10.1086/499510.

Leeson, P., & Gochenour, Z. (2015). The economic effects of international labor mobility. In B. Powell (Ed.), *The economics of immigration* (pp. 11–37). Oxford University Press.

Lewis, D., Kanji, N., & Themudo, N. S. (2021). *Non-governmental organizations and development*. Routledge.

Lomasky, L. E., & Tesón, F. R. (2015). *Justice at a distance*. Cambridge University Press.

López, E. J., & Leighton, W. A. (2012). *Madmen, intellectuals, and academic scribblers: The economic engine of political change*. Stanford University Press.

Maguire, S., Hardy, C., & Lawrence, T. (2004). Institutional entrepreneurship in emerging fields: HIV/AIDS treatment advocacy in Canada. *Academy of Management Journal, 47*(5), 657–679. https://doi.org/10.2307/20159610.

Marktanner, M., & Wilson, M. (2015). Pancasila: Roadblock or pathway to economic development. *ICAT Working Paper Series*.

McCloskey, D. N. (2019). *Why Liberalism Works: How True Liberal Values Produce a Freer, More Equal, Prosperous World for All*. Yale University Press.

McCloskey, D. N. (2022a). *Bettering Humanomics*. Centre for the Study of Governance and Society; King's College London. https://csgs.kcl.ac.uk/podcast/bettering-humanomics-in-conversation-with-deirdre-mccloskey/.

McCloskey, D. N. (2022b). *Beyond positivism, behaviorism, and neoinstitutionalism in economics*. University of Chicago Press.

Moses, H., & Letnes, B. (2004). The economic costs to international labour restrictions: Revisiting the empirical discussion. *World Development, 32*(10), 1609–1626. https://doi.org/10.1016/j.worlddev.2004.05.007.

Munger, M. C., & Villarreal-Diaz, M. (2019). The road to crony capitalism. *The Independent Review, 23*(3), 331–344. https://www.independent.org/pdf/tir/tir_23_3_02_munger.pdf.

North, Douglass. (1981). Structure and Change in Economic History. New York: Norton.

Nowrasteh, A., & Powell, B. (2020). *Wretched refuse?: The political economy of immigration and institutions*. Cambridge University Press.

Olson, M. (2008). *The rise and decline of nations*. Yale University Press.

Olson, M. (2009). *The logic of collective action*. Harvard University Press.

Ostrom, E. (2010). Beyond markets and states: Polycentric governance of complex economic systems. *American Economic Review, 100*(3), 641–672. https://doi.org/10.1257/aer.100.3.641.

Ostrom, E. (1990). *Governing the commons: The evolution of institutions for collective action.* Cambridge University Press.

Ostrom, E. (2014). A frequently overlooked precondition of democracy: citizens knowledgeable and engaged in collective action. In D. Cole, & M. D. McGinnis (Eds.), *Elinor Ostrom and the Bloomington School of political economy: Polycentricity in public administration and political science* (pp. 337–352). Rowman and Littlefield.

Owen, N. (1993). Economic and social change. In N. Tarling (Ed.), *The Cambridge history of Southeast Asia* (Vol. 2, pp. 467–528). Cambridge University Press.

Palmer, T., & Warner, M. (2022). *Development with dignity.* Routledge.

Pennington, M. (2011). *Robust political economy.* Edward Elgar Publishing.

Rodrik, D. (2006). Goodbye Washington consensus, hello Washington confusion? A review of the World Bank's economic growth in the 1990s: Learning from a decade of reform. *Journal of Economic Literature, 44*(4), 973–987. https://doi.org/10.1257/jel.44.4.973.

Rodrik, D. (2005). Growth strategies. In P. Aghion & S. Durlauf (Eds.), *Handbook of economic growth* (pp. 967–1014). Elsevier

Sachs, J. (2014). The case for aid. *Foreign Policy, 21.* https://foreignpolicy.com/2014/01/21/the-case-for-aid/.

Sandel, M. (2012). *What money can't buy: The moral limits of markets.* Macmillan.

Schumpeter, J. A. (1942). *Capitalism, socialism, and democracy.* Harper & Brothers.

Seale, J. (2022). *The Whistleblowers: Inside the UN review—a horrific tale of misogyny, rape and 10,000 deaths.* The Guardian. https://www.theguardian.com/tv-and-radio/2022/jun/21/the-whistleblowers-inside-the-un-review-a-horrific-tale-of-misogyny-and-10000-deaths.

Shirley, M. (2005). Institutions and development. In C. Menard & M. Shirley (Eds.), *Handbook of new institutional economics* (pp. 611–638). Springer.

Somin, I. (2020). *Free to move: Foot voting, migration, and political freedom.* Oxford University Press.

Storr, V. H. (2012). Why the market? Markets as social and moral spaces. *Journal of Markets & Morality, 12*(2), 277–296.

Sullivan, L. (2015). *In search of the red cross' $500 million in Haiti relief.* NPR. https://www.npr.org/2015/06/03/411524156/in-search-of-the-red-cross-500-million-in-haiti-relief.

Thelen, K., & Conran, J. (2016). Institutional change. In O. Fioretos, T. G. Falleti, & A. Sheingate (Eds.), *The Oxford handbook of historical institutionalism.* Oxford University Press.

Tomasi, J. (2012). *Free market fairness.* Princeton University Press.

Wagner, R. E. (2005). Self-governance, polycentrism, and federalism: Recurring themes in Vincent Ostrom's scholarly oeuvre. *Journal of Economic Behavior & Organization, 57*(2), 173–188. https://doi.org/10.1016/j.jebo.2004.06.015.

World Bank. (2021). Trade (% of GDP)|Data. World Bank Data. https://data.worldbank.org/indicator/NE.TRD.GNFS.ZS?end=2021&start=1980.